LAW *and* THEOLOGY
in JUDAISM

Let the words of the Torah be sharp in your mouth, so that if someone asks you a question you will not stammer and finally speak to him, but you will speak to him at once, as it is written, "Say to Wisdom, you are my sister" [Prov. 7:4].

B. Kiddushin 30a-30b.

What principles should guide us in interpreting Jewish law today? Interpreting law presupposes a mental picture of what we are doing and why we are doing it. What is it we do when we interpret law? To what authorities do we turn for guidance? To what extent are we influenced by them?; and in case of conflicting opinions how do we choose between them? . . . These are problems in philosophy.

Boaz Cohen, Law and Tradition in Judaism, p. 56.

LAW *and* THEOLOGY
in JUDAISM

by DAVID NOVAK

Foreword by
LOUIS FINKELSTEIN

KTAV PUBLISHING HOUSE, INC.

NEW YORK

7/17/74

Library of Congress Cataloging in Publication Data

Novak, David, 1941-
    Law and theology in Judaism.
    Includes bibliographical references.
    1. Responsa—1800-   I. Title.
BM522.74.09   296.1′79   74-806
ISBN 0-87068-245-8

MANUFACTURED IN THE UNITED STATES OF AMERICA

CONTENTS

TO MELVA

"Have mercy on me and let me grow old with her."

Tobit 8:7

FOREWORD

Rabbi David Novak's present work, *Law and Theology in Judaism,* is a significant and valuable contribution to the literature on Judaism available to the English-reading public. In this fine work Rabbi Novak introduces the reader not only to the content of the specific halakhic decisions which he offers, but to the method by which learned rabbis for more than a thousand years have weighed precedents, the needs of the moment, and the problems which might arise from different interpretation of norms against one another, in order to reach conclusions about the obligation imposed on a Jew by the Divinely-inspired Torah.

The examples Rabbi Novak has chosen are all subjects of controversy among rabbis and scholars of our time. The one involving the marriage law is being bitterly debated in Israel at the present time, because Jewish marriage law is the law of the land for Jews there. It is necessarily subject there to interpretation and application only by rabbinic courts (as the marriage laws of other groups are subject to the decisions of their ecclesiastical authorities).

Rabbi Novak has with much assiduity gone through the literature on each of the subjects discussed. With meticulous care, he presents fairly the views of the various interpreters and a summary of the arguments. Sometimes, as in any other system of law, these are exceedingly complicated. But with rare literary skill, Rabbi Novak reduces these complexities to simplicity. In the end he presents in each instance his own approach, giving the reasons for his rejection of the view he finds he cannot accept.

The reader of this volume will thus be able to see how our tradition has grown. Its fundamental basis is, of course, the Bible—especially the Pentateuch. This is supplemented by the Oral Tradition, which, codified in the Mishnah and related works, Jews have accepted as authoritative for at least two thousand years.

The question of the relevance of Jewish law, no matter how interpreted, to life today has to be faced; and Rabbi Novak fearlessly meets the issue candidly and forcefully. The relevance of the problem in the State of Israel need not be argued. Much of Jewish law is enforceable in the courts there. But how can its relevance to life in the diaspora be established, especially in a permissive age? Judaism is a religion of rigorous discipline. Obviously, its discipline is inconsistent with the whole trend of thought and conduct which rejects the bonds of "oughtness" as archaic.

But quite aside from this conflict between Judaism and the prevailing permissiveness, is the type of permissiveness now prevalent in so many quarters, and urged in others, really a good? Apparently the wisest of men, no matter how they viewed life, did not consider unbridled permissiveness a good. Modern permissiveness turns out on examination to be essentially a queer and distorted version of what ancient, medieval, and some modern philosophers have called "hedonism."

No one can really doubt that human happiness is good and human misery evil. "But," we are assured by the eminent psychologist, Professor George A. Miller, "no one who has argued for hedonism—Epicurean, Stoic, Utilitarian, Freudian—has ever argued for purely sensory pleasure." Two researchers at McGill University in Montreal discovered that by pushing two electric wires into a certain region of the brain of a rat, the rat could be made so happy that it would stimulate the lever activating this mechanism rather than another which would provide it with food. The full significance of this remarkable discovery has still to be studied. But perhaps it can be taken for granted that, even if it should be found that human beings could also be made to feel supremely happy through such electrodes in the brain, no one will urge their widespread use to overcome the fact of real human misery.

Rabbi Akiba regarded pain as no less a good than pleasure. One does not have to go that far to recognize the important role which pain has played in the preservation of the human species and the development of individual personality. The human race would long ago have become extinct if mothers were not willing to suffer the pains of parturition and of child-rearing for the sake of the joys of parenthood. Man would still be a cave-dweller if some individuals did not sacrifice the satisfaction of immediate and even enduring personal joys in order to gain insight into truths of science, or discover regions of the earth, or invent better technological tools. Which great work of art or literature has been created, except by human beings willing to suffer pain and hardship in order to achieve such creations?

Judaism, like other systems of law, under certain conditions, demands of its devotees sacrifices for the attainment of specific, clearly understood, quite intelligible goals. These goals include, among others, the recognition of the dignity of every individual person—no matter what his background or personal status might be, the establishment of peace among individuals and groups, above all the sanctity of the life of each person, and the sanctity of the home.

Thus, while the self-denial of fasting on the Day of Atonement makes that a supremely valuable day for communion with the Spiritual, one must violate the fast if it involves danger to one's life. If a person's life is in danger, one must violate the Sabbath to save him. One may not delay doing what has to be done for any reason. One should not try to evade the issue by asking a gentile or a child, not yet fully subject to the commandments, to perform the necessary task under such circumstances. It must be done by adult Jews as soon as the peril is discovered.

Protection of the sanctity of the home may be especially important in an age when the survival of the family may be threatened by widespread permissiveness, perhaps as never before in the history of civilization.

The rabbi, who has to decide issues which may seem technical and ritualistic to the uninformed, will have to weigh in the balance the different considerations which must enter into a decision of what is right under particular circumstances.

In making this evaluation, the rabbi will, of course, be influenced in large part by his theological commitments. Do the expressions "communion with the deity," or "sanctity of the home," or "sanctity of life" have real meaning for him?

That is why Rabbi Novak's discussion of theological issues today is so relevant in this work so largely devoted to legal decisions.

The congregation which is fortunate enough to have Dr. Novak as its Rabbi is, like him, to be congratulated on the appearance of this work, which will doubtless become the subject of discussion among his colleagues and lead to further studies of the issues he has raised. In the end, one of the most important results of this publication will be the enrichment and broadening of the study and practice of Torah in our time.

Louis Finkelstein

August 1973

PREFACE

This book is the result of my rabbinic ministry in the deepest sense. A rabbi today is many things his earlier counterparts were not; however, he is still *dayan*—interpreter of Jewish law—and *darshan*—interpreter of Jewish theology. He is these things if he loves Halakhah and Aggadah and chooses to share what he loves with those in his care. This I have tried to do in my brief career. I am continually gratified by the interest of the Jews and even the non-Jews with whom I come into contact. This book, then, follows the traditional rabbinical format of publishing one's responsa.

The essays in this book are all responsa I have written over the past few years, with the exception of "Belief in God," which is an expanded version of a paper written for my late revered teacher, Professor A. J. Heschel, in the spring of 1964. This, too, follows traditional procedure in that books of responsa usually conclude with investigations into more theoretical matters. Such investigations reveal the author's more general concerns, which form a background for the specific questions under analysis. After all, no questions or group of questions can ever fully tap the sources. No investigation or group of investigations can exhaust them either; however, one's own questions should be the basic motivation in answering the questions of others. This is what distinguishes a scholar from a computer.

The introductory essay, from which *Law and Theology in Judaism* takes its name, was originally a paper read at the annual Kallah of Texas Rabbis held in Dallas in March 1971. Later it was published in *Tradition* in the Summer 1972 issue. The essay in this book is an expanded version of that article. I am grateful to the editors of *Tradition* for their kind permission to use this article.

The essay, "A Jewish View of Abortion," was originally a paper I read at a symposium at the University of Oklahoma in April 1972. Earlier that year I had testified before the State Senate of Oklahoma against a liberalized abortion bill.

xiii

The essay, "Suicide in Jewish Perspective," was written as a result of my doctoral dissertation, which dealt with suicide in philosophical perspective.

The essay, "A Jewish View of War," was written in the fall of 1966 at the suggestion of my late revered teacher, Professor A. J. Heschel, as we were picketing in front of the White House protesting American involvement in Indochina.

The rest of the essays in this book are all expansions of questions I answered in the bulletins of Emanuel Synagogue in Oklahoma City, Oklahoma, from 1969 to 1972, and Beth Tfiloh Congregation in Baltimore, Maryland, from 1972 to the present. Some of these essays are only minor adaptions of my original responsa. Others, such as the essay on the agunah problem and the essay on funerals in the synagogue, are major reworkings of much shorter responsa, because I believed that these questions involved deeper issues than those immediately evident.

All of the essays in this book demonstrate its central thesis; namely, that Halakhah (law) and Aggadah (theology) are not only indispensable elements of Judaism in and of themselves, but that their interrelationship is equally important. Because of this I decided not to write a general introduction presenting the theoretical assumptions behind my responsa. Rather, I have stated these assumptions in the immediate context of their meaning. To have done otherwise would have contradicted my thesis about the *interrelationship* between Halakhah and Aggadah. This interrelationship is much more specific than general.

Maimonides advised us to "listen to the truth from whomever has said it" (*Shemonah Perakim,* introduction). Because of this, and the objective nature of Jewish legal and theological thought, I have not hesitated to utilize the work of any scholar who has some light to shed on any of the problems with which I am dealing. This utilization does not imply endorsement or rejection of the religious positions of these authors, any more than my personal consultations with other scholars implies either my endorsement of their positions or theirs of mine. To regard Judaism, especially Halakhah, as the exclusive program of one's own ideology is to take a giant step towards a sectarian fragmentation of the Jewish people. Even the Pharisees and Sadducees, who were in some ways more disparate than the groups within religious Jewry today, still reasoned together. This did not compromise their religious differences. Apparently the Pharisees, whose successors we are, believed that their view of Judaism was strengthened, not weakened, by intellectual contacts, outside their fold. Surely history proved them correct.

"From all my teachers I learned, for Thy testimonies were my conversation" (Ps. 119:99). It has been my privilege to have studied under gifted teachers. This book owes its larger inspiration to three of them.

My revered teacher, Professor A. J. Heschel, departed this world less than a year ago. I deeply mourn the loss of the man who taught me Jewish theology in depth. Every moment I was with him, and during the years 1964-66 this was almost daily, I learned. He was a living Torah. His love of God, his love of Israel the people of God, his love of man the image of God, coupled with his penetrating intellect, made any encounter with him memorable. I will never forget his many kindnesses to me; his sharing with me and many others his great heart and mind.

The late Professor Boaz Cohen, unlike Professor Heschel, was not a man of personal magnetism; thus, many of his students did not appreciate the gifts he had to offer. Nevertheless, Professor Cohen taught me more than anyone else what "Historial Judaism" means. His vast knowledge of the classical world of Greece and Rome, especially Roman law, made any lesson in Talmud or Codes a banquet of erudition. This knowledge was given freely and modestly. With him the indispensability of history for the understanding of Halakhah became clear and evident. Even witnessing him direct the writing of a divorce was always an occasion to learn something new and important. His teaching was a vital supplement to the technical talmudic skills I aquired from my Seminary professors, Saul Lieberman, Moses Zucker, and Seymour Siegel, and from my earlier teachers in Chicago, the late Rabbi Julius Weissbach and Rabbi Curt Peritz, now of London.

Finally, there was the influence of a non-Jew, the distinguished Roman Catholic philosopher, Professor Germain G. Grisez, now of the University of Saskatchewan, Canada, under whom I pursued my graduate studies in philosophy at Georgetown University in Washington, D.C. Professor Grisez, unlike most professional ethicians today, taught me the necessity for bringing the rigor of philosophical method to bear on practical moral issues such as abortion, capital punishment, and war. From him I also learned how faith and reason can nurture each other in their common quest for truth.

I am grateful to the staff of the Library of Congress, Hebraic Section, especially my friend, Rabbi Eli Subar; to the library of the Baltimore Hebrew College and its librarian, my Seminary classmate, Rabbi George L. Berlin, and his assistant, Mrs. Betty K. Sachs; and to the libraries of the Jewish Theological Seminary of America and the University of Oklahoma.

My thanks are due to my emeritus colleague in Beth Tfiloh Congregation, Dr. Samuel Rosenblatt, for sharing with me the riches of his unequaled private library. I am grateful to my friend, Rabbi Benjamin Bak, for sharing with me his library and also his vast erudition in the Codes and the responsa literature. In addition I thank the following friends and colleagues who answered specific queries and offered other help: Dr. Louis May, Dr. Warren Poland, Chancellor Gerson D. Cohen of the Jewish Theological Seminary of America, Rabbi Jacob Ruderman of the Ner Israel Rabbinical College, Rabbi Byron Sherwin of the Spertus College of Judaica, Rabbi Samuel Vitsick, Dr. W. Gunther Plaut, and Mr. M. F. Garfinkel. Moreover, I have benefited from many stimulating exchanges with my student, Mr. Jonathan I. Rosenblatt.

No small measure of gratitude is due to the members of Emanuel Synagogue in Oklahoma City and of Beth Tfiloh Congregation in Baltimore, my present pulpit. These good people, with their questions, stimulated my own research, which enabled me to answer them in the bulletins of these two congregations. Furthermore, they appreciated that scholarship is something to be expected of a rabbi.

To my wife Melva I owe my home and all that this sacred word implies. Without her I would not have had the emotional endurance needed for serious intellectual work.

My children, Marianne and Jacob, are too young to have offered any tangible help. However, they have given me such joy in just being their father that I cannot resist mentioning them at the time of any accomplishment. I look forward to learning with them.

My final and most important gratitude is to Him who has privileged me with the opportunity to study His Torah and to be in the company of the disciples of the wise. From the days He guided me to the Bet Midrash of my youth and to pious and learned teachers, until the present time, He has lightened my darkness.

DAVID NOVAK

Baltimore, Maryland
Sivan, 5733
June, 1973

CHAPTER 1

LAW AND THEOLOGY IN JUDAISM

1. Halakhah and Aggadah

THROUGHOUT THE HISTORY OF JUDAISM we see the development of legal precepts—that is, statements prescribing what Jews are to do—and of theological concepts—that is, statements describing those experiences which define what Jews are. Both the precepts and the concepts of Judaism involve a Jew's relationship with his own people, the external world, and the transcendent God. There has been no period in the history of Judaism when either precepts or concepts have been emphasized at the total expense of the other. Moreover, it is no accident that in every age Judaism has had expositors who excelled in the interpretation of both precepts and concepts: R. Akiba, Maimonides, and R. Kook, to name a few outstanding examples. Thus Judaism, and not just the Judaism of the rabbinic period, is composed of Halakhah, *law*, and Aggadah, *theology*.[1] These comprise the elementary propositions of Judaism.[2] Judaism revolves on an axis whose poles are the legal point of Halakhah and the theological point of Aggadah. Throughout this book I will use *law* and *Halakhah, theology* and *Aggadah*, as interchangeable synonyms.

To understand the relationship between Halakhah and Aggadah is a task of Jewish philosophy. Philosophy is distinct from both the immediate legal prescriptions of Halakhah and the immediate theological descriptions of Aggadah. Halakhah and Aggadah are the content of Judaism; philosophy is a method of inquiry subsequently employed for the sake of essential understanding. *Philosophy*, as I use the term in this chapter, is the systematically intelligent inquiry into the essential structures of an object, those intelligible prerequisites which make the existence of the object possible. Since Judaism is inconceivable without

1

either Halakhah or Aggadah, they comprise its indispensable prerequisites, the interrelationship of which it is the task of Jewish philosophy to understand.

The question of this relationship is of more than speculative interest; it has practical import for contemporary Jewish life, and for modern rabbis whose task is to interpret Judaism to today's Jews. It is not enough, for practical purposes, to teach the precepts and the concepts of Judaism unsystematically. The religious effectiveness of the rabbinical vocation depends on *how* the rabbi understands the essential interrelation between law and theology in specific cases. For whereas the layman must make the practical moral *decision* to either do or not do that which the law commands, the rabbi must make the practical moral *judgment* about what the law intends. Judgment is the presupposition of an act of intelligence for conscious and coherent action. As such, rabbinical judgment must take into consideration the interrelationship of Halakhah and Aggadah, which is essential in Judaism, if it is to be fully intelligent and not just mechanical. The rabbi must be the practical philosopher of Judaism. As my teacher, the late Dr. A. J. Heschel once wrote:

> The interrelationship of halacha and agada is the very heart
> of Judaism. Halacha without agada is dead, agada without
> halacha is wild.[3]

2. *Theories of the Interrelationship of Halakhah and Aggadah*

If the relationship of law and theology is so important for the understanding of Judaism, where ought the rabbi begin his examination of the question?[4]

The first suggestion might be to identify the basic principles of Judaism and then see how these principles are applied in various situations. This methodology has been suggested by three modern Jewish philosophers whom one would not normally associate together philosophically. All three seem to assume a general theological basis for Jewish law which admits of schematization in specific cases.

The first, Dr. J. B. Soloveitchik, describes the halakhic process as follows:

> When halakhic man approaches reality he comes with his
> Torah, given to him from Sinai, in hand. He connects himself
> to the world with set precepts and precise principles. Halakhic
> man draws near to the world ... with an a priori relation.
> His approach begins with an ideal construction and finishes

with a real one. To whom may he be compared?—To a
mathematician who fashions an ideal world and then uses it
in order to establish a relation between it and the real world
. . . There is no phenomenon, being or creature to which the
a priori Halakhah does not truly apply its ideal standard.[5]

The second, Dr. Max Kadushin, describes Halakhah in terms of the
nomenclature he has devised for the understanding of rabbinic texts:

Haggadah made the value-concepts vivid, and by means of
sermons nurtured and cultivated them. The other product of
the Rabbis, Halakhah, had an altogether different function.
It prescribed ways for the concretization of the concepts in
day-by-day living.[6]

Finally, the late Dr. Leon Roth presented the issue as follows:

A principle, clearly articulated and firmly grasped, enables us
not only to judge. It enables us to correct and improve . . .
Basically, the problem is that of the *translation of Aggadah into
Halachah* . . .[7]

All of these thinkers deal with the relationship between law and
theology on the basis of what I would call an "apodictic assumption."
All of them see law as the specific end-product derived from more
general theological grounds. For Soloveitchik the general ground is the
"ideal Torah" or "a prior Halakhah"; for Kadushin it is the "value-
concepts"; for Roth it is the "principle" or "Aggadah." Each one of
them posits an explicit theological substratum for the various precepts
of Judaism.

Nevertheless, this apodictic assumption is questionable. For if law and
theology are indeed related in such apodictic fashion, then it is strange
that none of the Codes, from the specifically legal sections of the Written
Torah to the Mishnah to Maimonides' *Mishneh Torah* and all the Codes
that succeeded it, none of them deduce specific laws from general
theological principles. Even in the *Mishneh Torah,* the most systematic
Jewish Code ever written, topics are interrelated, but the various laws
themselves have their own specific grounds. Maimonides affirms, as
did the Talmud before him, that the Halakhah is from revelation, but
neither he nor anyone else can show *how* this derivation is systematically
constructed.[8] If one wishes to see a work where specific precepts are

derived from general principles systematically, he ought to carefully study the second section of Thomas Aquinas's *Summa Theologica*. I know of no work in the literature of Judaism that is constructed or could be constructed in this way. Therefore, despite the impressive contributions these three thinkers have made to our understanding of Judaism, it might be helpful to look for another methodological assumption in our quest to understand the relationship between law and theology in Judaism.

In his great work on Don Hasdai Crescas, Dr. H. A. Wolfson provides another methodological assumption when he describes Crescas's method as that of the traditional Talmudist.

> And there is a logic underlying this method of reasoning. It is the very same kind of logic which underlies any sort of scientific research, and by which one is enabled to form hypotheses, to test them and to formulate general laws. The Talmudic student approaches the study of texts in the same manner as the scientist approaches the study of nature.[9]

Wolfson has designated this method as the "Talmudic hypothetico-deductive method of text interpretation."[10] What he has described is not a relationship in which one thing is derived from another apodictically. Rather, he has described a method more akin to the empirical sciences, which speculatively construct a hypothesis or model and then test it against the data at hand. The interrelationship between the model and the data requires that the perspective of each be affected by the other. Examination of the model from the perspective of the data (experimentation) requires modification of the model in order to be more accurately descriptive. And examination of the data from the perspective of the model (categorization) requires that the data be regarded as part of a system which itself is not explicit therein.

If we apply Wolfson's analogy to the question of Halakhah and Aggadah, we can say that Halakhah is the data, and that Aggadah is the model that widens the perspective found in the data. However, the relationship is not apodictic in the sense that law is derived from theology any more than data are derived from models. The intelligibility of this relationship lies in the relationship itself rather than in any one of its poles.[11] The task, then, is to see how this relationship functions. The theological model will require modification in the light of the legal data, and the legal data, being viewed from the perspective of the model, will yield a meaning they alone could not possibly give.

3. *Law and Theology in Jewish Marriage*

Let us see the validity of this methodology. I have chosen an example that very clearly exemplifies the relationship of law and theology in Judaism and which is also especially relevant to the vocation of the rabbi. I hope to show, in conclusion, how a deeper understanding of the relationship of law and theology in this specific case might actually alter the common practice of many rabbis.

There is no role of the rabbi that cries for a deeper understanding of the interrelationship of Halakhah and Aggadah than his role of celebrant of marriage (*mesader kiddushin*).

The Talmud emphasizes the importance of this role in the following manner:

> R. Judah said in the name of Samuel, "Whoever is not expert in the legal aspects [*teeb*] of divorce and marriage, let him have no jurisdiction [*asek*] therein." R. Assi said in the name of R. Johanan, "Those [incompetents] who do so are more dangerous to the world than the generation of the flood."[12]

Rashi points out that the Talmud is specifically referring to the celebrant of the marriage in his legal role of judge.[13] However, the Talmud is doing more than just that, for only the Babylonian tradition in the name of Samuel is a specifically legal statement. The Palestinian tradition in the name of R. Johanan, on the other hand, is a theological statement describing the cosmic status of the laws of divorce and marriage. The most heinous sin of the generation of the flood was sexual immorality, especially adultery. Maharsha points out that remarriage without proper divorce would create an adulterous situation, the very same state of affairs Scripture sees as the cause of the breakdown of both the social and natural orders. This is one reason he gives for mentioning divorce before marriage.[14] One can thus see the Talmud's juxtaposition of these two traditions on the same subject—the one legal, the other theological—as evidence of the close relationship between law and theology.

The task of the marriage celebrant, in our day the rabbi, is not only to supervise the proper enactment of the precepts of marriage. He is not only a dayan, who prescribes; he is also a darshan, who describes in theological perspective to the parties involved how Jewish marriage constitutes the Jew's most fundamental social relationship, and how it also constitutes the context of his sexuality, the biological substratum of human personality. The Talmud, then, presents a clear paradigm

of the rabbi's role in marriage proceedings; he must both prescribe
and describe, judge and teach. Is this not what any rabbi who values
his vocation does under the huppah? The marriage ceremony would
be incomplete if a rabbi merely presided over the giving of a ring and
the recitation of the formula of betrothal. And it might well be invalid
if a rabbi were careless about the precise prescriptions involved in Jewish
marriage and merely delivered a discourse about the meaning of marriage.[15]

What, then, is Jewish marriage? How do we define its essential properties. How does the interrelationship of law and theology enable us
to reach some conclusions for both understanding and practice?

At this point we must take notice of a very significant fact; namely,
that in rabbinic discussions of the institution of marriage the phrase
"divorce and marriage" (*gittin v'kiddushin*) is used, rather than the more
logical sequence, "marriage and divorce." We have already seen this
above. In the order of the tractates of the Talmud, *Gittin* comes before
Kiddushin. Maimonides, in his introduction to the Mishnah, explains
that this order is based on the order of Scripture: "She shall leave his
house and go and be unto another man" (Deut. 24:2).[16] Moreover, in
the talmudic elaboration of this scriptural *sequitur* we find that it is not
only used to explain an order of presentation, as in other cases, but
it is used to explain essential properties of the institution of marriage
itself.[17] To infer the positive from the negative is an accepted principle
of rabbinic exegesis.[18] Since we are to infer the institution of marriage
from that of divorce, if we ascertain what are the essential grounds
for the dissolution of marriage we can thereby determine on what
grounds marriage stands.

4. *Grounds for Divorce*

The grounds for divorce, the dissolution of marriage, are set forth in
the following Mishnah:

> The School of Shammai stated: "A man is not to divorce his
> wife unless he has found something *sexually abhorrent* about
> her, as the Torah says, '. . . because he has found something
> obnoxious about her,'" (Deut. 24:1). The School of Hillel stated:
> "Even if she burned his food, as the Torah says, '. . . because
> he found *anything* obnoxious about her.'" R. Akiba stated:
> "Even if he found one more attractive than her, as the Torah
> says, '. . . and if she did not find *favor* in his eyes.'"[19]

The Talmud in its discussion of this Mishnah indicates that the Shammaite position is based on the word *ervat* ("sexually abhorrent"), with its accepted connotation of sexual immorality. The Hillelite position is based on the word *dabar* ("anything"), with its wider connotation.[20] Thus the Shammaites derive their legal conclusion from the maximum standard the verse prescribes, whereas the Hillelites derive their legal conclusion from the minimum standard the verse prescribes. This type of exegetical difference between the two schools is found in other places as well.[21]

So far our discussion has been on the legal level. Nevertheless, the early codifiers accomplished a remarkable *tour de force* when they indicated that despite the legal ruling being according to the Hillelites, one ought to morally act according to the Shammaite view. Maimonides, although acknowledging in his commentary on the Mishnah that the law is according to the Hillelites, writes in the *Mishneh Torah*:

> A man ought not to divorce his first wife unless he has found something sexually abhorrent about her.[22]

Thus Maimonides in his two treatments of the question—that is, in the commentary on the Mishnah and later in the *Mishneh Torah*—establishes two criteria for divorce: (1) Divorce must be for objective reasons, hence the purely subjective reason offered by R. Akiba in the Mishnah is totally inadmissible.[23] (2) Divorce ought to be for reasons of unfaithfulness alone.

Inasmuch as the Halakhah follows the School of Hillel,[24] as Maimonides himself acknowledges, this second criterion is not legal; it is rather theological. As the *Tur* points out,[25] this second criterion is based on the following Aggadah:

> R. Eleazar said, "Whoever divorces his first wife even the altar of God weeps for him, as the prophet stated, 'And thus do you do further, you cover the altar of the Lord with tears, with weeping and sighing, so much so that He no longer considers the offering, neither does He receive it in good will from your hand. And you say, "Why?" Because the Lord has borne witness between you and the wife of your youth, against whom you have dealt with treachery, and she is your companion, and your convenanted wife' " [Mal. 2:13-14].[26]

Thus we see that the reason such strict grounds of divorce are encouraged, although not legally enforceable, is because marriage is understood to be an institution involving God's personal interest and concern. This is the theological model used to explain the legal facts.

Apart from its application to the legal problem of the grounds for divorce, the notion that God is personally interested and concerned with marriage has a considerable theological development of its own. A famous Midrash, repeated many times, states:

> A Roman lady asked R. Jose bar Halafta, "Everyone agrees that God created the world in six days. From the sixth day on what has he been doing?" . . . R. Berakhyah said . . . he said to her that He arranges matches in His world. . . .She said to him that she could make a thousand matches in one day. R. Jose was silent and went on his way. So she brought a thousand male slaves and a thousand female slaves and paired them off. . . .However, when night came and they all came together fighting broke out among them. . . .She then sent for R. Jose and related the incident. He said to her that the matter of marriage might be insignificant to her, but for God it is as significant as the splitting of the Red Sea as Scripture states, "God settles the solitary in a home" (Ps. 68:7).[27]

Here we seem to have an imaginative exposition of the principle, "Marriages are made in heaven."[28]

However, it is at this point that the interrelationship of law and theology is so crucial for our understanding of the essential nature of Jewish marriage. The Aggadah has tempered the Halakhah by placing a limitation on the grounds for divorce. Its force has enabled the codifiers to reject altogether the subjective standard of R. Akiba. And, although the later Halakhah permits divorce on the more lenient grounds of the School of Hillel, it encourages one to follow the stricter grounds set by the School of Shammai.[29] Nevertheless, the philosophical question is: If marriages are determined by God in advance, then how can the Torah prescribe divorce at all?

Heretofore we have seen how the Aggadah has tempered the Halakhah; now we must see how the Halakhah tempers the Aggadah. Just as the Aggadah made it impossible for the Halakhah to accept subjective grounds for divorce, and difficult for the Halakhah to admit even lenient objective grounds, we must now see how the Halakhah tempers the aggadic tendency to see marriage as the inevitable result of God's predestination. For if we carried the aggadic tendency to its logical conclusion, we would be in direct contradiction of the Torah's prescription of divorce.

5. *Divine Causality and Human Freedom*

The conflict between the halakhic tendency prescribing free choice in divorce and marriage and the aggadic tendency describing predestination comes to a head in the contradiction the Talmud discovers in two statements of the Amora Samuel. It will be noted that the first statement is legal, the second theological.

> Samuel stated that it is permitted to betroth a woman during the Festival Week lest a rival suitor precede him. . . .But how could Samuel say, "lest a rival suitor precede him" when we have a tradition that R. Judah said in the name of Samuel that every day a heavenly voice goes out and declares, "The daughter of X is to be married to Y"? . . . However the reason is that lest a rival suitor anticipate him by means of prayer.[30]

However, the Talmud does not really resolve this contradiction but only deepens it.[31] The various attempts of subsequent commentators at a resolution are admittedly inadequate.[32]

The problem, of course, transcends the discussion in this one text. It is involved in the attempt to define the grounds for divorce, and is a fundamental conflict between legal prescription and theological description. Such conflicts call for philosophical analysis if there is to be any ultimate understanding of the full intent of the Torah. From the Halakhah alone we could infer an expansion of human freedom in the case of the marital situation in regard to both its termination and its initiation. In fact, the Halakhah specifies, even in the case of the levirate, an institution where the plain meaning of the Written Torah seems to indicate a predestined marriage, that it is contingent on the free choice of both the man and the woman.[33] From the Aggadah, on the other hand, one could infer a restriction on freedom of choice in both divorce and marriage.

As has been the case many times throughout the history of Judaism, we have here a conflict between theories concerning divine causalityand human freedom. However, whereas in the more specifically speculative treatments of the question the discussion has been on a metaphysical level, this discussion of the question has been on the practical level. Because of this practical context of the question, understanding is more likely for two reasons: (1) We are dealing with concrete rather than abstract situations. (2) Practical conflicts require practical solutions, and Judaism has demanded more uniformity in practice than in theory. Therefore, in order for the grounds of both Jewish divorce and Jewish marriage to be intelligible, the legal data of the Halakhah and the theological model of the Aggadah must be practically reconciled.

6. *Imitation of God*

Perhaps we can find some sort of reconciliation between these opposing tendencies by giving more careful attention to the Midrash quoted above concerning the conversation between R. Jose bar Halafta and the Roman lady.

It seems to me that there are two ways one could interpret this Midrash, and either interpretation must answer this question: Why is God a successful matchmaker whereas the Roman lady was a failure?

The first line of interpretation sees the Midrash speaking in terms of causality. God created the world in six days and since that time He has concentrated on less spectacular acts of creation, especially matching the right man with the right woman. These seemingly mundane acts are as great as the miracle He performed at the Red Sea. His success is due to His causal power, which infinitely exceeds man's. God's limitless knowledge makes Him a success in this delicate area; the lady's limited knowledge makes her a failure. Just as the natural world functions coherently because of God's omnipotence, so the world of human relations can function coherently because of God's omniscience. "Man sees appearances, but the Lord sees the heart" (1 Sam. 16:7). Thus R. Jose shows the lady that her failure is due to her arrogant assumption that her knowledge of human beings equals God's.

This line of thought is brought out by the continuation of the midrashic text.

> "He brings forth prisoners into prosperity" [Ps. 68:7]. *Bakoshorot* indicates that He brings them out from their houses against their will [*b'al korhan*] and unites them in marriage. *Bakoshorot* implies: if they are unworthy they weep [*bokhim*]; if they are worthy they sing [*meshor'rim*].

This continuation of the text, by emphasizing God's causal power, explicitly eliminates human freedom in this area.[34] The obvious problem with this interpretation, however, is that human experience teaches us that many marriages are unhappy. How then is God a better matchmaker than the Roman lady?[35]

However, the Midrash continues and presents a second interpretation of the situation the verse from Psalms is describing.

> Another interpretation of "God settles the solitary in a home" is, If one marries *a wife suited to him,* God makes houses for the couple. "Solitary" denotes greatness. [Cf. Gen. 26:10; 2 Sam. 7:23]. And He causes their issue to be sons who are masters of Torah.'. . . . But if one does not marry a woman suited to him [*hagunah*] their issue will be Torahless [*amay ha'aretz*].

This addition, which is not found in any of the many parallels, introduces another line of interpretation in its explicit recognition of human freedom in the initiation of marriage. God's blessing of the marriage is now seen as subsequent to man's making the proper marriage choice.

This interpretation, if I am correct, changes the whole meaning of R. Jose's answer to the Roman lady. The lady did not essentially fail because she usurped God's prerogative in her assumption of equal omniscience. Rather, her failure was because of her lack of consideration for human dignity and freedom. Her slaves were used in an experiment in breeding, their needs and their desires were not taken into consideration. Because of being so inhumanly grounded, marriage, which is seen as the most serious of all human relationships, could not succeed. This is why she completely failed. God, on the other hand, not so much because of His causal power but because of His concern for His creation, is able to do better. This is certainly not saying that there are not plenty of unhappy marriages. However, it should be remembered that this interpretation of the midrashic text is not emphasizing God's causal power. It is emphasizing His concern with the human situation on earth, a concern initially manifested in God's compassion for Adam's loneliness in the Garden of Eden. This concern calls for a free human response.

There is, then, a fundamental difference between the authority God makes manifest in His decrees determining the mechanism of nature and the authority He makes manifest in His decrees directed to man, an essentially free, moral person. To marry and raise a family is not just an instinct God has built into human nature as He has built it into animal nature. This is why the command, "Be fruitful and increase" (Gen. 1:28), is repeated after God's unique creation of man. It is not something man automatically inherits with his physical constitution. This is why man requires a specifically human mate. "And the Lord God said, 'It is not good for man to be alone; I will make Him a helper according to his nature [*k'negdo*]' " (Gen. 2:18).[36]

Marriage, therefore, is a specific commandment to man based on the two statements in the first and second chapters of Genesis.[37] It is a mitzvah that man must freely carry out.

Here is where the Halakhah tempers the excesses of the Aggadah. For a mitzvah is grounded in God's concern for His uniquely free creation—man. Because human freedom is man's immanent dignity, it is the condition making a commandment from God to man possible. There could be no commandment without human freedom as its *conditio sine qua non.*[38] Man cannot participate in God's transcendent order as an automaton and still be man. Man's upholding of the commandment of God, in this case the commandment to marry a woman truly suited to his nature, enables him to freely participate in a reality that transcends the limits of human power and control.

The *grounding* of the commandment in a reality comprehended by God alone is what the Aggadah is emphasizing. Because this aspect of the mitzvah is beyond man's control it cannot be described by the usual means of ratiocination. It can only be apprehended through that aspect of man's nature which is also not under his control—his imagination. This is the greatness, I believe, of the seemingly unstructured and impressionistic theological method of the Aggadah. It attempts to apprehend the incomprehensible with the only appropriate means for such an endeavor, the imagination, whose vitality comes from the incomprehensible recesses of the unconscious. The significance of marriage as participation in God's transcendent order is what is emphasized here. The Aggadah portrays how any caprice in this relationship is destructive.[39]

The mitzvah, therefore, has two factors: (1) an aggadic factor emphasizing the *transcendent ground* of the commandment in a realm beyond man's comprehension; (2) a halakhic factor emphasizing the *immanent condition* of the commandment—human freedom. And, moreover, the important thing to bear in mind is that the immanent factor, the legal perspective, is taken into consideration before the transcendent factor, the theological perspective. Halakhah takes practical precedence over Aggadah.[40]

The Halakhah permits divorce. What the aggadic factor, the theological model, emphasizes, however, is that this freedom is for the sake of a reality beyond its grasp. Freedom is not an end in itself. Thus, if the fuller meaning of the commandment is apprehended, there can be only one true ground for divorce—namely, an act that essentially contradicts the meaning of that commandment. Since the fuller meaning of the commandment is not only to marry, but to marry one with whom one can fully respond to God's faithful concern,[41] the grounds for divorce must be the exact negation of the grounds for marriage; that is, unfaithfulness, adultery. This is what the School of Shammai is teaching us.[42]

This is why, it seems to me, the prophets compared the relationship between God and His people with the relationship between husband and wife. A Jew sinfully denies God's faithfulness by being unfaithful either to God Himself *or* to the people of Israel. Faithfulness to God, which could be called "transcendental faithfulness," is the ground of the faithfulness to one's covenanted fellow, which could be called "immanent faithfulness," whether that fellow is one's fellow Jew or one's spouse. God is not so much compared to man as man is commanded to imitate God.

Without God's faithfulness as the prior standard, interhuman faithfulness would have no real grounding. For faithfulness implies a constant presence: one must act as if the partner were always there. But the human partner is not always there. The body and its individual needs make mutual absence at times inevitable, just as the mind's limited powers of concentration make mutual mental absence, inattention, at times inevitable. Only God, who reveals Himself as unlimited, is constantly present. His presence alone is the only possible ground of total faithfulness in creation.[43] Therefore, man is only commanded to participate in God's faithfulness, not to equal it. God's faithfulness (*emunah*) is unilateral. It continues despite man's repeated lack of response to it. Man's faithfulness to his fellow, on the other hand, is mutual; it requires mutual inner-participation in order to participate in the transcendent ground.[44] That is why a man is to divorce his adulterous wife, even though God does not divorce his adulterous people. "Thus says the Lord, 'Where is your mother's bill of divorcement with which I sent her away?' " (Isa. 50:1).[45]

In terms of the practice of the rabbi, an understanding of the relation of Halakhah and Aggadah in Jewish marriage and divorce ought to affect his role in these cases. On the one hand, the Halakhah is according to the School of Hillel and the rabbi cannot refuse to grant a get if there are any objective grounds whatsoever. There is a certain practical wisdom, it seems to me, in the Hillelite law over and above its exegetical underpinnings. If we only granted divorces in cases of adultery, the theological desideratum, then we might very well find that unscrupulous couples would actually stage semipublic acts of adultery in order to create the grounds for divorce. We all know that such practices were not at all uncommon in New York State before the repeal of its "adultery only" divorce laws.

Nevertheless, despite the technicalities of divorce being Hillelite, ought not the intelligent exposition of both divorce and marriage be Shammaite? It seems to me that the proper understanding of the relation of law and theology in matters of *gittin v'kiddushin* ought to motivate the rabbi not only to emphasize the immanent element of free choice in the ceremonies of marriage and divorce, which is the halakhic requirement, but to be equally motivated to emphasize the transcendent element of faithfulness as grounded in God's faithfulness. In other words, the aggadic dimension requires the rabbi to make the very ceremony of marriage be seen by its participants as an act most pleasing to God, a true celebration of faithfulness. And this same aggadic dimension requires the rabbi to make the ceremony of divorce be seen by its participants as an act most abhorrent to God, a true tragedy of unfaithfulness: if not to each other by an act of adultery, then to God, in that the marriage partners took the divinely grounded covenant too lightly.

The judgment as to how to carry out the commandment, in both its legal and theological aspects, cannot be generally made. Every situation calls for a specific judgment made in awareness of the particular circumstances of the parties involved. This is what the rabbi's learning and piety ought to prepare him for. However, once understanding is arrived at, intelligent judgment cannot very well be avoided. The very nature of the rabbinical vocation calls upon the rabbi to become a practical philosopher of Judaism. This is why the responsibility is so awesome. For without the precise perspective of Halakhah, without the insightful perspective of Aggadah, and without the philosophical understanding of their interrelationship, how can one discover the true intent of the words of the Living God?

CHAPTER 2

WHO HAS NOT MADE ME A WOMAN

Question: IN A TIME WHEN MANY WOMEN are demanding liberation from traditional roles they believe to be degrading, and when they regard the source of this degradation to be traditional conceptions about them, it is inevitable that the Jewish liturgy would come under scrutiny. For among the blessings recited at the beginning of each morning service, there is the one prescribed for men, which states: "Blessed art Thou, O Lord our God, King of the universe, Who has not made me a woman." Is this not insulting to the entire female sex? Is it indicative of Judaism's attitude towards women?

Answer: As was explained in the preceding chapter, Judaism expresses itself in two forms: Halakhah (law) and Aggadah (speculative thought). Halakhah is normative; that is, the community always decided which legal opinions were binding on its members and which were not. Aggadah, on the other hand, is mostly nonnormative; that is, an opinion could be accepted or rejected as one saw fit.[1] Only certain aggadic opinions became binding on the whole community as *dogmas*. The thirteen principles of faith which Maimonides (d. 1205) spelled out in his commentary to the mishnaic tractate *Sanhedrin*, and which were later presented in the popular hymn Yigdal, are such binding dogmas. Thus, within the framework of traditional Judaism, no one could deny such dogmas as the existence of God, the revelation of the Torah, and the resurrection of the dead, although varying interpretations were always possible and acceptable.[2]

This distinction is important to bear in mind when dealing with such a question as the Jewish attitude towards women. In the Aggadah there

15

are many different opinions expressed about women. Some are highly
flattering; others are highly insulting. Nevertheless, despite the fact that
aggadic speculation most certainly had a very important influence on
Jewish law, it does not itself have the force of law; that is, it is not
binding on the community. Therefore, Jewish apologists are unconvincing if they attempt to present "the Jewish view of women" by quoting
such aggadic accolades as, "A righteous woman was married to a wicked
man and made him righteous, thus showing that everything depends
on the woman."[3] This is unconvincing because it is just one case (ma'seh)
and is not necessarily of universal applicability. Furthermore, it does
not give women any special rights.

On the other hand, feminists are equally unconvincing if they quote
such statements as, "Women are to kindle lights for the Sabbath because
Adam was the light of the world, for 'the light of God is the soul of
man [adam]' [Prov. 20:27], and Eve contributed [g'ramah] to his death.
Therefore, the mitzvah of kindling lights for the Sabbath was given
to women."[4] This is also unconvincing because Maimonides states that
both men and women are to kindle lights for the Sabbath, but the mitzvah
is more feminine because women are usually in charge of the home.[5]
Furthermore, if a woman is not at home, the man must kindle the
lights. It would seem that Maimonides' reason is the essential one and
that the Palestinian Talmud is engaging in speculation.

At a time when the role of women is being widely discussed, a serious
consideration of the place of women in Judaism would benefit from
an examination of the legal sources. Inasmuch as we are bound by the
Halakhah, we are responsible for its positions. However, we are not
responsible for the speculative opinions of individual sages, no matter
how appealing or unappealing they may be. This point was most convinc-
ingly made by Nahmanides (d. 1270) in his famous debate with the
apostate, Pablo Christiani.[6] As the late Professor Louis Ginzberg wrote:
"It is only in the Halakah that we find the mind and character of the
Jewish people exactly and adequately expressed."[7]

In all the many legal discussions in the Talmud concerning the role
of women, two major principles go to the heart of the question before
us. One of these principles concerns criminal and civil procedure; the
other concerns ritual matters.

Concerning civil and criminal rights and responsibility, the Talmud
stated that the Torah made men and women "equal" (hishva haKatub)
in all matters of (1) personal liability (onshin), (2) civil liability (dinin),
and (3) capital punishment (meetot).[8] The same applied if the woman
were the victim of violations in any of these areas of law. Thus women

could function equally in that area where "equality" is a meaningful concept. This is especially true in the economic sphere because money is an abstraction from real property and equality, being a mathematical concept is also abstract.[9]   In this realm concrete sexual differences are irrelevant. Even a married woman, who was to a large extent under the economic authority of her husband, could opt for economic independence in her marriage by antenuptial agreement.[10] Even without such specific agreement, the institution of the marriage contract (*ketubah*) protected her rights. Equality in the area of criminal law is not a mathematically inspired concept but, rather, a theologically inspired concept; namely, the equality of the worth of human souls before God.[11]

However, in the ritual domain we are not dealing with either abstract or transcendental issues, but with real differences between human beings; differences which are part of the experience of everyone. Here we come across our second major principle: "For all positive commandments [*mitzvot asseh*] that are dependent on a specific time, men are obligated and women are exempt [*peturot*]."[12] In fact, in the talmudic text we quoted about the role of women in civil and criminal law, it is stated, "A man is involved in commandments [*bar mitzvah*]; a woman is not [*lav bat mitzvah*]." The "commandments" spoken of are, of course, positive commandments.

Both men and women are held responsible for all negative commandments. Thus, for example, men and women may not desecrate the Sabbath or eat forbidden foods. Moreover, women are responsible for positive commandments having no time specification, such as love of God, honor of parents, and giving charity.

Some have held that the reason women are exempt from many commandments is due to the fact that they are often busy with household duties and caring for children, activities which are unpredictable in their demands.[13] In other words, women have little and irregular leisure. My own opinion is that this exclusion is due to a much deeper fact —namely, that time is different for women and for men in that women "tell time" by the feminine rhythm of their bodies. There is a whole area of exclusively feminine law dealing with this (*niddah*). A false sense of prudery today removes this area of Judaism from the thoughtful analysis it deserves. Men are men and women are women—*Vive la différence!* as the French say.

Nevertheless, there are so many exceptions to this rule that the Talmud takes it to be a general description (*k'lalut*), which one cannot use to draw any specific conclusions. For example, women are obligated to eat matzah on the first night of Passover even though this commandment has a specific time.[14] Maimonides requires women to pray informally, but whenever they choose.[15] In terms of the formal prayer services, women are not obligated to participate, although the option (reshut) is theirs if they so choose. There are several other exceptions to this "rule."[16]

However, the area of greatest interest concerns those laws where women were originally excluded and by their own persuasive efforts convinced the men in power that their rights required changes in the law.

The earliest example of this is in Scripture. The daughters of Zelophehad petitioned Moses to inherit the property of their father, who did without male children. Moses took their case before God, who approved their petition (Num. 27:1-11). However, since God's reasons are not humanly known, His thoughts are not ours (Isa.55:8-9); this may not be a valid precedent.[17]

"Women's Liberation," namely, demanding and getting changes in accepted traditions, has definite precedent in the Talmud, which is a humanly written work.

> It is taught that Michal, daughter of King Saul, used to put on tefillin and the sages did not stop her, and that the wife of the prophet Jonah used to make the Festival pilgrimage [olah l'regel] and the sages did not stop her . . . because they probably held the opinion of R. Jose who taught that women had the option [reshut] to do so if they wanted.[18]

The reason R. Jose gave for the compliance of the sages is that they wanted to "please" (nahat ruah) the women.[19] Obviously they did so because they accepted the women's motivation as sincere and pure.[20] On the basis of this, Rabbenu Tam (d. 1171), the leader of Franco-German Jewry, permitted greater female participation in religious services, even though he had some difficulty in reconciling this with strict precedent. He held that women could not only perform male commandments, but could also recite the blessing and this was not to be considered "taking the Lord's Name in vain."[21]

In the Temple at Jerusalem men and women sat separately on all occasions. The Talmud sees the reason for this in that frivolity (kalut rosh) was to be strenuously avoided.[22] For the same reason women were not called to the Torah—it was considered undignified for a woman to parade herself in front of a male gathering.[23] Nevertheless, on Yom Kippur day the High Pirest read the Torah portion, according to Rab Hisda, in the women's section (ezrat nashim). The reason for Rab Hisda's opinion is that the sources seem to indicate that the High Priest was sitting just before reading the Torah, and sitting was only permitted in the women's section.[24] However, could this not be another example of a practice designed to please women? For this reason I permitted, in the face of some opposition, the Torah to be carried through the women's section of my synagogue on the Sabbath and Festivals.

With this background we can now intelligently examine the blessing, "Who has not made me a woman."

The blessing is one of three negative blessings whereby a man thanks God for not having made him (1) a non-Jew, (2) a slave, and (3) a woman. What do non-Jews, slaves, and women have in common? All of them have fewer religious obligations than adult Jewish males. Non-Jews are only bound to keep the seven moral laws of Noah.[25] Slaves—that is, non-Jewish slaves of Jews—were required to keep all negative commandments and all positive commandments not connected with a specific time.[26] Therefore, by negation, the adult male Jew thanks God for his status.

Nevertheless, women and slaves, who are both considered to be under the authority of someone else, are to say, 'Blessed art Thou, O Lord our God, King of the universe, Who has made me according to His will [she'asani kirtzono]." As one male author puts it, "It is as our sages said that one should bless God for the bad as well as the good."[27] Another male author wrote, "Even though she is a full Jewess, she is excempt from the study of the Torah and from positive commandments dependent on a specific time."[28]

All of these apologetics, none of them by women, would be unnecessary, however, if the man would simply say, "Blessed art Thou, O Lord our God, King of the universe, Who has made me a Jew [she'asani yisrael]." This formula implies one is not a non-Jew, a slave, or a woman, without actually specifying anything that might be explicitly offensive. The late historian, Abraham Berliner (d. 1915), urged the adoption of this reading and argued that if this were done no apologies would be required for the offending blessing.[29]

Of course, to actually change the text of the prayerbook is not for one rabbi or group of rabbis to undertake. As Dr. Philip Birnbaum, an eminent Jewish liturgist, wrote in the introduction to his edition of the traditional Ashkenazic prayerbook:

> The Siddur should never become a source of contention among any segments of our people. . . . Editors of the Siddur should not take liberties with the original, eliminating a phrase here

and adding one there, each according to his own beliefs. Such a procedure is liable to breed as many different kinds of public worship as there are synagogues and temples. The danger of rising sects is obvious, sects that are likely to weaken still more our harassed people.[30]

However, I would suggest the following procedure. If this blessing is really offensive to Jewish women, and I have never met even a pious woman who could honestly accept it, they ought to insist it not be read. Such omissions (*sheb v'al taaseh*) were accepted when human dignity (*kabod haberiyot*) was at stake.[31] Certain far more important Jewish religious institutions were modified in the face of popular Jewish needs.[32] If the Jewish people are not prophets they are the children of prophets;[33] that is, when the Jewish people are sincerely striving to do God's will, their practices and aspirations have a degree of sanctity. If today's Jewish woman desires greater participation in religious life, then statements offensive to her ought to be played down. After all, for the sake of peace between a man and woman, God Himself modified a statement in the Torah.

> Bar Kappara said that peace is so great that something was contrived [*b'duyyim*] to bring about peace between Abraham and Sarah. . . . Scripture did not quote Sarah's exact words, "My husband is too old" [Gen. 18:12] to Abraham, but it said, "I am too old" [Gen. 18:13].[34]

At that time a statement was changed that insulted Abraham; today we have a statement that surely insults Sarah.[35]

CHAPTER 3

RIDING ON THE SABBATH

THERE WAS A TIME IN JEWISH HISTORY when it was assumed that the vast majority of Jews kept the Sabbath. The effects of this collective Sabbath not only extended to human lives but even to the natural world. There are stories about rivers that would not flow on the Sabbath and oxen who behaved towards the human beings around them differently on the Sabbath than on any other day.[1]

Today the Sabbath-observer is in a minority. Although it is true that many contemporary Jews have partial Sabbath experiences, whether synagogue attendance, lighting candles, or eating special foods, fewer have experienced what the prophet described:

> If because of the Sabbath you turn away your foot from pursu-
> ing your business on My holy day, and you call the Sabbath
> a delight and make it honored . . . then shall you find delight
> in the Lord . . . (Isa. 58:13-14)

The reasons for the weakening of Sabbath-observance, especially among modern American Jews, are seemingly economic and demographic.

Earlier in this century, when large masses of Jews were immigrating to this country from Eastern Europe, economic conditions made Sabbath-observance an extreme hardship for many of these people. With the breakup of the semiautonomous communities in which these Jews had lived for centuries, the centrifugal forces of emancipation had economic as well as religious and cultural consequences. In Europe Jewish artisans and petty traders to a large extent controlled the market in which they operated. The non-Jewish peasants came to them. Thus the economic

21

patterns of life were a function of the community as a whole, a community regulated by Jewish religious norms. In America these Jews were thrown into an open-market situation controlled by economic and cultural forces outside their community. As such they now had to go to the non-Jewish world to sell their goods and services.

However, the phenomenon of the American five-day week, although not affecting such occupations as retailing, has indeed affected many other Jews, especially with the gradual broadening of the occupational involvement of American Jews. Most people are no longer required to work on Saturday.

Nevertheless, as regards Sabbath-observance, the lessening of the economic problem has almost simultaneously coincided with the development of a demographic problem. With the availability of the automobile to virtually every American family, housing patterns have arisen that have all but eliminated walking as a practical means of locomotion in a community. Religious considerations aside, how many suburban housing-developments have sidewalks? Therefore, the notion of "neighborhood" as previously understood has been radically altered. Most modern synagogues serving suburban areas are beyond reasonable walking distance for a large number of their members. This is why the question about riding on the Sabbath is probably asked more often than any other question of Sabbath-observance. Indeed, the popular definition of a "Sabbath-keeper" (*shomer shabbat*) is usually expressed in terms of, "Does he or she ride on the Sabbath or not?"

Question: What is the source of the prohibition of riding on the Sabbath?
Answer: In Jewish law there are two irreducible sources of perennial authority: (1) the Written Torah, the Pentateuch; (2) the Oral Torah, the traditions ascribed to Moses (*halakhot*), which were kept *as if* written in the Torah, even though their specific prescription could not be found in the text of the Pentateuch.[2] These two sources were always regarded by normative Judaism as revelations of God's will.

All other legislation is secondary. It has had to justify itself as either: (1) direct interpretation of Scripture (*derash*); (2) indirect interpretation of Scripture (*asmakhta*); (3) protection of scriptural laws by "fencing" them with additional laws (*gezerot*); or (4) adjustment of specific laws in the interest of greater priorities (*takkanot*).

In the area of Sabbath-observance, the Mishnah classifies thirty-nine specific acts (*abot melekhah*) as subsets of the general prohibition: "On the seventh day, a Sabbath unto the Lord your God, you shall do no work . . . " (Exod. 20:10).[3] These thirty-nine acts were determined by carefully analyzing the different kinds of labor involved in the building of the Sanctuary (*mishkan*) in the wilderness under the direction of Moses. Since the penalty for working on the Sabbath is directly juxtaposed (*semukhim*) in the Torah to the detailed description of the building of the Sanctuary, the rabbis concluded that this was meant to specify just what the Torah meant by "work" in relation to the Sabbath.[4]

Furthermore, the juxtaposition accomplished two things: (1) It demonstrated that the Sabbath as a "Sanctuary in time" had priority over the building of the physical Sanctuary in space. As important as the building of the Sanctuary was, it did not surpass the observance of the Sabbath. This idea was profoundly developed by my late revered teacher, Professor A. J. Heschel, in his book, *The Sabbath*.[5] (2) It established an objective historical criterion for work, which applied to all Jews since the entire people of Israel, men and women, participated in the building of the Sanctuary (Exod. 35:25-26). The only other criterion would be the highly subjective category, "exertion," which would obviously vary from individual to individual. The Sabbath was meant to be a social institution.

Nevertheless, our sages, although using a historical criterion, were interpreting a law whose source is transhistorical. Despite the fact that the labors involved in the building of the wilderness Sanctuary are the paradigm for the labors prohibited on the Sabbath, there was certainly a recognition that the situation in the wilderness was not in every respect identical with subsequent Jewish history.[6]

The revelation of the law in a particular time and place might very well influence its initial meaning, but it certainly did not confine its ultimate meaning. As the Torah states, ". . . from the day the Lord commanded and henceforth for your generations" (Num. 15:23).[7] To limit the prohibition of work only to labors performed in the Sanctuary would have the effect of relativizing the concept of work on the Sabbath. Such limitation would shrink the hegemony of the law with each new technological innovation or change. Therefore, derivative acts (*toldot*), which are clearly related to the primary acts (*abot*), although not in themselves identifiable with the construction of the Sanctuary in the wilderness, were also prohibited.[8] Since the number of such derivative acts is potentially infinite, their affirmation saves the hegemony of the law from becoming contingent on historical circumstance. Thus the principles of the law, in our case the Sabbath law, are seen as transcending *any* finite period *within* Jewish history, and, therefore, are applicable to *all* Jewish history.

Now there is no specific prohibition of riding on the Sabbath in either of the primary sources of Jewish law. In other words, there is no explicit "You shall not ride on the Sabbath" in either Torah or tradition. Therefore, the prohibition of riding is either a derived prohibition (*toldah*), or a rabbinic "fence" built to protect the Sabbath (*gezerah*).

1. *Automobile Driving*

The first case of riding to be considered is that of driving an automobile, since this is the most common way most of us ride today. Driving an automobile, although obviously not directly prohibited in sources first published centuries ago, involves three main areas with which the sources most definitely did deal: (1) combustion of fuel; (2) locomotion over distances not normally covered by walking; (3) various preparations required for travel.

Concerning combustion of fuel the Written Torah states, "You shall not kindle fire in any of your dwelling places on the Sabbath day" (Exod. 35:3) "Dwelling places" refers to anywhere one happens to be.[9] Every time one starts his automobile he is igniting the gasoline in the motor.

In 1950 three members of the Rabbinical Assembly presented a responsum that attempted to legally justify riding on the Sabbath, if one's destination were the synagogue. The responsum created a sensation within the Conservative rabbinate and far beyond. What is much less known, however, is that dissenting papers were prepared by Dr. Robert Gordis and Dr. Ben Zion Bokser.[10] These papers, learned and well written though they were, did not really show the halakhic fallacy upon which this whole dispensation (*heter*) was based. They were, rather, elaborations of the dissenters' theological objections.

Since I was only eight years old in June of 1950, I was not personally involved in the heated discussions that accompanied this responsum or the *ad hominem* attacks that were inevitable in such a charged atmosphere. Therefore, I believe that I can be more objective than my predecessors of twenty-three years ago in showing the fallacy of permitting riding on the Sabbath, especially driving an automobile.

The three rabbis (Dr. Jacob B. Agus, Dr. Theodore Friedman, and the late R. Morris Adler) argued that kindling is only prohibited when there is a need for it *as there was a need for it in the construction of the Sanctuary.* Since combustion for energy was not needed in the building of the Sanctuary, this analogy would rule that combustion for energy is not a prohibited form of kindling on the Sabbath. This is presented as the view of the Tanna, R. Simon, as interpreted by R. Isaac the Elder (Ri)[11]

> The combustion of gasoline to produce power is a type of work that obviously could not have been prohibited before its invention. All acts of burning are prohibited only when

performed for specially described purposes such as: cooking, heating, lighting or the need of its ashes. Burning for the sake of power was not included in this list . . . . The combustion of gas in the carburator is therefore the type of work classed as *m'lachah shaina tz'richah l'gufa* [work not needed for itself] . . .[12]

This reasoning is halakhically inadmissible for the following reasons:
1. Even if this is a correct interpretation of the position of R. Simon, the law is not according to him.[13]
2. Even according to R. Simon the act is certainly rabbinically prohibited (*assur*) even if not actually liable according to scriptural law (*patur*).[14]
3. R. Simon's view concerns removing something on the Sabbath for a negative rather than a positive purpose. Rashi states:

> It is an act not performed for its own sake, but only to remove something from the actor . . . for it did not come to him out of choice and he had no need of it, therefore it is not a premediated act [*melekhet mahshabat*] according to R. Simon.[15]

Thus, according to Rashi, even R. Simon would hold that any act performed for a positive purpose is scripturally prohibited (*hayyab*).
4. The Tosafists point out that an act was prohibited when it was done to accomplish something that would not have existed before (*l'taken yoter mimah shehayah batehilah*).[16] Unless one accepts the position of the ancient Greek physicist Zeno that locomotion does not exist, a position successfully refuted by Aristotle, igniting an engine to drive an automobile certainly accomplishes something.[17]
5. Moreover, it should be noted that even though the Mishnah holds that only *constructive* acts violate the Sabbath in the scriptural sense (*d'oraita*), the Talmud includes one who injures a fellow man where injury, a negative act, is the motive. Maimonides holds that the reason for this is that the person did something positive; namely, he appeased his anger.[18] Therefore, a seemingly negative act had a positive end (*veharay hu k'metaken*). If a purely subjective state of mind is considered a positive end, how much more is combustion for the sake of locomotion, which is an objective fact?
6. It is surprising that these rabbis, who so emphasized that the Halakhah was never "a frigid and frozen mold,"[19] should base their reasoning on a view that, if accepted at face value, would rule out

any expansion, which is a positive aspect of the development of the Halakhah. As often happens, extremes look alike. What looks like progress is at times regression.

In short, this whole line of reasoning is unacceptable because it violates the two cardinal principles of all reasoning: the principle of contradiction and the principle of sufficient reason. The position of the three rabbis contradicts itself on the one hand by calling for the development of Jewish law, and on the other hand by presenting a standard that would make the definition of work dependent on conditions in the time of Moses. And their position is based on an insufficient use of the sources, in that they present a minority interpretation of a minority opinion.[20]

As regards combustion for the sake of locomotion, if it is not "kindling" (habarah) in the original sense (ab), then it is certainly "kindling" in the derived sense (toldah).[21] Practically, there is no difference between the two. The only difference between the two categories concerns the sacrifices brought for their unwitting (shegagah) transgression.[22] The sacrificial system has been inoperative for almost two thousand years.

2. Riding in a Vehicle Driven by Someone Else

The next question involved in riding on the Sabbath is the matter of traveling distances not normally covered by walking. The Torah states, "Let everyone remain in his place; let no one go out from his place on the seventh day" (Exod. 16:29). Now what is considered a person's place (mekomo)?

The Karaites, a group of Jewish biblical literalists, over a thousand years ago interpreted this verse to mean that on the Sabbath one's place is restricted to home and synagogue.[23] However, in the rabbinic tradition, of which we are the heirs, one's place is interpreted as the normal space of one's community and its outlying areas. These were determined to be the limits of one's city plus two thousand cubits (three thousand feet, or approximately a half-mile).[24] This area is known as the tehum. If one wanted to walk beyond this distance he had to make special provision (erub) for the extension of this limit another two thousand cubits in any given direction.[25] Because of the great areas of space covered by our metropolitan communities, this is rarely a problem today. Nevertheless, I remember the son of Grand Rabbin Fuchs of Lorraine telling me that his father has to make this special provision regularly in order to travel on foot from his seat in Colmar to visit outlying towns on the Sabbath.

We can thus see that the intention of the law is to keep one in the vicinity of his or her own neighborhood—"neighborhood" being the area of normal walking distance.

However, a question does arise as to the use of public transportation on the Sabbath under the following conditions: (1) the vehicle is driven by a non-Jew; (2) the vehicle makes regular stops irrespective of the presence of Jewish passengers; (3) its route is confined to the municipal limits; (4) one is not required to pay his fare on the Sabbath (or Festival).

Practically this would be a possibility if one had a pass attached to his or her clothing, enabling the person to ride on a bus, streetcar, or similar public conveyance. The late Sephardic Chief Rabbi of Israel, R. Ben Zion Uziel (d. 1954), addressed himself to this question in a responsum written over thirty-five years ago.[26] He admitted that such travel was legally permissible, especially to attend synagogue services. He pointed out that earlier prohibitions of riding were based on the fact that animals were being used to work on the Sabbath, something the Torah explicitly forbade. Nevertheless, more general theological concerns influenced him to refuse to allow this halakhic leniency in actual practice.

His main point was that the Sabbath must be kept in the spirit of the law as well as in its letter. This desire to extend the physical and spiritual rest of the Sabbath was behind the rabbinic institution of *shebut*—the prohibition of acts resembling work, even though not work in the technical legal sense. R. Uziel quotes both Maimonides and Nahmanides on this general point. More specifically, he quotes the leading nineteenth-century authority, R. Moses Schreiber of Pressburg (Hatam Sofer, d. 1839), who prohibited such travel because it creates both physical and mental tension inconsistent with the spirit of Sabbath rest.[27] Nevertheless, R. Uziel points out that the anxiety meant is that of a business trip, and this would not be the same as a trip to the synagogue for Sabbath worship. On the basis of this distinction he dismisses R. Schreiber's prohibition and permits such riding, provided the other preconditions are present. R. Uziel claims that if tension is the key factor (*gufo na ve'nad*), then travel on foot ought to be prohibited too. However, I would say that in our day the mere experience of being in traffic creates far more tension for the rider than for the pedestrian, irrespective of what his purpose in riding is.

In a subsequent edition of his responsa published twelve years later, R. Uziel emphasized to a rabbi in Bombay that anyone who "fears and trembles for the word of the Lord" ought not ride in *any* vehicle on the Sabbath and Festivals, irrespective of the conditions.[28] Why R. Uziel so abruptly changed his view is unknown to me. I can only suspect that his dispensation met with strong rabbinical opposition and that he yielded, "inclining after the majority."[29]

The problem with this kind of travel is that public transportation in our day inevitably involves direct payment and other preparations not in keeping with the Sabbath. The Talmud states, "One is not to ride on an animal on the Sabbath lest he go beyond the limits of travel [tehum] and even more so lest he cut a twig to prod the animal."[30] The limits of travel were marked for pedestrians, but, as Rashi pointed out, one riding may overlook them.[31] Furthermore, various auxiliary acts, such as carrying money, identification, and automobile-repair tools, are the modern equivalents of "cutting a twig to prod the animal." This point was brought out in the bitter criticism of several members of the Rabbinical Assembly following the presentation of the responsum of the three rabbis in 1950.[32]

Moreover, there is the problem of the Jew who drives his or her car to the synagogue on the Sabbath to attend services. Should this person be told to stay home? Here one must know who is asking the question about riding to the synagogue on the Sabbath.

If the person is already a Sabbath-observer, I do not hesitate to inform him or her not to ride to the synagogue. In one particular case, an observant man in my congregation fractured his leg before Rosh Hashanah. The only way he could attend the synagogue services to hear the blowing of the shofar was to ride. I told him that he should not ride even if this meant he would not hear the blowing of the shofar. After all, our sages prohibited the blowing of the shofar on a Rosh Hashanah coinciding with the Sabbath lest people carry the shofar.[33] In other words, the restraining sanctity of the Sabbath or Festival takes precedence even over a postive, Torah-ordained institution.[34] As it happens, God helps those who desire to do His will,[35] and the injured man heard the shofar blown in his home by a teenage member of the congregation. One can always have the full Sabbath at home even without the synagogue, but one cannot have the full Sabbath at the synagogue without the home.

On the other hand, there are many people who if told not to ride to the synagogue on the Sabbath would continue riding everywhere *but* to the synagogue. For them the synagogue's influence would be lost altogether. Therefore, it is wiser not to condemn people who are unprepared as yet to become full Sabbath-observers. As the Talmud puts it,

R. Iylaa said in the name of R. Eleazar ben R. Simon that just as one is commanded to say something which will be heard, so one is commanded not to say something which will not be heard.[36]

However, once such people begin to seriously ask about the Halakhah of riding on the Sabbath they are usually at a level where they are ready to translate the synagogue Sabbath experience into their own personal action. I know several people who came by automobile when they began attending Sabbath services. Later, as they came closer to God and the Torah, they stopped riding to services. In some cases this involved purchasing or renting a house or apartment closer to the synagogue. One chooses where to live on the basis of his or her life-priorities. If Sabbath-observance is high on the list of those priorities, one will make it his business to live in the neighborhood of the synagogue. If Sabbath-observance is not high on one's list of priorities, choice of a home will be determined by other considerations. The late Professor Louis Ginzberg (d. 1953) was entirely correct, it seems to me, in refusing to endorse innovations in Jewish Law designed to exonerate Jews "most of whom had long ago denied its authority."[37]

Finally, a fundamental spiritual problem was overlooked by those who felt that they were saving the Sabbath by permitting people to ride to the synagogue. The assumption underlying this dispensation ignores the possibility of repentance (teshubah). To tell people who are not living according to the law of the Torah that what they are doing is correct is to close the door of return in their faces. It places a "stumbling block before the blind."[38] The same is true, on the other hand, if we fail to see that riding to the synagogue, although not permissible, is spiritually on a higher level than driving to business or to a place of amusement. In other words, driving to the synagogue may be the beginning of a true return for persons who have never known any other kind of Sabbath.

In practice I have come to the following conclusions:

1. Driving an automobile is prohibited according to scriptural law in a derived sense (toldah), if not in an original sense.

2. Riding on a public conveyance where no other preparations are necessary and in a non-Jewish area is almost too remote a possibility to rule on.[39] Moreover, because of the tension and anxiety involved in any vehicular travel today, such travel is inconsistent with the spirit of the law. The whole institution of shebut (rabbinically pro-hibited activities on the Sabbath) is the practical outcome of speculating on the deeper meaning of the Sabbath.

3. Observant Jews should be warned of the prohibition of travel on the Sabbath, even in order to attend synagogue services. Nonobservant Jews should be dealt with more cautiously lest their contact with the synagogue be severed and they be further alienated from the Torah.[40]

CHAPTER 4

THE AGUNAH, OR THE CASE OF THE UNCOOPERATIVE HUSBAND

1. The Agunah Problem

NO OTHER QUESTION HAS VEXED modern students of Jewish law more than the question of the agunah or "bound wife"—that is, the woman who is still legally tied to an absent husband.

A woman can become an agunah in one of two ways.

First, a husband is lost on a trip or in battle and, although presumed dead, is not legally dead because his death has not been witnessed. In order to save the wife from becoming an agunah the rabbis ruled that virtually *anyone* could be accepted as a witness in such a case. Normally the rules of evidence were much stricter.[1] Nevertheless, a witness was still required; without one the wife would be an agunah. Easing the laws of evidence helped in some cases, but in many others it did not.

Another solution was the giving of a "conditional" (*tenay*) divorce. By this procedure a husband who knew that he might be lost in some remote or obscure place gave his wife a bill of divorce (*get*), stipulating that if he did not return within a certain period of time his wife was retroactively divorced.[2] This would help matters when the husband could either foresee the possibility of becoming lost, or was willing to take these precautions so that his wife might not become an agunah.

Despite these two protective measures, the first type of agunah will always be a Jewish problem because Jewish marriage is a sacred covenant. As a sacred covenant it presupposes the All-Presence of God even if the parties themselves are not present to each other. The presence of God is always assumed, whereas the presence of the human parties cannot always be assumed. The marital covenant transcends "living

31

together."[3] A sacred covenant is a total commitment, involving far greater risks than, let us say, a business contract where virtually every situation can be stipulated in advance. Only death or divorce severs the marital covenant.

Without this theological reality in mind, the fact that there should be an agunah problem at all would appear to be an example of immoral caprice. Although Jewish law is interpreted by humans for human situations, its sources are given by God. Many human abuses have crept into Jewish matrimonial law and we are morally obligated to correct them. Nevertheless, all our efforts must be directed towards correcting human deviations; before the law of God we can only be corrected. Therefore, before we correct human error we must accept the perfect authority of God. Laws of the Torah may be restricted by interpretation, but they can never be permanently uprooted without our being false to the Torah system as a whole.[4] Jewish moral zeal to right legal wrongs is self-defeating if it eclipses the transcendent authority of the law itself. Unfortunately, many contemporary students of the agunah problem have not recognized its full theological implications.[5]

The authority of the law itself is directly involved in the second way a woman can become an agunah.

According to Jewish law, just as marriage must be initiated under specifically religious conditions to be considered valid, so must it be terminated under specifically religious conditions. Thus the Torah states,

> If a man marries a woman . . . and she does not find favor in his eyes because he has found in her an unseemly thing, then he shall write for her a bill of divorcement and place it in her hand and send her forth from his house. (Deut. 24:1)

From this verse it is clear that it is the man's prerogative to divorce his wife. The rabbis were aware of the phenomenon of mutually given divorce. However, they rejected it from Jewish consideration, stressing the initiatory role of the Jewish husband in both marriage and divorce[6]

Nevertheless, this does not imply absolute privilege for the man. A man must have grounds for divorcing his wife.[7] Furthermore, a woman was entitled by the Torah to food, clothing, and conjugality. If the husband did not provide these marital rights, then the woman could sue for divorce by petitioning the court to *force* her husband to give her a divorce.[8] Thus we see that as long as the husband consented to give his wife her divorce, even under the pressure of a Jewish court, his own lack of initiative was not an insuperable obstacle. In other words, the court (*Bet Din*), empowered to interpret and apply Jewish law, was held to possess an authority greater than the personal privilege of an uncooperative husband.

In most cases we assume that the Jewish husband is law-abiding and will voluntarily comply with the decree of the Jewish court. If he does not, compliance is forced. The problem today is that Jews in the diaspora are part of a wider society than just the Jewish community. Anonymity and mobility enable an individual Jew to defy a Bet Din and still be able to live a normal life, socially, economically, and even religiously. Should, then, a Jewish woman have no protection from a husband who is in clear defiance of Jewish law?

This type of agunah *ought not be* and no theological justification is here possible, because in this case a divorce is *obliged*. The problem is: How do we carry out what Jewish law has *already* obliged?

A woman who refuses to accept her husband's justified get can be divorced against her will on the assumption that the court can act on her behalf *(al yeday zikkuy)*—that is, the get frees her from being an agunah. Without it she could not remarry and celibacy is looked upon as disadvantageous.[9] However, the court cannot do this for a husband who refuses to give a get to his wife either out of spite or for purposes of blackmail.[10] For should he decide to himself remarry without having given a get to his former wife, he is guilty of polygamy but not adultery. A woman who remarries without a get from her former husband is an adulteress. It is obvious that practically speaking we have before us a "double standard."

It is with this clear "loophole" in the practical power to effect a divorce *on behalf* of a woman that modern Jewish scholars have wrestled. The literature on the subject is enormous. What I propose to do is to critically analyze some of the major modern proposals. Finally, I will offer my own modest suggestion, which is not original but only a slight modification of an earlier proposal of one of my teachers. This proposal is more conservative than the others and I will present it after dealing with some of the more radical suggestions.

Any proposal should stand up to four criteria: (1) Does it comply with Jewish law? (2) Does it strengthen the sanctity of marriage? (3) Does it strengthen the unity of the Jewish people? (4) Does it offer a genuine relief to the suffering agunah?

2. *Abrogation*

The first approach to the agunah problem would be to take the path of least resistance and simply recognize that the marital bond has been severed by a civil divorce decree. Thus the American Reform movement in 1869, at their Philadelphia Conference, followed the lead of the radical German reformer, Samuel Holdheim, who in 1843 advocated just that. Led by the radical American reformer, David Einhorn, they declared,

> A judgment of divorce pronounced by a civil court has full validity also in the eyes of Judaism, if the court documents reveal that both parties to the marriage agreed to the divorce.[11]

However, this approach is based on the Reform rejection of the binding character of the law of the Torah (both Written and Oral), which for traditional Jews makes the difference between a truly objective Jewish norm and a situation where "a person does whatever is right in his own eyes" (Deut. 12: 8). Aside from the theological problem involved in denying a cardinal principle of Judaism—namely, the divine revelation of the Torah—this abrogation involves a sociological problem—namely, by allowing remarriage without a get they are sanctioning a situation whereby the children of any subsequent remarriage of the woman will be illegitimate (mamzerim) and may not marry other Jews.[12] Thus, abrogating the requirement of a get has the effect of making Reform Judaism a denomination separate from the whole Jewish people as it has historically defined itself. This is clearly the most radical solution to the problem.

As is to often the case with "easy" solutions to profound human problems, the Reform solution creates more difficulties than it solves. Many desperate traditional Jews, impatient with traditional marriage and divorce procedures, have turned to Reform rabbis. However, marriage only has meaning within the context of a community, hence the marriage formula: "Behold you are consecrated unto me *according to the law of Moses and Israel.*"

By continued adherence to this abrogation, the Reform movement, emphasizing individual desires over community norms and holding the secular realm to be authoritative in Jewish familial matters, indicates its historical origins in the Romanticism and assimilationism of the early nineteenth century. All of this has been at the expense of Jewish unity. Thus, one of the most perceptive and learned Reform theologians today, Professor Jakob J. Petuchowski of the Hebrew College in Cincinnati, recently wrote:

It is thus the Halakhah dealing with "personal status" which guarantees the underlying unity of the "holy community." But it is precisely the legislation governing "personal status" which Reform Jews and some Conservative Jews, particularly in America, have largely chosen to ignore. They . . . must be prepared to conform to the law at least in this respect. For, only if the "holy community" remains undivided on the basic level of its existence, only if there can be an unqualified acceptance of one another as fellow Jews, can there be room for differences in individual piety and congregational practice.[13]

Even more recently, certain Reform rabbis, especially in Canada, have been calling for a return to traditional marriage and divorce requirements.[14]

3. Annulment de Facto

The Reform abrogation of Jewish divorce adds to the number of agunah women *only* if we assume that Reform marriages are initially valid and, hence, that remarriages of Reform Jews after civil divorces are invalid. However, if neither their divorces *nor their marriages* are valid, then the whole problem largely evaporates as regards remarriage and the legitimacy of subsequent children. Children merely born "out of wedlock" are not illegitimate (*mamzerim*).[15] This leades us into the question of annulment as a second solution.

The Halakhah recognizes "erroneous" marriage—namely, that a marriage improperly initiated can, under certain circumstances, be annulled (*ayn kiddushin tofsin*). The marriage is declared non-existent. Thus, for example, a marriage initiated without witnesses, or where the article of value given by the groom to the bride is less than the value of a perutah, a coin of low worth, may be considered null and void. In the tractate *Kiddushin*, which is devoted almost exclusively to marital matters, numerous cases of questionable marriages are discussed, including many which seem to be terribly far-fetched.[16] However, if one remembers that an annulled marriage, unlike most marriages severed by divorce, did not entail any postmarital problems, especially the payment of the cash settlement stipulated in the marriage contract, one can see why, in an age when marriage rites were less ceremonial and more spontaneous, the grounds for an annulment rather than a divorce would be quite varied and thus more easily available.

Therefore, if many marriages can be shown to be null and void at their inception, the problem of securing a Jewish divorce from an

uncooperative husband will be less acute, inasmuch as in many cases
his cooperation, unlike for a divorce, is not required at all.

The ease with which annulments were being granted by some rabbis
prompted the great Conservative student of Jewish matrimonial law,
the late Dr. Louis M. Epstein of Boston (d. 1949), as early as 1928
to write:

> In the last few years we have heard too often of easy and
> ready relief offered to Jewish women in matrimonial difficulties
> by rabbis who have established their reputation in that
> specialized field, relief from the Jewish marriage bond by the
> annulment of their marriages ... one has a right to suspect
> some irregularity in the procedure, when he finds rabbis mak-
> ing a profession of it, and when, contrary to Jewish usage,
> they act single-handed, consult none of their colleagues, and
> publish no responsa in support of their action.[17]

Since 1928 a good deal has transpired, especially in the denomi-
nationalization of Jewish life and the erosion of the desire for
traditional Jewish marriage on the part of many Jews. Thus the question
of annulment in our time has become a question of the *auspices* under
which the marriage ceremony was conducted. The two types of marriage
most suspect have been civil marriages and Reform marriages.

In 1928 Dr. Epstein criticized the clandestine approach of those grant-
ing annulments. However, in 1961, R. Moshe Feinstein of New York,
considered one of the leading halakhic authorities in the world today,
and an acknowledged spokesman for right-wing Orthodoxy, published
a widely acclaimed collection of responsa. In this he dealt with both
civil and Reform marriages.

Concerning civil marriage, no one could hold that the formalities
of its ceremony constitute a valid Jewish marriage. The question arises
concerning the talmudic principle, "It is assumed [*hazakah*] that one
does not engage in intercourse as an act of fornication [*be'ilat zenut*]."[18]
In other words, it seems that people who are commonly known to be
living together as husband and wife are indeed married. What we have
then is a tacit recognition of common-law marriage *ex post facto*.

However, R. Feinstein is quick to point out three crucial exceptions
to this rule: (1) The assumption is only valid when it is known that
the couple is totally observant, including the laws governing sexual intimacy (*niddah*). He bases this on the opinion of R. David ibn Zimra
(Radbaz) and others.[19] (2) Intercourse, if known to have taken place for

the sake of initiating marriage, is valid, although strongly discouraged. However, since the couple *assumes* that their civil marriage is already binding, they will not regard any subsequent act of intercourse as initiating their marriage (*l'shem kiddushin*). (3) Finally, considering the sort of lives such persons lead, we cannot assume proper witnesses of their "married life" together.

Many other fine legal points are involved in R. Feinstein's responsa on the subject; however, it is his basic assumption that a marriage is only valid when the ceremony was religiously correct to begin with, or when the parties were *totally* observant of Jewish family law after the fact. In conclusion he writes:

> Practically one should try to find the husband and obtain from him a get. If this is impossible one may permit the woman to remarry without a get. But if the woman does not accept upon herself the laws governing sexual intimacy we should not become involved so that in the end we are helping a transgressor ... [20]

Concerning Reform marriage R. Feinstein basically presents the same arguments. However, he is even more vehement in his disapproval.

> It is clear and evident ... that every Reform rabbi does what he pleases and says it is "marriage" [*kiddushin*] ... even if there were valid witnesses present ... they are not witnesses to a marriage conducted according to the Torah.[21]

Of course, R. Feinstein has saved many Jewish women from being in the category of agunah. Furthermore, no one could question his mastery of the rabbinic sources. Nevertheless, what do his responsa do for the sanctity of marriage and the unity of the Jewish people?

The problem today is far broader than whether Jewish women observe the laws governing sexual intimacy, or even whether the marriage ceremony is conducted properly with valid witnesses. The problem today is that many persons, especially the young, who are most likely to marry, are opting for relationships that are nonmarital by anyone's standards. They believe formal marriage ties entail more difficulties than rewards. Therefore, any marriage, whether civil or Reform, no matter what the halakhic inadequacies, is better than no marriage at all. Automatically annulling two whole categories of marriage in which many Jews are bound will not bring such Jews to a realization that they must have a proper Jewish marriage—instead, it will drive them further away into complete sexual anarchy. Rather than do this, we should recognize the validity of both types of marriages *ex post facto* and encourage the parties to further ground their marriage by having a traditional Jewish marriage ceremony and *all* that it implies. I have done this on several occasions with couples with whom I had become close. Of course, no one would make this an impediment to helping an individual woman overcome the sorrow of being an agunah. However, to annul what many Jews believe is better and holier than "living together" can only make sexual anarchy more attractive and encourage worse transgressions such as intermarriage, which threatens the very survival of the Jewish people. Moreover, how ironic it is that R. Feinstein and the Reform movement, practically speaking, come to the same conclusion, albeit for different reasons—namely, that both Reform and civil marriages do not need Jewish divorces![22]

A leading Conservative halakhist, Dr. Isaac Klein of Buffalo, long ago wrote about the acceptance of common-law marriages only for "proper" people (*kasherim*)—that is, people who are fully observant Jews:

> It is obvious that we cannot adhere to this criterion today not only among those who dispense with religious marriage, but also among those who are very scrupulous that the marriage be performed strictly according to the requirements of Jewish law. Our experience is that the moral standards of those who have become united through civil marriage . . . compare favorably with the standards of those who have had the benefit of a religious ceremony.
> According to the law, then, our decision is that in the case of civil marriage, a *get* is necessary.[23]

Dr. Klein is willing to make exceptions in agunah cases, but there are other issues besides the agunah problem. It is with these issues that he, like his predecessor. Dr. Epstein, deals as well. The main point is that those having civil or Reform marriages are not doing so for the sake of "fornication" (*be'ilat zenut*). The moral climate of our times, unfortunately, is very much like the moral climate before the giving of the Torah, as described by Maimonides; that is, those who engage in nonmarital sex can do so without any "formalities" at all![24]

Finally, concerning civil marriages only, an interesting new approach was proposed by the late Dr. Jehiel J. Weinberg (d. 1966), formerly rector of the Orthodox Rabbinical Seminary in Berlin.

After briefly reviewing the various opinions, both those requiring a get and those that do not, he quotes Maimonides, who reiterates the talmudic teaching that Noahides—that is, humanity in general—are responsible for the sin of adultery (*arayot*). Since divorce is a legitimate non-Jewish institution, when does it take effect for non-Jews? In other words, when is a Noahide woman still married so that any subsequent liaison is adulterous, and when is any subsequent liaison legitimate because she is a divorcee?

> When is someone else's wife [*eshet habero*] like our divorcee [*gerushah*]? It is when she is removed from his house and is sent on her own [*l'atzmah*].[25]

Now according to Dr Weinberg, non-Jewish marriage is a civil matter and not marriage in the Jewish sense (*ishut*). He classifies a Jewish woman civilly married as a "concubine" (*pilegesh*), and as such, he says, she is on no higher level than a non-Jewish wife of a non-Jewish man. Therefore, if formal separation (*perishah*)—that is, civil divorce—is sufficient to terminate a non-Jewish marriage, then it ought to be sufficient to terminate a civil marriage between two Jews.[26]

This argument he presents against the late R. Joseph Rosen of Dvinsk (Rogochover Gaon, d. 1936), who held that civil marriages require a get on Jewish civil as well as Jewish matrimonial grounds. However, the point is of more than technical value alone, for it reflects a tacit recognition (although not approval) of the legal reality of a secular system of marriage, initiated and terminated on its own grounds. Thus we have a middle ground between liaisons that are obvious fornication, on the one hand, and the sanctity of Jewish marriage (*kiddushin*) on the other hand. Of course concerning Reform marriages this line of reasoning could not be followed because these marriages are religious not civil. Indeed, in another responsum Dr. Weinberg was much more conservative in dealing with them.[27]

Practically, Dr. Weinberg urged that such civil marriages be annulled before three outstanding experts. He suggested that the late Dr. Isaac H. Herzog (d. 1958), the Ashkenazi Chief Rabbi of Israel, use his position of preeminence in Jewry to convene a court to handle such matters.

4. Annulment de Jure

The type of annulment heretofore dealt with has concerned marriages improperly initiated. I have called this annulment *de facto* because, not

only does the law in principle make such annulments possible, but there
are numerous rabbinic precedents for this as a practical legal measure.
However, there have been suggestions that the power of annulment
be extended to include marriages *properly* initiated but *improperly* terminated; that is, by a civil divorce only.

In 1951, the President of Conservative Judaism's Rabbinical Assembly,
R. David Aronson of Minneapolis, made the following suggestion:

> ... in the very form of the marriage formula the man accepts
> the condition that the rabbis have the power to determine the
> form of divorce. In other words, the rabbinic authority to reg-
> ulate the marital status, in its inception and termination, is
> one and indivisible. As the authority includes the power to
> determine the forms of marriage it will validate, so it has the
> power to determine the forms of divorce.[28]

> ... it is essential that the right to initiate divorce proceedings,
> presumed to be the prerogative of the husband, be vested in
> a rabbinic court.[29]

In a learned and well-written article published in 1970, Dr. Simon
Greenberg, Vice-Chancellor of the Jewish Theological Seminary in New
York, elaborated on the notion of annulment (*afka'at kiddushin*), coming
to much the same conclusions as R. Aronson.[30]

However, let us look at the talmudic background for this type of
annulment.

The principle, "The rabbis removed the bond of marriage from him,"
is found in six places in the Talmud. Nevertheless, we can narrow the
discussion down to four cases, and these four cases, in turn, down to
two fundamental acts.

In one instance we are dealing with a case where a man kidnapped
a young bride and betrothed her before her wedding with another man.[31]
In the other instance a man kidnapped a woman and by torture forced
her to consent to marriage with him.[32] Both situations constitute one
case. The rabbis annulled the "marriages." Here, however, since the
marriages were improperly initiated, we simply have two more examples
of annulment *de facto*. In this spirit, the thirteenth-century French authority, R. Isaac ben Sheshet (Ribash), goes so far as to suggest,

> Where a community agreed that no one could initiate marriage
> without the consent of the leaders of the community . . . if some-
> one violated that ruling his marriage is null and void.[33]

Nevertheless, this is only a theoretical suggestion and R. Isaac explicitly states that without universal consent he himself would not put it into actual practice.

The second type of annulment involving the principle of *afka'at kiddushin* involves a situation where a man nullified his divorce to his wife *after* he had sent it to her through an agent. Rabban Gamliel the Elder ordered that this practice, although scripturally permitted, be prohibited for the sake of the common good (*tikkun ha'olam*). If left unchecked it would certainly wreak havoc with the whole system of Jewish divorce.[34] The Talmud subsequently asked how the court of Rabban Gamliel could remove a scripturally based right. The answer given is that marriage and divorce are subject to rabbinical supervision (*adaata d'rabbanan*).[35] This means that just as marriage must be *initiated* under rabbinically approved methods, so divorce must follow the same sort of procedure. By nullifying his get the husband defied rabbinic authority. The validity of the original marriage is not the precipitating cause of this annulment.[36] Therefore, the nullification of the get is invalid and the divorce stands. In other words, we have here a support for rabbinically supervised and approved divorce. This is anything but an institution of annulment *de jure*, for it is definitely *not* an annulment in *place of a divorce*.

The rabbis also refused to nullify a conditional divorce when the man wanted to break the condition but was accidently prevented from doing so (*ayn ones b'get*).[37]

Of course, if the court has the right to declare the article of value (*kessef kiddushin*) null and void (*hefker*) long after the actual transfer, then theoretically it can annul *any* marriage it chooses to annul. Nevertheless, in the light of the talmudic examples of *afka'at kiddushin* it is understandable why both R. Joseph Karo and R. Moses Isserles in effect ruled this out of practical consideration.[38] If this has been the accepted opinion, even about marriages initiated under questionable circumstances, then certainly annulment of marriages properly initiated is out of the question.

Such a major innovation should have the universal consensus Ribash desired for his proposal. The Conservative movement, which prides itself on perpetuating Solomon Schechter's concept of "Catholic Israel," should be the last group to cause further fragmentation of the Jewish people. Indeed, Dr. Simon Greenberg cautions:

> In the final analysis it is the woman who should decide whether she wants to take upon herself whatever psychological and religious consequences which may follow and whatever practical risks are involved. For there are such risks. She should be

told, for example, that the *get* thus granted would not be recognized as binding by a rabbi or a court which is governed by the currently accepted traditional interpretation of the *halakhah*, and therefore would not be recognized in the State of Israel . . . [39]

I believe Dr. Greenberg himself has given the best reason for the practical inadmissibility of this solution.

5. *Conditional Marriage*

The validity of certain marriages initiated under specified conditions is dealt with as early as the Mishnah:

> If a man says to a woman, "Be wed to me on condition [*al m'nat*] that I am this or that (for example, a *kohen*)" and it is found that he misrepresented himself, even if the woman thought at the time, "I would marry him regardless of what he is,"—nevertheless, the marriage is null and void.[40]

Therefore, it has been suggested that the marriage formula include a stipulation that if the marriage is civilly terminated and a get does not follow within a certain period of time, then the marriage is retroactively annulled. This would certainly avoid some of the other problems associated with annulment, which we have seen above.

The main proponent of this view has been an Orthodox scholar, Dr. Eliezer Berkovits of the Hebrew Theological College in Chicago, and a leading disciple of the late Dr. Jehiel J. Weinberg, under whom he studied and taught in Berlin. However, Professor Berkovits's proposal is only theoretical. Thus he stipulated,

> It is not our desire to suggest here what the precise form of the condition ought to be . . . but for the sake of God and the sanctity of the Jewish people we are obliged to deliberate anew on this matter at this time because of the severity of the current problem . . . and perhaps with God's mercy a solution will be found. [41]

The question of conditional marriage arose in 1907 when the French rabbinate devised a means for solving the agunah problem in future cases. They proposed that all marriages be initiated with the following conditional formula:

Behold you are consecrated unto me in a manner that precludes your becoming an agunah on my account. If the civil judges decree a divorce then the marriage will be annulled [*lo yahulu ha'kiddushin*] and the woman shall be released and be free to remarry with regular Jewish marriage rites.[42]

Before putting this extraordinary measure into actual practice the French rabbis sought the approval of other rabbis throughout the world. The response was almost universally negative. The various responses were ultimately published in a book entitled *Ayn Tenay b'Nissuin* (There are no conditional marriages!).[43] In the face of this united opposition the plan was withdrawn. Many specific objections were raised, but the underlying assumptions behind this rejection were: (1) This proposal presents a condition designed to get around the laws of divorce set down in the Torah. (2) It took a matter subject to Jewish jurisdiction and made it subject to civil jurisdiction. (3) In contradiction to the Torah's prescription, it enabled the woman to initiate her own divorce. These were the legal grounds for rejection.[44]

Furthermore, I believe, there were historical considerations implicit in the vehemence with which the French proposal was attacked. How ironic it must have appeared that exactly a century earlier, in 1807, Napoleon had convened the rabbis of the French Empire in a "Sanhedrin" and at that time they gave their approval to civil marriage and divorce, reserving for themselves only a ceremonial function.[45] Of course in traditional circles this was regarded as Jewish capitulation to a secular regime, however well intentioned the rabbis of 1807 may have been. It must have appeared in 1907 that history was repeating itself, that a further erosion of Jewish religious authority was being fostered in the very same country where the centrifugal forces of Emancipation began.

Dr. Berkovits was well aware of the opposition to conditional marriage and the universal rejection of the French solution to the agunah problem. What he tried to do in his very detailed and lucid book, *Tenay b'Nissuin ubaGet* (Conditional marriage and divorce), was to show that his proposal was not the same as the French proposal of 1907 and, therefore, that the objections against the earlier solution do not apply to his own.

Historically the Berkovits proposal has two interesting precedents. The first is the fact that there was a second French proposal after the first one was so roundly condemned. In this later version the marriage became null and void *only if the husband refused to give his wife the get to which she was entitled.*[46] In other words, the second version escapes all of the previous objections. (1) It is no longer a proposal to get around Jewish divorce law. (2) It no longer gives the civil courts jurisdiction in Jewish matrimonial matters, for it is the Jewish court that now determines the grounds for the dissolution of the marriage. (3) It is now the Jewish court, not the woman herself, that initiates the dissolution of the marriage. The action of the husband causes the court to intervene.[47] Moreover, the criteria for this action are Jewish ethics, not the divorce standards of secular society.[48]

The second precedent for the Berkovits proposal is the fact that in 1924 the rabbinate of Turkey instituted conditional marriage. Although the Turkish proposal was subsequently rejected by the Palestinian rabbinate, led by the late Sephardi Chief Rabbi Ben Zion Uziel, the rejection was not based on the strong legal obstacles to the French proposal, but, rather, on a practical reluctance to endorse such an innovation. [49] Dr. Berkovits is of the opinion, however, that the anarchy prevalent in the Jewish world today, especially in matrimonial matters, calls for such an innovation. He believes he has amply demostrated its legal validity. Although the Talmud states, "There are no conditions in marriage," he astutely points out that this is a description of the facts during the talmudic period, not a prescription of what necessarily ought to be then or now.[50]

Dr. Berkovits closes his study with a plea to world Orthodoxy to implement his suggestion. To my knowledge no such implementation has yet come forth. However, the Conservative movement took the Berkovits proposal virtually *in toto* and put it into practice.

In a responsum published in 1968 the following antenuptial agreement was drawn up:

> *The groom made the following declaration to the bride:*
> "I will betroth you according to the laws of Moses and the people Israel, subject to the following conditions:
> "If our marriage should be terminated by decree of the civil courts and if by expiration of six months after such a decree I give you a divorce according to the laws of Moses and the people Israel (a *get*), then our betrothal (*kiddushin*) and marriage (*nissuin*) will have remained valid and binding;
> "But if our marriage should be terminated by decree of the civil courts and if by expiration of six months after such a decree I do not give you a divorce according to the laws of Moses and the people Israel (a *get*), then our betrothal (*kiddushin*) and marriage (*nissuin*) will have been null and void."

The bride replied to the groom: "I consent to the conditions you have made."[51]

Furthermore, to insure that this annulment does not become a substitute for divorce the Conservative responsum closed as follows:

> Let it be clearly understood that the decree of nullity will be considered only a last resort to prevent *iggun.* Accordingly, it is recommended that when a decree of nullity is issued to a wife, a similar decree *not* be issued to the offending husband. Further, he should not be granted any permission to remarry until he gives a *get* to his wife . . . . This should act as a further encouragement to the husband to comply with the wife's request for a *get.*[52]

This is a definite deterrent, considering that after the ban of Rabbenu Gershom against Jewish polygamy (ca. 1000), a man without a get is in virtually the same predicament as a woman without a get: neither of them can remarry.

Of course, one could argue various technicalities *ad infinitum.* The greatest problem is that the positive initiatory role of the husband is removed. However, this is only required in cases of divorce, not of annulment. Moreover, the institution of the "forced get" (*meuseh*) considerably compromised that initiatory right.[53] There are a number of other significant examples in the history of the Halakhah of personal rights removed or modified in the interest of the common good.[54] Finally, the point remains that Dr. Berkovits has established his case, he has cogent answers for all the objections raised against him, and his proposal is an extension, not a diminution, of the authority of Jewish matrimonial law. Moreover, he has provided a solution for women who are in the agunah predicament because of their husband's *unlawful* refusal to give a get. The only remaining problem is that this proposal has not yet received universal rabbinical consent. However, I would be very interested to see a responsum by a rabbi who opposes the Berkovits proposal, giving specific arguments in a particular case of annulment due to a conditional marriage, that the woman involved was still married to her original husband.

The only real objections to the Berkovits proposal are practical rather than legal.

Dr. Simon Greenberg criticized this proposal and the proposal of Dr. Louis M. Epstein, which we will examine shortly, with the following words:

> In the first place, these suggestions have been unequivocally
> rejected by the overwhelming majority of the Orthodox rab-
> binate whose consent they were intended to win. In addition, . . .
> they involve the psychologically repulsive act of requiring the
> bride and groom, in joint action at the time of their marriage,
> to provide for its dissolution. [55]

This proposal in effect turns the entire wedding ceremony into a prelude
for divorce. Although divorce is a major problem, marriage is even
more of one. Even though the Torah permits divorce, it is regarded
as a tragedy in God's eyes, for marriage is considered to be a matter
in which God takes personal interest. Marriage must be strengthened
even before divorce is facilitated. This general concern must be recognized before any solutions to more specific problems in matrimonial
law are accepted.

6. *Prearranged Divorce*

The earliest American solution to the agunah problem to be based on
the halakhic sources was the proposal of a man of great intellect, learning,
and compassion, Dr. Louis M. Epstein. Upon his untimely death his
teacher, Professor Louis Ginzberg, wrote: "He was . . . like a devoted
son . . . Dr. Epstein was such an unusual man . . . "[56] Louis M. Epstein
dedicated the last twenty or so years of his life to solving the agunah
problem and defending his solution against considerable opposition and
ad hominem attacks.

In 1930 he introduced his solution to the convention of the Rabbinical
Asssembly:

> We have . . . one objective, to invest the court with the power
> of granting a divorce to the wife without the consent and in
> the absence of the husband. We find that this is possible on
> the basis of the existing halakah. It may be achieved by the
> husband's making out an instrument at the time of the marriage
> authorizing the court to grant his wife a divorce in his absence
> and appointing the necessary witnesses and agents for this pur-
> pose. [57]

Dr. Epstein suggested that this authorization for divorce by proxy (*minui
shelihut*) be included as part of the ketubah, the marriage contract. Just
three years earlier, in 1927, he had published a study of the institution

of the ketubah, *The Jewish Marriage Contract*, wherein he showed how the ketubah was developed to protect the Jewish wife from being divorced without a substantial monetary settlement.[58] Undoubtedly he believed that the ketubah, which today is purely ceremonial, could once again be made an institution fulfilling its original purpose of protection of the wife.

As we have seen earlier, Dr. Epstein was a man of great modesty who did not want to act unilaterally in such a weighty matter; therefore he solicited the opinions of the rabbis in Europe and elsewhere, hoping their responses would enrich research and action in this area. He was well aware of the opposition that would arise against any innovation, no matter how theoretically cogent. Nevertheless, he believed that a trend was developing in favor of his type of solution and that sooner or later a solution, either his own or one quite similar, would be found.

The chief legal difficulty with his solution is that the husband must personally appoint the scribe and witnesses for the divorce.[59] This is quite unfeasible. And, although some authorities hold that this appointment can be made in writing rather than in person, Dr. Epstein believed that the weight of halakhic precedent ruled out this more liberal view and held that there would be no point in pursuing it. Therefore, he suggested that the husband appoint his own wife as his agent to write for herself her own bill of divorce with rabbinical approval and under rabbinical supervision. After debating various points, he came up with the following formula:

> I do hereby appoint and authorize my wife _____ in her presence and _____ in their presence, both by verbal appointment and by means of this written document, that any one of them shall write a divorce for my wife . . .
>
> I further declare that I grant this authorization for the writing of the divorce only if at any time I disappear or fail to support her or fulfill my conjugal duty for a period of three years or if we are divorced from each other by the action of the civil court.[60]

Dr. Epstein was well aware of the lack of rabbinical consensus for his proposal, but he urged his Conservative colleagues to band together and influence Jewish public opinion. As an astute historian of the Halakhah he knew, I am sure, that the force of public opinion—that is, the opinion of a public commited to law, not anarchy—had affected rabbinic attitudes more than once in the past.[61] In other words, he did not ignore the requirement for consensus, but he saw that consensus can and does change in the face of good reasoning and fundamental moral concerns.

Aware of the universal rejection of the conditional marriage proposal of the French rabbinate in 1907, Dr. Epstein believed his proposal was halakhically more cogent and urged his colleagues *"not* to accept a conditional marriage for any purpose."[62] Nevertheless, just as the earlier suggestion prompted the publication of a series of condemnations in pamphlet form, so the Epstein proposal prompted the publication of a similar pamphlet, *L'Dor Aharon* (To the later generation) by the Orthodox rabbinical organization Agudat HaRabbanim in 1937. In this pamphlet the same type of invective used in the rejection of the French proposal was directed against Dr. Epstein. The issue became a direct confrontation between Orthodoxy and Conservatism.[63]

As with the later Berkovits proposal, many technicalities could be argued *ad infinitum*. Nevertheless, here too the point remains that Dr. Epstein's suggestion cannot be dismissed by one or even several legal arguments. The opposition was explicitly rooted in an innate conservatism and a resistance to any change, legally grounded or not. Aside from his philosophical differences with the Orthodox rabbinate, Dr. Epstein accused them of being more concerned with castigating the Conservative movement than with alleviating the plight of the hapless agunah.[64] Whatever the respective motives of either side, it is clear that there is no point in reviving this suggestion, which would lead to the intensification of what many believe to be the curse of denominationalism in modern Jewish life. In fact, Dr. Epstein indicates that it was decided in 1936 to withdraw the suggestion for fear of further aggravating the problem.[65] Nevertheless, he cautioned that his generation may be the last one to be seriously concerned with the problem since both Reform and civil marriage offer a ready-made way out for the agunah. In other words, he believed that unless the law is modified, as is clearly possible, its authority would be taken seriously by fewer and fewer people.

The chief practical problem with the Epstein proposal, it seems to me, is the same as with the Berkovits proposal, namely, it makes the marriage ceremony a prelude to divorce.

Furthermore, both proposals are based on the fundamental assumption that in the process of the development of the Halakhah the privileged position of the husband was progressively limited in the interest of justice for the woman. Both proposals are presented as further developments of that process to close the loophole of the agunah, the woman matrimonially paralyzed by her husband's obstinate refusal to give her a get. Nevertheless, such a process of development presupposes the universal consent of adherents without which no law has any practical authority. I believe that this point underlies the refusal to accept the proposals of either Epstein or Berkovits, even by those sympathetic with their aims, impressed by their scholarship, and respectful of their integrity.

7. Strengthening the Bet Din

The most conservative of all the contemporary proposals about the agunah problem was made by my teacher, Professor Saul Lieberman of the Jewish Theological Seminary in New York, a man generally reputed to be one of the greatest Talmudists of our time. In the early 1950s he proposed an additional clause in the ketubah whereby both husband and wife agree to be bound by the decision of the rabbinical court (Bet Din) of the Rabbinical Assembly and the Jewish Theological Seminary of America. This is in keeping with the institution of the ketubah, which protects the woman from being totally dependent on the caprice of her husband. As the Talmud authoritatively states,

> R. Meir stated that it is forbidden for a man to remain with his wife for even one hour without a ketubah. His reason is so that she not be regarded as easy to be rid of. [66]

Professor Lieberman's proposal restores the force of the ketubah on behalf of the woman. In its present state the traditional ketubah has no practical force.

The additional clause reads:

> And in solemn assent to their mutual responsibilities and love, the Bridegroom and Bride have declared: As evidence of our desire to enable each other to live in accordance with the Jewish law of marriage throughout our lifetime, we, the Bride and Bridegroom, attach our signatures to this Ketubah, and hereby agree to recognize the Beth Din of the Rabbinical Assembly and The Jewish Theological Seminary of America, or its duly appointed representatives, as having authority to counsel us in the light of Jewish Tradition which requires husband and wife to give each other complete love and devotion, and to summon either party at the request of the other, in order to enable the party so requesting to live in accordance with the standards of the Jewish law of marriage throughout his or

her lifetime. We authorize the Beth Din to impose such terms
of compensation as it may see fit for failure to respond to
its summons or to carry out its decision. [67]

This proposal helps curb the current anarchy (*hefkerut*) in Jewish matrimony in two ways.

First, a couple pledges themselves to be bound by the authority of
Jewish law and the authority of a Bet Din, without which the law would
have no practical force. Marriage is presented in its necessary communal
context, which is what is emphasized by the words, "according to the
law of Moses and Israel." By committing themselves to the ruling of
a particular court their marriage formula takes on concrete practical
significance. From my own rabbinical experience I have found that discussing all of this with a prospective couple in the premarital interview
adds a note of seriousness often lost in the face of all the superficialities
of a modern wedding, which *seem* to be so essential. Professor Lieberman's
proposal is one of the most effective devices for premarital education
I can think of. It helps the rabbi bring home the point that in Judaism
marriage is more than a mutual commitment between a man and a
woman. It is also a commitment to live according to God's law in the
Torah—hence the use of God's name in the blessings, and a commitment
to the Jewish people—hence the minimal two witnesses, preferably a
quorum (*minyan*) of ten or more Jews, [68] and a commitment to the ongoing
authority of the rabbis to interpret and apply the law—hence the ketubah.

The second effective aspect of the insertion of this new clause is that
the couple is bound by a civil agreement to accept the decision of the
Bet Din. This is brought out in a later English version of the clause,
which reads:

> ... and if either spouse shall fail to honor the demand of
> the other or to carry out the decision of the Beth Din or its
> representatives, then the other spouse may invoke any and
> all remedies available in civil law and equity to enforce com-
> pliance with the Beth Din's decision and this solemn
> obligation. [69]

This obliges the couple civilly to comply with whatever the Bet Din
rules in their particular case. The Bet Din, it could be argued in a
civil court, has been designated by the parties as a panel of arbitration
whose decision has been accepted in advance as binding.

All of this is based on the following Mishnah:

A get forced [*meuseh*] by Jewish authorities is valid [*kasher*] by non-Jewish authorities it is invalid [*pasul*]; However, if the non-Jewish authorities force him and say, "Do as the Jewish authorities bid you," it is then valid. [70]

The Gemara subsequently notes that a forced get is valid when the *grounds* for it are valid; namely, a man is obliged to divorce his wife and pay her the ketubah settlement, or the woman is obliged to be divorced by her husband without her ketubah settlement (*assurah lo*). [71] Moreover, the Talmud recognized that when the Jewish court has no practical power to enforce its own decisions it could use the non-Jewish authorities to do its bidding. It recognized a crucial distinction between a non-Jewish court being used *in place* of a Jewish court, which is invalid, and a non-Jewish court being used as an *extension* of a Jewish court, which is valid. Originally only courts of fully ordained (*semikhah*) rabbis in the Land of Israel could have such legal authority. However, the Babylonian Amora, Rab Joseph, who lived after the time ordination had fallen into disuse (ca. 350 C.E.), claimed an extension of such authority (*shelihut*) for his own generation. Use of non-Jewish authorities for purposes of enforcing Jewish decisions is part of this general process of extension. In other words, there is recognition of the phenomenon of a Jewish court with a gentile bailiff as it were. [72]

Maimonides raises the crucial question of how we can possibly approve an act commited under duress (*ones*), whether that duress is applied by Jews, by non-Jewish agents of Jews, or by non-Jews at their own bidding. He answers that duress is only invalid when the person is forced to do something not prescribed by the Torah. However, to force someone to do what the Torah does prescribe is not duress, because a person normally wants to be law-abiding and it is only temporary obstinancy (*takfo yitzro hara*) that prevents him from doing what ought to be done. [73]

Practically, the merit of the Lieberman proposal is that it helps alleviate the plight of many agunah women. First of all, some obstinate men will come to honor their earlier commitment to accept the authority of the Bet Din. Secondly, other obstinate men will comply if threatened with civil action. This I have personally done in one case with success. Thirdly, even if the matter comes to the civil court and it indicates that the husband is required to give a get in accordance with his acceptance of the ketubah, on grounds of, let us say, mental cruelty, the get given cannot be suspected of having been improperly coerced (*amatla*). [74]

The only practical change that I have made in the Lieberman proposal

is to limit the clause to an antenuptial agreement concurrent with but
outside the actual Aramaic text of the traditional ketubah. This change
does not affect the force of the original proposal on behalf of the possible
agunah and quiets the objections of anyone who will not accept an actual
innovation (takkanah) in the text of the ketubah itself. [75]

Nevertheless, despite the cogency of Professor Lieberman's proposal
and its simple elegance, despite his unquestioned mastery of every phase
of rabbinics, the proposal came under attack on technical as well as
practical and philosophical grounds.

In a well-documented article published in 1959, R. Norman Lamm
of New York presented an Orthodox reaction to the conservative proposal. Happily this attack was objective and not ad hominem in nature.
R. Lamm attempted to show that,

> The essential fault of the Conservative proposal with regard
> to all these phases and definitions of asmakhta is its extremely
> indeterminate nature, a vagueness which Jewish law cannot
> tolerate as the proper basis for legal negotiations. [76]

Asmakhta is the talmudic designation of an agreement whose conditions
are either vague or unlawful. Such an agreement is invalid. [77] R. Lamm
accuses the clause in the new ketubah that stipulates "compensation . . .
for failure to respond to its summons or to carry out its decision," as
being an example of asmakhta and therefore making the agreement
invalid.

However, R. Lamm is in essential error. The inserted clause is not
a contract between husband and wife comparable to a contract between
business partners. Furthermore, the husband is not obligating himself
to give a get, which might suggest duress; that is, at the time of the
actual preparation of the get he is not bound by an earlier promise.
No, the agreement is one where the parties agree to accept the authority
of a designated Bet Din, which may or may not order a get. The key
word in the Aramaic version of the ketubah is pitzuyin, which means
"alloted share." [78] A Bet Din has the right to impose penalties upon
those under its jurisdiction to bring about compliance with its decisions. [79]
Since the bride and groom voluntarily placed themselves under the jurisdiction of the Bet Din of the Rabbinical Assembly and the Jewish Theological Seminary, this can be considered an example of arbitration (pesharah)
where the respective parties accept a panel of either rabbis or laymen
to settle their differences as the panel sees fit. Arbitration is valid in monetary matters; hence the English version of the clause translates pitzuyin

as "compensation."[80] The whole point is that in a time or place where we can assume that the practical power of the Bet Din is in force we do not need any specific stipulation of that authority. In a time and a place where, on the other hand, we cannot make such an assumption, specific stipulation of authority is necessary.

Furthermore, since the subsequent English paraphrase stipulates "any and all remedies available in civil law and equity," the couple have accepted the authority of the civil court to carry out the ruling of the Jewish court. Therefore, according to R. Moses Isserles (Rema), as R. Lamm himself points out, such a monetary agreement is valid on the principle of "the law of the kingdom [dina d'malkhuta] is the civil law for Jews [dina]."[81] By making the clause a document separate from the traditional ketubah, I believe I have strengthened its civil validity. Actually, the subsequent English paraphrase renders the deliberately vague pitzuyin as "any and all remedies." By avoiding the term compensation, any hint of a problem with the monetary concept of asmakhta absolutely disappears.

In summary, all that Professor Lieberman's proposal has done is to strengthen the hand of the Jewish court. The proposal is just as effective if, for whatever reasons, another Bet Din is designated. The fact remains that this proposal does not give women the power to effect their own divorces, nor does it enable a get to be written in the absence of the husband.

On practical grounds R. Lamm objected that "at this tender moment of marriage . . . there is no serious contemplation at this time of marital controversy . . ."[82] This might be R. Lamm's experience, and that might be the way it was back in 1959; however, my rabbinical experience some fourteen years later is different. Considering the divorce rate among young couples today, I am convinced that the possibility of controversy or incompatibility is very much on the minds of the engaged couple. What they need to know is that their compatibility or incompatibility is objectively dealt with by the norms of Judaism. This might be less romantic but it is more truthful, and truth is the very essence of Jewish marriage.

The only other objection to the Lieberman proposal was that it would not stand up in a civil court of law. This was argued in a pamphlet issued by Yeshiva University in New York, and it was also argued by some members of the Rabbinical Assembly.[83] I know of no actual test case in the American courts.

It is true that the new ketubah of Professor Lieberman is not one hundred percent effective; but, I believe, it is the best solution we will have until a Sanhedrin, or a court having Sanhedrin-like consensus, is established in the Land of Israel. In the State of Israel there is much less of this type of agunah problem because there the religious courts do have sole jurisdiction in matrimonial law with the full backing of the coercive power of the government.[84] Perhaps this problem, like the problem of the second day of the Festivals, is the price we pay for living in the diaspora.[85] Nevertheless, there are problems other than the agunah problem, yet similar to it, which call for solutions by the centralized authority of the rabbinate of Israel.[86] In the meantime we do the best we can. At least about us it should not be said, "My vineyard I did not protect" (Cant. 1:6)—be that "vineyard" our Torah or our women.

CHAPTER 5

THE SPORT OF HUNTING

QUESTION: One of the happier phenomena of modern Jewish life is that despite the centrifugal forces of secularism, which have lured many away from the life hallowed by the Torah, a significant number of young people, whose parents or even grandparents and great-grandparents were drawn away, are being drawn back by the stronger centripetal forces of Torah and Jewish tradition. For those of us privileged to witness and actually help those returning, it is nothing less than an incident of God's providence (*hashgahah*) in the world. God has not abandoned His people.

It is questionable whether such "returnees" to Judaism are really in the category of the penitent baalay teshubah. After all, to "return" implies that one is coming back to a way of life which he once lived and away from which he subsequently strayed. The baal teshubah, therefore, is not returning to something new but, rather, to something old. Thus the classical statement of return is: "Return us unto Thee, O Lord, and we will return; *renew* [*hadesh*] our days as of old [*c'kedem*]" (Lam. 5:21).[1] The original alienation from the Torah was not so much a lack of knowledge as a failure of will.[2]

However, these young people are not regaining something that they once had and subsequently lost. They are discovering what they never had. As such their alienation from the Torah is rooted in a lack of experience and knowledge, not a failure of will. Theirs is more than a decision; it is, rather, a whole process of education of the spirit. As the Latin insight says, *Nihil volitum nisi praecognitum*; that is, one cannot will what he does not already know. Therefore, these people are in the category of the "kidnapped child" (*tinok she'nishbah*).[3] The Halakhah prescribes for them a gradual process of re-entry into Judaism, a process that requires, it seems to me, an even greater awareness of the psychology of the individual person than for a returnee to his earlier faith.[4]

A young man came under my influence. Without any overt pressure, for this is not my nature, but by his own attendance at the synagogue and participation in the classes in Scripture and Talmud, he became an observant Jew. He made his kitchen kosher and ceased working on the Sabbath. Later, when he married, he and his wife began living a fully observant life together.

He was glad to give up his former ways, except that he very much enjoyed riflery and hunting. He took great pride in his impressive collection of guns. However, he had some inner inkling that these practices might be in conflict with Judaism. One Sabbath afternoon, as he was walking with me to the synagogue, he asked me about the propriety of these sports. For him I prepared the following response.

Answer: It all depends on what is hunted and how it is being hunted.

In ancient times it was the practice to hunt animals and tear off a limb while the animal was still alive and eat it. Scripture states: "Surely living flesh you may not eat" (Gen. 9:4). The Talmud called this practice *aber min ha'hay* and included it among the seven laws for which all mankind was held responsible, not only Jews.[5] It was felt that this type of hunting was so dehumanizing that no human person should engage in it. The notion of "reverence for life" (*Erfurcht vor allem Leben*), so profoundly developed by the Christian philosopher Albert Schweitzer, well expresses, I believe, the concept behind the prohibition of aber min ha'hay. This must be kept in mind in any discussion of hunting, because it illustrates the difference between nature as a means for man's finite needs, and nature as a means for man's infinite lust. This is our inheritance from the Noahide law, an inheritance the receiving of the Torah did not annul, but one which it improved upon—very much in the sense of the German philosophical term *Aufhebung*, that is, something lifted from a lower level and included on a higher level.[6]

As for the specific question itself, one must distinguish between three types of hunting: (1) hunting to protect life and property, (2) hunting for profit, (3) hunting as a sport.

1. Hunting to Protect Life and Property

Despite a reverence for all life, which the Torah certainly teaches in many places, in cases of conflict between human life and nonhuman life, human life and safety always take priority. Thus the Talmud states, "When a wild cat came and tore off a child's hand, Rab went and proclaimed the law that it is permitted to kill and forbidden to raise these dangerous animals."[7] It will be noticed that Rab, the judicial authority in the community of Sura, gave official *permission* to hunt these dangerous animals.

Even though, in another talmudic discussion of the subject, R. Eliezer stated about dangerous animals, "Whoever kills them first is meritorious in the eyes of heaven,"[8] the law is not according to him. Rather, we follow the interpretation of Resh Lakish, which holds that this only applies to animals that have *already* killed. In other words, wild animals are considered the property of someone (*yesh lahem tarbut*) and, therefore, may only be killed if shown to be a definite public menace. In our day, even wild animals are not totally "wild" (*hefker*) but, rather, are under federal or state protection. Furthermore, these animals are to be "judged" in a court of law; that is, the right to kill them on the grounds that they are known killers must be entrusted to a court or its agents.[9] Thus in our case there would have to be an official declaration of the public menace of certain animals. This would be like, for example, the bounties that were offered for the killing of mountain lions or coyotes, which were dangerous to life or property. On the other hand, some animals were considered by the Talmud to be so dangerous that one was to kill them even on the Sabbath, even if they were not actually chasing anyone.[10]

Considering, however, that today many species of wild animals are being threatened with extinction, and conservationists are pressing for stricter hunting laws, I hardly think that any Jew I know of can find permission (*heter*) to hunt on the grounds that human safety calls for it.

2. *Hunting for Profit*

Hunting for profit—for example, hunting animals for their furs or hides—can be halakhically justified. Obviously, hunting for food would be hard to justify inasmuch as a gunshot would make the animal "torn" (*terefah*); that is, nonkosher. One could, of course, trap an animal, such as a deer or a wild ram, and then slaughter it according to the kosher method of *shehitah*. However, such a probability is so remote that the law need not rule on it.[11] The two objections to hunting seem to be that it violates the law prohibiting "wanton destruction" (*bal tash'hit*) and the law prohibiting cruelty to animals (*tza'ar ba'alay hayyim*). Hunting for profit seems to be excepted from both of these prohibitions.

Concerning wanton destruction Maimonides writes,

> When the Torah states you shall not destroy any fruit tree
> [Deut. 20:19] this includes all wanton destruction such as
> one who burns or breaks things for no reason. [12]

Hunting for purposes of obtaining valuable furs and hides would not
be wanton destruction because its purpose is lawful, namely, earning
one's livelihood (*parnasah*). Destruction of something is involved in constructive activity. To rule out anything destructive *qua* act would make
human life impossible. Therefore, wanton destruction can only be judged
in terms of its end rather than its means.

Concerning cruelty to animals the Talmud infers that it is a scripturally
(*d'oraita*) prohibited practice on the basis of several more specific scriptural laws prohibiting various acts that would cause an animal pain.[13] The
phrase *tza'ar ba'alay hayyim* seems to describe several mitzvot rather than
being a specific commandment itself. Nevertheless, the Tosafists, in their
notes to the Talmud in two different places, emphasize that if there
were any conflict with human need this prohibition does not apply. [14]

Furthermore, R. Ezekiel Landau of Prague (d. 1793), in an important
responsum on the subject, which deals with most of the sources I have
already discussed, points out that a Jew need not hunt for hides inasmuch
as,

> . . . there are many hides already prepared, many from ani
> mals who died natural deaths . . . let not a Jew himself kill ani
> mals for no reason other than to pass his precious time in
> hunting . . . [15]

3. *Hunting as a Sport*

It seems, therefore, that the question before us is that of hunting for
sport. R. Landau considers it a waste of time, even if one subsequently
uses the hides. Moreover, he regards it as un-Jewish, noting that in
Scripture Nimrod (Gen. 10:9) and Esau (Gen. 25:27) are described as
hunters. Esau, of course, became the prototype of virtually everything
Jews were to avoid. [16]

It is interesting to note that R. Landau's response was to a question
about a wealthy Jew who owned a large estate containing wild animals.
It is important to remember that this period in Jewish history was the
beginning of the Emancipation, with its ready temptations of assimilation.
Undoubtedly, this particular Jew was anxious to imitate the ways of
his non-Jewish landowning neighbors. Hunting, of course, was a sport
of the aristocracy. Being a man of great wealth, the Jew in question

certainly did not need the hides of the animals he wanted to kill for his livelihood (*parnasah*). Furthermore, hunting involves one exposing himself to danger and the Torah prohibits this: "You should very carefully guard your lives" (Deut. 4:15). Finally, R. Landau emphasizes that hunting is a practice that brutalizes (*akhzariyut*) those who engage in it. In others words, even though one can get around the objective prohibitions of wanton destruction and cruelty to animals, the subjective effects of this "sport" cannot be gotten around. This is the very essence of the opposition of R. Ezekiel Landau. [17]

In most cases, hunting can be prohibited on the objective grounds of wanton destruction and cruelty to animals. Nevertheless, R. Landau opened up the whole question of the psychology of the hunter when he introduced the concept of brutalization. Following this lead we can carry the discussion further, I believe.

Why do certain persons hunt for sport? What sort of pleasure do they get out of killing animals? Why has so much literature glorified the hunter, from the *Odyssey* of Homer to the novels of Ernest Hemingway?

Without going into the various psychological theories concerning aggression, it seems as though hunting enables one to express his mastery of those powerful impulses which otherwise seem to master him. The hunter always exaggerates his peril, as when Esau said to Jacob, "I am at the point of death!" (Gen. 25:32).

Our sages recognized that destructive acts are committed in order to give one a sense of control over himself. For example, striking another person on the Sabbath is considered a *positive* prohibited act, because it was done to assuage one's own rage. [18] The problem is not how to eliminate destructive drives, which may be impossible, but, rather, to rechannel them into constructive acts. In other words, the problem is one of sublimation. The Talmud discusses this problem in the following passage:

> A person born under the sign of Mars [the *red* star] will be a shedder of blood. Rab Ashi said this means either a bloodletter [*makeez dam*] or a murderer, or a slaughterer [*tab'ha*] or a circumciser [*mahola*]. Rabbah said I am under that sign. [19]

Now on the surface this passage seems to be an exercise in astrology. However, on the very same page we learn of the view that the Jewish people are not under the influence of constellations (*ayn mazal l'Yisrael*). Although an opposing view is mentioned, Maimonides tried very hard to show that the weight of Jewish teaching rejects astrology.[20] Therefore, the sixteenth-century theologian, R. Samuel Edels (Maharasha), interprets this passage as follows:

> It is only decreed that one is to be a shedder of blood. But it is within man's free choice if this shedding of blood is a permitted option [*reshut*] like bloodletting [*that is, surgery*]; a prohibited option [*issur*] like murder; or a mitzvah like circumcision.[21]

Thus we are shown that although one's personal tendencies might be innate, one's use of them is his own free choice.

Because of this I advised the young man who questioned me that although he must give up hunting animals, he could continue enjoying riflery in such forms as shooting at targets and at clay pigeons. Of course, it is well known that our sages advised study of the Torah as a sublimation of excessive sexual drive,[22] and, perhaps, it might work for the sublimation of agression in certain cases. However, the questioner was not a person of scholarly temperament and I had to "educate the young man on his own individual level" (Prov. 22:6).

"The Creator of the earth, who made it and established it, did not create it to be a waste but rather made it to be a dwelling" (Isa. 45:18). The Torah helped make one hunter come to accept the world as his dwelling place from God rather than a wilderness in which he had to be afraid.

CHAPTER 6

FINE ART IN THE SYNAGOGUE

QUESTION: Appreciation of fine art is considered by most people in our culture to be an index of one's taste or lack of it. No home whose inhabitants have any pretension to sophistication would be without pictures, sculpture, and other *objets d'art*. A rabbi is usually not asked about the propriety of various forms of art for the homes of the members of his congregation. However, when the adornment of the synagogue becomes a question, then someone usually remembers that maybe all art is not acceptable by Jewish standards, that maybe Judaism does not accept all art willy-nilly. It is here that the question arises: What are the standards for fine art to be placed in the synagogue?

Answer: What first comes to mind in dealing with this question is the admonition given at Mount Sinai: "You shall not make for yourself any statue [*pesel*] or picture [*temunah*]" (Exod. 20:4). Now one can understand the plain meaning of this text in two ways: either as a prohibition of all representative art in general, or as a prohibition of only specifically idolatrous art.

The first alternative was the interpretation of the ancient Jewish historian, Josephus. Addressing himself to a non-Jewish readership and writing in Greek, he said:

> Now Pilate, the procurator of Judea, . . . took a bold step in subversion of the Jewish practices, by introducing into the city the busts of the emperor that were attached to the military standards, for our law forbids the making of images [*eikonōn*].[1]

Although various scholars have debated the meaning of Josephus's words,[2] it is clear that he is making a general statement designed to impress upon his Graeco-Roman readers the unique position of Judaism in regard to representative art.

The second alternative seems to be that of many aesthetically minded Jews today, who accept all art and relate to it in a purely secular way. Many modern synagogues have not hesitated to make use of all types of fine art. The matter is further confused by comparisons with Christian houses of worship. On the one hand, synagogues have never been decorated with art as explicit as that found in the Roman Catholic or Eastern Orthodox churches. On the other hand, synagogues have never been as starkly unadorned as the churches of such groups of biblical literalists as the Seventh-Day Adventists, the Mennonites, or the Jehovah's Witnesses.

The position of Jewish law seems to lie somewhere between these two extremes. The Talmud states:

> Likenesses of the heavenly bodies are not to be made, nor the likenesses of the four-faced creature mentioned in the first chapter of Ezekiel [having the combined features of an ox, man, lion, and eagle], nor the three-dimensional image [*partzuf*] of man.[3]

Maimonides clarifies the last point by stating:

> It is forbidden to make images for aesthetic purposes [*l'noy*], even though there is no idolatry involved, in order that no one one mistake them for idolatry. However, this only applies to a human figure [*tzurat adam*].[4]

Thus we can see that some art is viewed as being essentially idolatrous and other art is seen as basically secular.[5]

The late Professor Louis Ginzberg explained the three prohibited art forms as follows:

> Not only was the human form the most favored by the Greeks and other nations of antiquity for the representation of their gods, but the Jews had not forgotten their suffering because of their refusal to pay divine honors to the statues of the living or dead Caesars . . . the fear that Gnostic and syncretistic sects might interpret the symbolic vision of the Prophet Ezekiel led the rabbis to prohibit the representation of the four figures in the Divine throne. And finally, the old astral worship was not quite dead among large numbers of Gentile inhabitants

of Babylonia and Palestine and hence the unqualified prohibition against representation of the heavenly bodies.[6]

The question of the four-faced creature of Ezekiel's vision is not at issue today. Therefore, even though the ban remains in effect, there is no need to probe into the deeper reasons for its being promulgated. The same seems to be the case for the ban on astral figures.[7]

The issue still very much with us is the question of human figures. Thus the *Tur* states:

> We only prohibit the figure of a man in full form with all the parts represented, hence the figure of a head is not included in the ban.[8]

Thus in terms of practical application, no fully formed human sculpture may be used.

Sculpture of the full human figure is an art form that has perennially interested artists. If idolatry in its classical manifestations no longer seems to be a living issue, then why should we still insist on the ban on human sculpture?

The human figure has always intrigued man. In our culture, while we do not find worship of sun, moon, and stars, we do find much worship of man. Our culture is basically anthropocentric; that is, man-centered and man-oriented. We are taught to believe that the very mysteries of life and the universe lie within the conscious or unconscious mind of man. However, the man we look upon as divine is not the ordinary human being with all his failures and weaknesses. Rather, we construct an *ideal* man or woman, one who embodies the perfection we want to create for ourselves. This idealization of the human form finds its deepest expression in sculpture.

Judaism, conversely, is theocentric; that is, God-centered and God-directed. "I am the first and I am the last, and there is no God beside Me" (Isa. 44:6). Man's position in the universe is determined by his relationship with God. Man is made in the "image of God" (*tzelem Elokim*). Now the Septuagint renders the phrase in Gen. 1:26 as *kat' eikona theou*, "according to the symbol [*or icon*] of God"! This point was significantly presented by my late revered teacher, Professor A. J. Heschel:

> And yet there is something in the world that the Bible does regard as a symbol of God. It is not a temple nor a tree, it is not a statue nor a star. The one symbol of God is *man*,

every man. God Himself created man in His image, or to use
the biblical terms, in His *tselem* and *demuth*. How significant
is the fact that the term, *tselem*, which is frequently used in
a damnatory sense for a man-made image of God, as well as
the term *demuth*—of which Isaiah claims (40:18) no *demuth* can
be applied to God—is employed in denoting man as an image
and likeness of God![9]

However, since "no man can see My face" (Exod. 33:20)—that is,
since God cannot be depicted—so also the true reality of God's image,
the human person who is His unique relational partner, also cannot
be truly depicted. Man is more than a physical form; his true significance,
like that of God Himself, is invisible.[10] Thus the Talmud connects the
invisibility of God with the invisibility of man as the basis of prohibiting
the making of an image of *either* God *or* man. It justifies the ban on
human sculpture by this analogy:

> A baraita teaches that all full forms are permitted except the
> full form of man [*partzuf adam*]. Rab Huna the son of Rab
> Idi said that at one of Abaye's lectures he heard the following
> interpretation: "You shall not make with Me [*itti*] gods of
> silver, or gods of gold" [Exod. 20:20] should be rendered
> as if it were written, "You shall not make My symbol [*otti*;
> *ot* means symbol], namely, man, gods of silver, or gods of
> gold."[11]

Therefore, it is as futile to attempt to capture the true reality of man
in sculpture as it is to attempt to capture the true reality of God in
an idol. Man's uniqueness is his intimate sharing of the mystery of God.
The ban on full human sculpture is a *realistic* reverence for the mystery
and sanctity of the human person.[12] I think the ban is most timely
in our own age, which couples the extremes of unrealistic idealization
of man and a brutal disregard for his very real needs. We want man
the space-traveler, the man or woman in the bloom of youthful vigor,
not man the catatonic mental patient, or man the baby deformed or
mongoloid!

When idolatry is seen as the creation by man of his own idealized
self, we can see that it is in essence a perennial temptation of the human
spirit, and that a change in its historical manifestation does not alter
this fact.[13]

Furthermore, the refusal to accept idealized images of God and man is related to the refusal to accept facsimiles of the Temple in Jerusalem. The rebuilding of the Temple will be the result of the direct intervention of God in history, namely, the sending of the Messiah. [14] Therefore, all of our prayers for the rebuilding of the Temple are *hopes* directed to God, not ideals suggested to ourselves. This is why we cannot by ourselves recreate the Temple or any of its objects. For were it not for the fact that the Temple and its objects were ordained by God's command, they themselves could be construed as having idolatrous intent. The fact that our synagogues are *not* taken to be *the* Temple (*Bet HaMikdash*) helps us remember this. On the very page where the Talmud prohibits the three art forms described earlier, it states:

> One should not build a house in the form of the Temple . . .
> a table in the form of the altar, nor a candlelabrum in the
> form of the Menorah, but he should make it with five, six,
> or eight branches. [15]

All we can do is attempt to have the *spirit* of the Temple in our synagogues.

> "And I will be for them a sanctuary in miniature" [Ezek.
> 11:16]—these are the synagogues and houses of study. [16]

Here again we see Judaism's emphasis on the greater importance of the spirit than of physical form. [17] The Temple and other Torah-ordained objects are required because man is a historical being having an imagination and a need for visual associations. [18] However, the God who ordained these things is beyond history and therefore beyond the imagination of even His closest creature. [19] Indeed, the true reality of the human person, the image of God, and of Israel, the people of God, is something no eye but God's has ever seen. [20]

CHAPTER 7

MAY A PHYSICIAN PERFORM A CIRCUMCISION?

QUESTION: A physician in my congregation, who is an observant Jew, attended a circumcision ceremony (*brit milah*) and was surprised to see a fellow physician performing the operation with a rabbi reciting the prayers. He asked me whether the services of a religious professional in this area (*mohel*) were necessary.

Answer: Circumcision is the oldest Jewish rite. It began when Abraham our father, the founder of our people, answered God's command and circumcised the male members of his household (Gen. 17:23). When his son Isaac was born he circumcised him on the eighth day. Later the Torah made circumcision on the eighth day a perpetual obligation for every Jewish male (Lev. 12:3), unless illness would make the operation too hazardous.[1] Circumcision is so important that it is even to be performed on the Sabbath or Yom Kippur. According to R. Joseph Karo, in the *Shulhan Arukh*, it is the most important positive commandment.[2]

Although an uncircumcised male is still a Jew by birth,[3] circumcision initiates the child into the covenant of Abraham. Therefore, if for whatever reason a child was not circumcised by his father (or at his father's arrangement), when he reaches his majority he is obligated to have himself circumcised.[4] Furthermore, circumcision is a *conditio sine qua non* for a male convert entering Judaism.[5]

Circumcision, then, marks the physical transition into Judaism. For this reason, of all the explanations given for why circumcision is to be performed on the eighth day, the explanation I like best is the following:

When David entered the bathhouse he saw himself naked and

66

he said, "Woe is me that I am naked [that is, bereft] of the mitzvot." When he looked at his circumcision he began to praise God with the psalm, "For the leader, on the *eight stringed instrument* [*ha'sheminit*], a psalm of David" [Ps. 12:1][6]

R. Eleazar Azkari explains that circumcision is the *eighth* commandment inasmuch as the sons of Noah—that is, mankind—were already given the seven Noahide laws.[7] Circumcision marks the transition of a son of Noah into a son of Abraham.

Preferably, a father ought to circumcise his own son as Abraham circumcised his sons, Isaac and Ishmael.[8] Nevertheless, just as all fathers are not capable of teaching their own sons and hence hire teachers to fulfill this obligation, so all fathers are not capable of circumcising their own sons and hence hire others to fulfill this obligation too.

Preferably, a father ought to engage a circumciser who is religious, expert, and righteous.[9] This is why the mohel is a professional certified to have the above qualifications.

Nevertheless, Jewish tradition does recognize situations where the services of someone other than a mohel might have to be secured. The Talmud reports:

A non-Jew is not to circumcise a Jewish child because they are suspected of bloodshed—according to R. Meir. The other rabbis held that a non-Jew may do so if other Jews are present, but not privately ... A city where no Jewish physician is found but where there is a non-Jewish physician, he may circumcise.[10]

Two considerations would bar a non-Jewish physician: (1) if his intention were to harm the Jewish child; (2) if his intention were to perform a non-Jewish religious rite. However, R. Johanan held that concerning a recognized non-Jewish physician (*mumheh*), there would be no question of his using the operation of circumcision as a pretext for injuring the Jewish child, for he has his medical reputation at stake.[11] Moreover, circumcision is a Jewish rite, so we do not suspect the gentile physician of performing a rite of another religion.[12] To insure this is why there is insistence on Jewish supervision.

It is interesting to note, however, that R. Johanan's opinion was formed before the rise of Islam. In Islam circumcision does have a religious significance. Nevertheless, in our society the probability of using a Muslim physician for a circumcision is so remote that it need not be ruled on.[13]

All of this is possible because circumcision, unlike certain other religious operations, does not have to have direct religious intention (*lishmah*) in order to be valid.[14] This is why the prayers and blessings recited at the circumcision are not a *conditio sine qua non (ikkub)* for the subsequent validity of the act itself.

However, all of the above applied only to exceptional circumstances (*sh'at ha'd'hak*). Jewish tradition also tried to adhere to the following:

> R. Judah said that circumcision by a non-Jew is invalid as Scripture states, "And *you* shall keep my covenant" [Gen. 16:9].[15]

Thus it is only after the fact (*diabad*) that a proper circumcision *on the eighth day* by a non-Jew is accepted. Furthermore, some authorities also require that in such cases the ritual of "taking a drop of blood" (*hatafat dam brit*) be performed by a mohel afterwards.[16] Finally, non-Jewish circumcision is never initially permitted (*l'khat'hilah*) when a qualified mohel is available.[17]

In larger Jewish communities it is certainly not a problem to secure the services of a qualified mohel. In these communities there is no excuse whatsoever for using anyone other than a pious, learned, and expert mohel. This is especially important considering that circumcision is a medical operation performed on most non-Jewish children as well. As standard hospital procedure, purely medical circumcisions usually take place earlier than the eighth day. In fact, I always advise mothers of newborn boys to explicitly instruct the hospital authorities *not* to circumcise their sons medically as they will have their own brit milah either in the hospital or at home. Because of all of this the significance of brit milah as religiously prescribed circumcision must be emphasized, if anything even more than in the past. For this reason I do not "co-officiate" with a physician at a circumcision wherever the services of a mohel are available, nor do I condone those rabbis who do so.

Nevertheless, when serving as a rabbi in a remote community, I had to take advantage of the exceptional provisions in the law lest the mitzvah or circumcision be altogether forgotten. Rabbis who serve as military chaplains face the same problem.

There is a fascinating precedent in the Talmud, which throws considerable light on this problem. It will be recalled that one of the most enigmatic episodes in the Pentateuch is the encounter between the Lord and Moses when Moses' wife, Zipporah, intervenes and circumcises their son, touching his feet with the foreskin (Exod. 4:26–26). The passage troubled the commentators, who wondered why the Lord sought to kill Moses. The usual rabbinic explanation is that Moses, in his anxiety to reach

Egypt and lead his people out of bondage, neglected the *immediate* mitzvah, namely, the circumcision of his own son.[18] Zipporah understood this and took matters into her own hands.

Moreover, the incident raised a halakhic problem for the authority who held that a woman may not function as a mohel because she herself cannot be the subject of circumcision (*lav bat milah hi*). If so, how did Zipporah assuage the Lord's anger when she herself performed an act which is to be done by men only? The Talmud gives two answers: (1) She only *arranged* for the circumcision but another man actually performed it. (2) She only began the act but Moses completed it.[19] The first interpretation not only is a rather forced interpretation of the text itself, but does not help us in our problem with a non-Jewish physician at a circumcision. However, the second interpretation is of great help to us because it indicates that if someome else began the circumcision, and the father of the child *completed* the operation in some way, then it is as though he himself performed the entire operation.[20] This was my practice in those cases where only a non-Jewish physician was available.

Of course, as R. Jehiel M. Epstein (d. 1908) pointed out, after the fact (*diabad*) the circumcision is valid even if the non-Jew performed the entire operation from beginning to end.[21] However, it is preferable before the fact (*l'khat'hilah*) for a Jew, optimally the father himself, to complete the act. The question now arises: At what point in the operation must the father take over in order for it to be considered that he himself completed it (*v'agmarah*)?

Circumcision consists of three steps: (1) *milah*: the cutting of the foreskin; (2) *periah*: the cutting and pulling down of the corona, the membrane covering the head of the male organ; (3) *metzitzah*: the drawing of blood. R. Epstein held that since milah without periah is invalid, the milah can be performed by someone not originally acceptable (*pasul*) and the periah by someone who is originally acceptable (*kasher*).

The issue today is that most physicians use a device called the "Gamco Clamp," which performs the operation of *both* milah and periah simultaneously. Two questions now arise: (1) Is this device permitted in general? (2) At what point would the father perform the act of periah when the Gamco Clamp is used?

The late Secretary to the Committee on Law and Standards of the Rabbinical Assembly, Dr. Michael Higger, wrote an unpublished responsum on the question of the Gamco Clamp, which I have in my possession. On the basis of a passage from the Palestinian Talmud he infers that periah need only be a separate act when there is a need for a second

act to remove any remaining strands (*tzitzim*) of the foreskin or membrane.[22] Since the Gamco Clamp accomplishes both milah and periah
at once this is not a problem. Furthermore, he writes,

> Already in Gaonic times, the operation of circumcision was
> done by using an instrument which performed the Millah and
> Periah in one act, and the Gaonim permitted it.[23]

Furthermore, he quotes a leading Orthodox halakhic authority, R.
Joseph Henkin of New York,[24] who reluctantly permits the use of the
Gamco Clamp under the following conditions:

1. The mohel should make the dorsal slit and place the clamp
    on the organ.
2. The clamp should be kept in position only for two or three
    minutes, because if the foreskin is completely damaged by
    the clamp (*ad sheyamut or ha'orlah*) the mitzvah of circumci-
    sion has not been kept even *ex post facto*.

Dr. Higger adds that the first blessing is to be recited at the time
the dorsal slit is made so as to provide for the "covenantal drop of
blood" (*dam brit*) to be taken. Finally, Dr. Higger endorses the use of
the clamp, noting that it eliminates the danger of severing the artery
during circumcision and reduces bleeding to a minimum. Jewish law
advocates avoiding mortal danger or even possible danger (*hashash
sakanah*).[25]

On the basis of all this, in those cases where I had to permit the
use of a non-Jewish physician, I instructed the father to place his hand
with that of the physician when the clamp was placed on the organ
and the final incision was made. In this way he most definitely "completed" the operation.

In the case of a Jewish physician it would seem that it would be much
easier to permit him to circumcise Jewish children. Indeed the Talmud
refers to the mohel as a "Jewish physician" (*rofe Yisrael*).[26] In another
passage where the term *physician* is used, Rashi assumes it refers to
a mohel.[27] R. David Hoffmann of Berlin (d. 1921) held that a circumcision
by a nonobservant Jewish doctor was valid after the fact.[28] Furthermore,
circumcision as a medical practice was well-known in talmudic times;
however, a clear distinction is made between medical and religious circumcision.[29]

There was some question of whether a Jew could circumcise a non-Jew for health reasons. However, the Tosafists permitted any medical treatment of non-Jews by Jews on the grounds that it was necessary for advancing medical knowledge and, also, that general humanitarian needs (*m'pnay aybah*) required it.[30]

The phenomenon of the circumcised gentile was also well-known in talmudic times. In fact, if one referred to a person as "circumcised" the designation was by no means limited to Jews; it could mean a circumcised non-Jew.[31] Nevertheless, precisely for this reason, and in the face of the Christian dismissal of the spiritual necessity of circumcision, the Talmud goes to considerable lengths to emphasize the covenantal aspects of circumcision *qua* brit milah for the Jewish people.[32]

However, since Jewish physicians perform purely medical circumcision on *both* Jews and non-Jews, I believe they ought not function as mohalim even if they are pious and knowledgeable, because in the eyes of the general public they are functioning as physicians performing one more operation. I have heard that Dr. Immanuel Jakobovits, the Chief Rabbi of Great Britain, is of the same opinion, but I am unable to find any written statement of his position.

In conclusion I recommend the following practical points.

1. Circumcision should only be performed by a qualified mohel whenever such services are available.
2. If no mohel is available a Jewish physician should be used, preferably an observant Jew. The physician should make the blessing *al ha'milah*. A rabbi should be present to supervise the circumcision, taking especial care to see that the use of any surgical devices does not violate the acts of milah or periah.
3. If a non-Jewish physician must be used, then a Jew, preferably the father of the child, should assist in the operation so that it could be said that he "finished" it.
4. If the family feels that a physician should be in attendance *alongside* the mohel, in case of emergency, there is no objection whatsoever.

CHAPTER 8

MOURNING FOR A NON-JEWISH PARENT

IN AN AGE of great interchange between persons of varying ethnic and religious backgrounds, opportunities for changing one's inherited lifestyle are becoming increasingly available. This includes changes of religious commitment. For Jews this has a double meaning. On the one hand, there are numberous alternatives available for Jews who no longer wish to identify with the Jewish people and the Jewish faith. Conversion out of Judaism (*shmad*), although impossible according to Jewish law,[1] is nevertheless a practical reality in many different ways. Indeed this is one corollary of the centrifugal process of Jewish acculturation into the life of the non-Jewish world. For persons who have taken this step, the relationship with their Jewish family and associates, from *their* standpoint, is not the subject of the categories of the Halakhah, because the presupposition for the operation of these categories is no longer present. Halakhic questions concerning this relationship, such as their inheritance rights or burial privileges, can only be asked by those who have remained faithful to Judaism.

On the other hand, for Jews there is a second aspect to this process of acculturation: the significant number of non-Jews who are converting to Judaism. These persons have two areas of relationship that are of interest to the Halakhah. The first is their new relationship with their fellow Jews. There is much material on this subject in Scripture, and in the rabbinic and postrabbinic writings.[2] The Halakhah is also concerned with the relationship of the convert with his or her non-Jewish parents and associates. However, this area of relationship has received much less attention in the literature, primarily, I believe, because in the past conversion to Judaism involved such a social and cultural displacement that virtually all previous relationships were totally severed. In our society, on the other hand, change of religion is an accepted

72

phenomenon and the social isolation of Jews is less pronounced. There-fore, a non-Jew who converts to Judaism, although making a profound religious transformation, is making a less profound social transformation than in former times. This factual background is important to bear in mind in looking at the following question.

Question: A young man whom I prepared for conversion, who con-verted to Judaism for the purest of motives, experienced the loss of his non-Jewish mother. He came to me and expressed his dilemma as follows: "When I converted you told me that I was 'as a newborn child,' born again as it were; that all previous ties were no longer binding. Nevertheless, my feelings of love for my mother, who did not convert with me, are still with me. Indeed, she actually encouraged me to become a Jew. Am I being disloyal to Judaism, which means everything to me, if I mourn my mother's death?" He then proceeded to ask specifically about attending the funeral, the period of mourning, and the recitation of the Mourner's Kaddish.

Answer: As an integral part of the preparation for conversion I emphasize to all candidates the accepted Jewish teaching that "the convert who converts to Judaism is like a newborn child [*c'katan she' nolad dami*]."[3] This indicates that in becoming a Jew one becomes a new person.

This teaching has had a far-reaching effect in the Halakhah. For example, in the ancient rite for bringing the first fruits to Jerusalem on the Festival of Shabuot, the worshipper says, "I have come to the land which the Lord promised our fathers to give us" (Deut. 26:3). The Mishnah states:

> The following persons bring their fruits but do not recite the formula of Thanksgiving: The convert [*ger*] brings but does not recite because he cannot say "Which the Lord has promised *our fathers* to give us." If his mother is Jewish, he may do so. When the convert prays the Amidah privately he should say, "God of the fathers of Israel." When he is in the synagogue he should say, "God of *your* fathers." If one's mother is Jewish he may say, "God of *our* fathers."[4]

Nevertheless, the Talmud brings a contradicting baraita:

> R. Judah taught that a convert may indeed say "our fathers" because Scripture says Abraham became "father of a multitude

of nations" (Gen. 17:5) . . . R. Joshua ben Levi said that the
law is according to R. Judah; so also did R. Abbahu.[5]

This is based on the ancient notion that Abraham converted many gentiles
to his faith.[6] Indeed Abraham himself was a convert.

Maimonides codified the law according to the baraita rather than
the Mishnah. He elaborated on this question in his famous responsum
to Obadiah, the convert who was criticized in his own community for
reciting the words of the Amidah, "our God and *God of our fathers*."[7]

In two other places the Mishnah teaches that a convert who before
his conversion had contracted certain diseases, which entail ritual impurity (*t'umah*), did not carry the ritual stigma these diseases entailed after
his conversion.[8] In other words, the transformation is so complete that
it has physical as well as spiritual consequences. From all this it would
seem that *all* former ties are now broken.

Nevertheless, the phrase describing a convert states that he or she
is "like a newborn child." Being an analogy rather than an absolute
identification it admits of important exceptions.[9] For example, the Talmud asks whether a convert to Judaism has fulfilled the commandment
of procreation if he fathered children while still a non-Jew, R. Simon
ben Lakish says no, because as "a newborn child" his life begins again
and all former acts are nullified. However, R. Johanan says that we
cannot pretend that the children do not exist when they do (*d'ha havu
layh*). The law is according to R. Johanan, even in those cases where
the non-Jewish children did not convert along with their father.[10]

In another place the Talmud asks whether a convert may marry his
mother or sister (who of course were also converts) since their previous
biological ties seem to have been broken by their conversions. The answer
is that they may not practice what theretofore would have been incest,
lest it be argued that their conversion to Judaism was a moral descent
(*kedusha kalah*) rather than a moral elevation.[11] In other words, the rabbis
saw the acceptance of the Torah, by an individual or by the Jewish
people as a whole, not as an abrogation of the moral standards required
of all humanity, but, rather, as a process of going beyond them.[12] The
prohibitions of incest, adultery, and homosexuality, grouped under the
same rubric (*arayot*), are one of the seven areas of morality binding
on gentiles as well as on Jews [13] These prohibitions presuppose the
integrity of the family as a biological and social unity. Therefore, by
insisting that the religious fact of conversion does not annul the earlier
prohibition of incest, the rabbis were acknowledging the integrity of

the gentile family tie, even with the member who is now a Jew, holding that it is not totally canceled by conversion to Judaism.[14]

Furthermore, the Talmud rules that a convert may inherit his gentile father's estate, with the exception of any non-Jewish religious articles it might contain.[15] Strict logic would again seem to indicate that the convert, being "a new-born child," ought not claim his inheritance even if in non-Jewish law he were still regarded as his father's son and legal heir. Yet the Talmud states that the rabbis were exceptionally lenient (*akeelu bah*) and ruled as they did lest the convert "revert to his former ways" (*l'kilkulo, l'suro*). Now why would this be a problem at that time as opposed to any other time? Rashi indicates that if the rabbis did not permit this the convert might leave Judaism for the sake of gaining his inheritance.[16] In other words, the continued allegiance of the convert to Judaism was enough of a reason to stretch the logic of the law a bit.

Of course monetary considerations play an important role in motivating human action. Conversions for monetary reasons, whether to or away from Judaism, were not unknown to the rabbis.[17] Nevertheless, despite the serious consideration any interpretation of Rashi's calls for, I believe the leniency of the rabbis is based on psychological factors for which the monetary value of the estate might well be only symbolic.

At a time of personal loss, feelings of guilt are normal. Considering that the convert severed childhood religious ties by his or her conversion to Judaism, the emotional regression involved in the experience of parental loss might *temporarily* eclipse the mature decision to convert to Judaism. By permitting attendance at the funeral, although not permitting any direct participation in non-Jewish religious rites, we are helping the convert through a trying emotional period without demanding an inhuman test of his Jewish loyalty.[18]

Now this may be good psychology, but while a philosophical, historical, sociological, or psychological consideration may *condition* a halakhic decision, it cannot *ground* such a decision. Such grounds can only come from Scripture or tradition.

Happily, the Talmud itself deals with the problem of a convert's regression to former non-Jewish ways and this treatment involves psychological rather than monetary factors. A baraita reads as follows:

> It happened that a certain non-Jew in Sidon wrote Torah scrolls and Rabban Simon ben Gamliel permitted purchasing them from him.[19]

The Talmud then asks how Rabban Simon could possibly permit this when he himself requires that the criterion for a Torah scroll being valid (*kasher*) for Jewish use is that it be prepared with proper intention and purpose (*l'shmah*). Certainly this could not be assumed in the case of a non-Jewish scribe. Rabbah ben Samuel answers that the "non-Jew" in question was really a convert who had regressed to his former gentile ways (*hazar l'suro*), and we can, therefore, assume that he knew the requirements for preparing a Torah scroll. However, if this is the case, then the man in question is an apostate (*min*), whose knowledge might be sufficient but whose religious intention is disqualified by his very apostacy *ipso facto*.[20] Finally, Rab Ashi, one of the editors of the Talmud, says that the man was a convert who regressed to his former gentile ways out of fear (*m'shum yirah*). Rashi adds that he feared for his life.[21] In other words, he became a sort of Marrano because he feared for his life and safety at the hands of gentiles. A twentieth-century authority, R. Israel Meir Kagan (Hafetz Hayyim, d. 1932), stated that even though the convert should have laid his life down for his faith, he nevertheless remains a Jew because this was *under duress* (*ones*).[22]

The point in bringing in all this discussion is to show that if involuntary fear, albeit mortal terror, does not remove the Marrano-like convert from being a *bona fide* Jew, we can see why the rabbis were also lenient in the case of the convert at the time of the death of his non-Jewish parent. Certainly the emotions that grip him or her at this traumatic time are involuntary and overwhelming (*ones*). His fear at this time might well be that if he, the convert, did not attend the gentile parent's funeral (and accept his inheritance), he might be in everyone's eyes, even his own, like the despicable children in Shakespeare's *King Lear*, about whom their father cried: "How sharper than a serpent's tooth it is to have a thankless child! Away, away!"[23]

Inasmuch as we are commanded to love the convert over and above the love we are to have for our fellow Jews, the specific emotional needs of converts are to be taken into sensitive consideration.[24] The Talmud reports, "Rab reiterated the popular saying, 'One should not denigrate gentiles in the presence of a convert for even ten generations.'"[25]

Furthermore, Jews are required to aid non-Jews, especially in times of sorrow and need, for the sake of peace and goodwill (*mip'nay darkhay shalom*).[26] The convert (Jew) can aid his biological family (non-Jews) in their time of sorrow and need. This principle found many applications in the course of Jewish history. Peace and goodwill would hardly be the result if a child did not attend the funeral of his own mother.

Interestingly enough, Maimonides ruled that a convert need not mourn his non-Jewish parent.[27] R. Joseph Karo comments that the reason for this ruling is twofold: (1) Mourning is only required for the relatives for whom a kohen is dispensed from his restriction would seem at first glance that of contact with the dead (Lev. 17:1 ff.); (2) The convert is "like a newborn child." Nevertheless, R. David ibn Zimra (Radbaz) reports the view of an anonymous authority who rules that a convert ought to mourn his mother.[28] R. Shabtai HaKohen (Shakh) identifies this authority as R. Mordecai ben Hillel (Mordecai, d. 1298).[29] However, the actual text of *Mordecai* reveals that in a case of a convert whose mother *converted too*, R. Isaac ben Samuel (Ri, d. 1200) ruled that he should properly mourn (*l'hitabel*) her death.[30] The reason given by R. Mordecai, however, is that the maternal tie (*hayas*), unlike the paternal tie, is not broken. If this is the case, then the fact of whether the mother herself converted or not is irrelevant.

Nevertheless, in discussing the laws regarding honor of parents, Maimonides notes,

> A convert is forbidden to curse or abuse his non-Jewish father. He must not show him any disrespect so that it not be said that conversion to Judaism involves a moral descent ... but he should demonstrate a measure [*miktzat*] of honor.[31]

On the basis of this text, a 1933 responsum of R. Aaron Walkin of Pinsk is reported,[32] which rules that a convert may indeed mourn his non-Jewish parent, for honor of parents includes one's actions even *after* their death.[33]

It would seem at first glance that Maimonides has contradicted himself; however, the key phrase in this second text is "*a measure* of honor." In our case this would probably mean that the convert may observe *some* mourning practices, but not the full number required for one's own biological Jewish parent.

Actually, there is a direct scriptural precedent for formal mourning for a non-Jewish parent. The war bride, even if she converts to Judaism, is to mourn her non-Jewish parents because, as R. Abraham ibn Ezra (d. 1167) explained, "human reason dictates honor for one's parents whether they are alive or dead."[34] Moreover, even though honor of parents is not one of the seven Noahide laws binding on non-Jews, nevertheless the standards of sexual morality (*arayot*), which are binding on them, presuppose respect for the integrity of the family, which, of course, directly involves respect for parents. Indeed the classical talmudic example of respect for parents is that of the way a non-Jewish son acted towards his father.[35] And the Midrash explains that Abraham delayed his departure for Canaan so that it would not be said he abandoned his responsibility to his aged (non-Jewish) father, Terah.[36]

As for saying Kaddish for a non-Jewish parent, we must understand the purpose for saying Kaddish for a parent. The Talmud states that during the first year of bereavement a child should refer to his or her deceased parent as "my father (or mother), my teacher—I am the atonement for his (or her) repose."[37] It was believed that the child's behavior during this year affects the otherworldly status of the departed parent.[38] In other words, the test of a parent's influence is the life-style of his or her children.[39] Therefore, the children of the deceased are to engage in special mitzvot during the year of bereavement. Originally Kaddish was recited after a public lecture expounding the Torah.[40] The study of the Torah is the greatest mitzvah and, ideally, the mourner should engage in it even more during this year. However, since everyone is not a scholar, the custom gradually arose that the mourners themselves say Kaddish in an abridged form. Nevertheless, as early as the sixteenth century, R. Abraham Hurwitz emphasized that Kaddish is not a magical incantation on behalf of the dead, but, rather, one mitzvah among many that ought to be performed as evidence of good parental influence.[41]

Since Kaddish is a prayer that can be said by any Jew, I cannot see any reason to prevent the convert from saying it for his non-Jewish parent, if he believes that parent was a good influence on his life. Even though the convert is not obligated (*metzuveh*) to do so, he can take it as his own personal obligation.[42] The only reservation I would make is that the convert *not* follow the normal *dispensations* from various religious duties granted to one mourning for a biological Jewish parent.[43] In other words, one can add to but not subtract from the law. Also, R. Ephraim Oshry, formerly of Kovno and now of New York, in his collection of responsa quotes an earlier responsum, which ruled that Kaddish may be *periodically* recited for a non-Jewish parent, provided some distinction is made between mourning for a Jewish parent and mourning for a non-Jewish parent.[44]

Finally, in the particular case before us, the non-Jewish mother actually influenced her child to convert to Judaism, although never converting herself. Scripture tells us that Terah left Ur Kasdim with Abram, his son (Gen. 11:31). A rabbinic work, *Seder Eliahu Zuta*, states, "As reward for leaving with Abraham for the sake of God, God made Abraham a king during Terah's lifetime."[45] The Zohar, the "Talmud" of Jewish mysticism, teaches that it was Terah's original intention to make the whole trip with his son.[46]

Therefore, considering the question in general, and considering the particular circumstances of the convert who questioned me, I came to the following practical conclusions:

1. I permitted his attendance at the mother's funeral, emphasizing to him that he must not in any way participate in any non-Jewish religious ceremonies or prayers.
2. He may say Kaddish whenever he chooses.
3. He may not refrain from those mitzvot from which a regular Jewish mourner is excused.
4. He may observe whatever other mourning procedures he chooses, although I pointed out that this mourning should be private (*b'tzina*) rather than public.

Chapter 9

SUICIDE IN JEWISH PERSPECTIVE

1. *Jewish Ethics*

SUICIDE IS an inescapable problem for ethics. I know of no ethical system that has not dealt with it. To formulate a Jewish ethical approach to this problem, we must have some notion of ethics in general and of Jewish ethics specifically.

Every system of ethics must enable one to answer the most personal of all questions: What am I to do now? In ethics, theory is for the sake of practice. Jewish ethics epitomizes this practical emphasis and Judaism has taken great pride in its practical appeal.

> ... for that will be proof of your wisdom and discernment
> to other peoples, who on hearing of all these laws will say,
> "Surely that is a great nation of wise and discerning people."
> (Deut. 4:6)

In the medieval philosophical dialogue, *Kuzari*, by R. Judah Halevi, the pagan king of the Khazars finally embraces Judaism because, more than any other life system, it provides him with the most satisfying set of practical directives. [1]

Nevertheless, ethics is held together by intelligible principles, which enable a person to act intelligently. Theoretical structure distinguishes ethical action from a mechanical response. Philosophically one would say, *Nihil volitum nisi praecognitum* ("Knowledge must precede volition [and action]"). Jewishly one would say, "Great is the study of the Torah for it brings one to action." [2] Ethical action is the result of intelligent choice.

80

The theoretical principles of ethics arise from an understanding of the field of relations in which the human person finds himself. This field of relations is defined by three points: (1) the relationship with self; (2) the relationship with others in society; (3) the relationship with the transcendent. Although an ethical system must include all three points to be complete, its specific character is determined by its emphasis of one of the respective points as its fundamental base of reference. Ethical systems emphasizing self can be called "psychological"; those emphasizing society, "sociological"; those emphasizing transcendence, "theological."

The fundamental base of reference in Jewish ethics is the revelation of the will of God to the people of Israel in the Torah. Therefore Jewish ethics is essentially theological. The person's relationship with both self and society are ancillary to his or her relationship with God. However, the theological perspective is fundamental, not terminal; therefore, considerations of self and society are by no means eliminated from Jewish ethics. This is certainly the case in the ethical question of suicide.

A system of ethics grounded in revelation has often been dismissed as insulting to human intelligence. By emphasizing the will of God, Judaism is accused of providing an authoritarian rather than an intelligible foundation for human action: the person is *told* what to do rather than *discovering* what is to be done. This critique found its most famous spokesman in Immanuel Kant, who rejected *heteronomy* (external standards) in ethics in favor of *autonomy* (internal standards).

Nevertheless, this rejection of theological ethics falsely assumes that the revelation of the Torah is the same as the presence of an oracle. The difference between them, however, is considerable. Revelation is God's approach to man at a point in history. After that event man must attempt to comprehend the meaning of revelation as the fundamental ethical datum; that is, he must intelligently approach God. God and the human person are engaged in a mutual relationship of discovery. In the case of an oracle man approaches God in each particular situation. Although Scripture describes the working of the oracular *Urim veTumim*, it is clearly secondary to the authority of revelation.[3] After the destruction of the first Temple the oracle ceased to function altogether.[4] Furthermore, the oracle's function was strategic rather than ethical. Therefore, the theological process of discovering God's will is as intelligent a human enterprise as the psychological process of discovering the nature of the self or the sociological process of discovering the nature of society. Revelation is not an insult to human intelligence but only a threat to human pride. However, is not all truth a threat to human pride, for is not truth discovered rather than invented? Philosophically one would say, *Veritas est adaquaetio intellectus ad rem* ("Truth requires an adjustment of the subject to the object".) Jewishly one would say, "If the Torah seems empty, the emptiness comes from you." [5]

To understand suicide in Jewish perspective involves considerable intelligence because the sources seem rather ambivalent on the whole question. Jewishly speaking, the question itself breaks up into two questions: (1) May I commit suicide? (2) May society conduct normal burial and mourning rites for a suicide? The first question includes psychological considerations; the second sociological considerations. We shall see that these two questions are logically related.

2. *The Nature of Suicide*

It would seem that suicide is prohibited by the sixth commandment of the Decalogue, "You shall not murder." Nevertheless, none of the classical rabbinic sources apply this commandment to suicide. [6] Instead the rabbinic tradition preferred to look elsewhere:

> A person is not to harm himself. There is a tradition concerning the scriptural verse, "For your life-blood, too [*akh*] I will require a reckoning" [Gen. 9:5], that R. Eleazar taught the following interpretation, "From you I will require a reckoning for your *own* life-blood." [7]

The reason for the choice of this verse instead of the prohibition of murder becomes apparent in the following:

> Does this ban on suicide [Gen. 9:5] include one like Saul? No, Scripture uses the limiting term *akh* to exclude such cases. Does this ban include one like Hananiah, Mishael, and Azariah? No, Scripture uses the limiting term *akh* to exclude such cases. [8]

It is clear that the second text builds upon the first. Suicide is prohibited, but persons in the same category as Hananiah, Mishael, and Azariah, or as King Saul, are not morally judged to be suicides. The exceptions enable us to construct a theory as to what constitutes the limitation of the ban on suicide. In other words, by discovering what suicide is *not* we can then discover what it *is*, and why it is inconsistent with our relationship with God. As I pointed out in an earlier study, to infer the positive from the negative is a fundamental principle of rabbinic exegesis. [9] This method will serve here as well.

It is evident that Gen. 9:5 was chosen over Exod. 20:13 (the sixth commandment) because its formulation admitted exceptions, something that could not as easily be inferred from the absolute-sounding, "You shall not murder." In fact, in the classical sources suicide is not called "self-murder" but is designated by a unique term, *ma'abed atzmo l'daat* ("willful self-destruction").[10] Suicide is treated in a different context than murder; its main treatment is in the laws of mourning rather than in the laws of homicide.

In determining the exceptions to the rule we have two distinct categories: those like Hananiah, Mishael, and Azariah, and those like King Saul. Indeed, it has been interpreted that this is why the Midrash repeats the limiting term *akh* in each case rather than lumping them together.[11] All the various situations dealt with in the subsequent literature can be subsumed under one of these two categories.

It is best to begin with Hananiah, Mishael, and Azariah, inasmuch as they were martyrs and Jewish tradition has some very definite guidelines for martyrdom. Unhappily, Jewish history often demanded that these theoretical guidelines be translated into practice.

3. Martyrdom

It will be recalled from the third chapter of Daniel that these three men, known in Aramaic as Shadrach, Meshach, and Abed-Nego, were Jewish officials ordered by King Nebuchadnezzar to worship a golden image he had erected. When they refused they were thrown into a fiery furnace, but they miraculously escaped harm. The Midrash assumes they were aware that their refusal to serve the idol would cause their death. Nevertheless, the commandment to place the sanctification of God's name over one's own life (*Kiddush Hashem*) is considered to be pleasing in God's eyes, even though the act, taken as behavior, is often indistinguishable from suicide.[12] Hananiah, Mishael, and Azariah are chosen to exemplify the fact that martyrdom and suicide are theologically distinct.[13] Israeli Justice Haim H. Cohn put it very well:

> Suicide is sharply to be differentiated from martyrdom, which under certain circumstances, is the greatest *mitzvah* of Judaism; a difference must also be made between letting oneself be killed and active suicide.[14]

An authoritative passage in the Talmud emphasizes that human life has priority over all the commandments of the Torah, except three: murder, sexual immorality, and idolatry.[15] Hananiah, Mishael, and

Azariah are the personal precedents for this last exception. They showed that the glory of God takes precedence over human life.

Martyrdom is not suicide because it is initiated by God not by the human subject. It is God who creates a situation where His glory and continued human life are mutually exclusive. However, this situation is not internal but external; that is, it is not that the subject himself *feels* that his or her life is inconsistent with God's glory, but, rather, that the decision is forced upon the subject by factors outside the control of his conscious or unconscious mind. The person confronts the situation outside himself. Thus martyrdom is a *public* act. Indeed, according to the continuation of the same talmudic passage, martyrdom requires the presence of the same number of *other* persons as a quorum for public worship. [16] It can thus be inferred, I believe, that suicide, as opposed to martyrdom, is a *private* act. By "private" I do not mean that suicide must be committed in solitude. Indeed, the verification of suicide, as we shall see below, requires witnesses. No, by a "private act" I mean an act for which the subject's *internal* state of affairs is the determinant. Even if others witness the suicide the drama is within the person committing the act. Thus the martyr, R. Hanina ben Teradyon, was burnt at the stake by the Romans for publicly teaching Torah. To risk one's life to *publicly* teach Torah is an act of sanctification for which one is to suffer martyrdom, if need be. However, R. Hanina refused to shorten his own *private* suffering, as suggested by his students, by opening his mouth to let the flames enter into his throat, reasoning, "It is better that He who gave life Himself take it back and let not a man destroy himself." [17] This reasoning is not based on any textual interpretation but is, rather, a general theological insight. [18]

It is relatively easy to exclude the three would-be martyrs in Daniel from the stigma of suicide because there are two nonsuicidal factors in their favor: (1) They were willing to die rather than commit an idolatrous act; the choice was inescapable. (2) Their deaths would not have been self-inflicted for they themselves did not jump into the fire.

4. *Suicide by Anticipation*

However, it becomes much more difficult to exclude from the stigma of suicide the talmudic case of four hundred boys and girls who were sent into Roman captivity. When they discovered that they were to be used as sexual objects they jumped into the sea, reasoning, "If we drown in the sea we will come to the life of the world-to-come." [19] Here, the forbidden act was not yet present but only anticipated; furthermore, their death was self-inflicted. Yet, despite all this, the Talmud relates the story approvingly. Indeed the story is immediately followed by the famous story of the martyrdom of Hannah and her seven sons. Both stories had an enormous influence on subsequent Jewish thought. [20] The medieval glosses, *Tosafot*, note that in a case where one fears that non-Jewish persecutors will cause him or her to sin, suicide is an imperative. [21] Sin, in this explanation, must be understood in two senses:

1. The sin must be active; that is, one must fear that he or she will be forced to *commit* immoral acts rather than merely be *used* by others for immoral purposes. Queen Esther was seen as the passive victim of King Ahasuerus and, therefore, not liable to cause herself a martyr's death. [22] Indeed, if the suicide were committed for any lesser reason, such as fear of death or imprisonment, then Josephus's argument to the Masada suicides is in keeping with Jewish tradition: "And shall we then inflict upon ourselves certain death, to avoid an uncertain death, which we fear, at the hands of our foes?" [23]

2. The sin must be a public profanation of God's glory (*Hillul Hashem*). [24] If one of the boys or girls had submitted to the Romans, the example might very well have caused the others to despair and abandon Judaism altogether.

A third type of situation causes even further problems. There are a number of cases reported in rabbinic sources where suicides were the result of self-execution for sins entailing the death penalty. In other words, certain persons killed themselves in lieu of a formal trial and death sentence. [25] This type of exoneration is impossible to accept on the basis of Jewish legal tradition. Execution requires that (1) two witnesses not only witnessed the crime but also forewarned the criminal; (2) the criminal rejected their forewarning (*Hatra'ah*); and (3) the criminal had a public trial before a duly constituted court. Maimonides was suspicious that persons who confess to capital crimes might be mentally ill. R. David ibn Zimra (Radbaz) insightfully noted that if self-incrimination were permitted by Jewish law, then one could commit suicide by causing his own execution. Self-execution has no basis in the law itself. [26]

Nevertheless, the Talmud in several places records that a heavenly echo (*bat kol*) announced that certain such suicides are deserving of the bliss of the world-to-come and receive it as their reward. An old Midrash tells the story of the assimilated nephew of R. Jose ben Joezer, who ridiculed his uncle's plight as a martyr. Suddenly, after experiencing his uncle's great faith in the face of his doom, he became very remorseful and executed himself, utilizing all four means of Jewish capital punishment. When the rabbi saw his nephew's bier ascending heavenward, he exclaimed, "In but a short period of time this man has preceded me to the Garden of Eden"; in other words, by this one act he has merited eternal bliss ahead of one who devoted his entire life to good works. [27] It is difficult to accept as ethical precedents such cases of heavenly voices approving self-executions, inasmuch as a famous talmudic passage, treating an incident in which a heavenly voice contradicts what the sages of Israel have determined to be the law, indicates that "the Torah is not in heaven" but is, rather, to be interpreted by human authorities. [28] Clearly, self-execution is not legally valid in Judaism.

Later responsa carry the point further still and report cases of individuals known to be pious and learned who committed suicide. In order to exonerate these self-inflicted deaths from the stigma of suicide, several authorities assume that the deceased must have committed some capital crime for which, in all piety and learning, he was convinced he was deserving of death. [29] In other words, in the talmudic accounts the crime of the person is specifically known, or the commentators are quick to surmise what it was specifically. In these responsa the crime is not specifically known but only generally assumed. It would now seem that the principle of martyrdom has been stretched just about as far as it can possibly go, even in imagination, much less in actual law.

As a continuation of the discussion of the four hundred captured boys and girls and of Hannah and her seven sons, the Talmud introduces the statement of the sage Rava that a teacher should not demonstrate the laws of kosher slaughtering on himself. Rashi, in his commentary, assumes that the reason is that he might accidentally kill himself. [30] However, could not Rava's concern be deeper, namely, a wariness about a possible "ritual" suicide?

5. Mental Illness

At this point a new factor enters the picture; namely, the whole issue of mental illness. Indeed R. Moses Schreiber (Hatam Sofer), analyzing one such case in his famous responsum written in 1835, finally reasons that we can assume mental illness since the suicide under consideration was neither witnessed nor forewarned. However, R. Schreiber does not connect the suspicion of mental illness with the possible motive of self-execution. It is presented as an independent ground to be employed when every other exoneration fails. A late nineteenth-century authority, R. Jehiel M. Epstein, suggests that because suicide is an improbable act, every legal means should be used to exonerate it. [31]

Mental illness as the explanation for certain suicides, thereby ruling out their "willfulness," is brought out in the minor talmudic tractate *Semahot*, which deals with mourning procedures.

> A case occurred with the son of Gorganos in Lydda, who ran away from school and his father threatened to box his ears, so he went and killed himself in a pit. They came and asked R. Tarfon, who said that no burial dignity was to be withheld from him. [32]

Nahmanides, in his presentation of this earlier source, reasons that R. Tarfon ruled this way because the suicide was that of a child. [33] Asheri (Rosh) further notes that the real issue here is not so much that the suicide was that of a child but, rather, that the suicide was committed under unusual stress (*pahad*); namely, what we would call hysteria. [34]

Furthermore, Nahmanides, in his reworking of the earlier source, follows this example of the terrified child with these words about King Saul:

> Saul, king of Israel, was doomed to die, suicide was, therefore permitted to him [*mutar lo*] as indicated in *Bereshit Rabah* . . . the prohibition of suicide does not apply to one like Saul who is *pursued* [*nirdaf*]. [35]

This characterization of Saul as one "pursued" is not found in the rabbinic source as our text stands. It could very well be an independent insertion by Nahmanides. Anyway, it adds a new dimension to our understanding of why Saul is traditionally exempted from the stigma of suicide. [36] The Talmud was very solicitous of the honor of King Saul in a number of separate passages. In one place a heavenly echo (*bat kol*) announces that Saul, despite his alleged sins against the Gibeonites, was still "the Lord's chosen." [37] Elsewhere, the Talmud criticizes those who did not properly eulogize Saul. [38] The remark is directed against those who saw Saul's ordering the massacre of the priests of Nob (1 Sam. 22:18 ff.) as the basis of his sin against the Gibeonites, inasmuch as the priests of Nob were the chief source of their support. However, Nahmanides states that the Talmud's remark about improper eulogy of Saul is directed against those who would accuse Saul of committing suicide unlawfully. [39] A later authority attempts to exonerate Saul's suicide by arguing that (1) if he were captured many Israelites would have died in attempting to rescue him; (2) it would have been a profanation of God's name (*Hillul Hashem*) if the "annointed of the Lord" were killed by the uncir-

cumcised Philistines. [40] However, some earlier medieval authorities
refuse to exonerate Saul. In the same passage they also condemn an
overwillingness to die and to kill others in the face of possible forced
conversion. [41] This important dissent from a marked trend in Jewish
tradition is especially poignant when the memory of the Holocaust forces
us to rethink traditional Jewish martyrology.

We are left with the question: Why is Saul's suicide not explicitly
exonerated on the grounds of mental illness? Certainly there is ample
evidence in the scriptural accounts of his life that he was a paranoid
schizophrenic: his deep depressions; his lapses of memory; his unjustified
suspicions; his sudden personality changes; his homicidal defenses.
Indeed, in Scripture his obviously psychotic episodes, which became
more and more frequent as he grew older and sicker, are designated
afflictions by "the evil spirit from the Lord." [42]

The answer to this question is that psychosis was not distinguished
from imbecility. Only a person who was imbecilic (*shoteh*) was considered
mentally ill. However, a person of accepted piety and learning, certainly
the divinely chosen king of Israel, was not considered to be an imbecile,
hence he was not considered psychotic. In fact, so astute and sophisticated
a scriptural commentator as the fifteenth-century Spanish statesman,
Don Isaac Abrabanel, dismisses the suggestion that Saul's vision of the
prophet Samuel with the witch of Endor (1 Sam. 28:3 ff.) is evidence
of psychosis:

> Those imagining that they see things not having external reality
> are of imperfect intelligence and are very sick and lacking in
> strength ... but Saul was exceedingly intelligent, wise and per-
> ceptive and in excellent health. And he was constantly aware
> of his sin and pondered his fate many times. [43]

How ironic that a heightened sense of guilt and doom should be cited
as a proof of mental health! Nevertheless, the assumption underlying
such a pre-Freudian analysis is that psychosis and imbecility are identical.
Therefore, one having average or above-average intelligence could not
possibly be psychotic. On this assumption Abrabanel exonerates Saul's
subsequent bizarre death by arguing that he was fearful of his imminent
ignoble execution at the hands of the Philistines. [44] A later rabbinic
scholar compares Saul's fear to the fear of the four hundred captured
boys and girls who committed suicide out of fear of what would happen
to them at the hands of the Romans. [45] In other words, both are cases
of hysterical suicides.

Running the gamut of possible exonerations of suicide, from the relatively easy case of martyrs like Hananiah, Mishael, and Azariah, to the very difficult case of those like King Saul, we can see how the law concerning society's reaction to suicide was so precisely formulated.

> Who is considered a suicide? It is not one who went up to the top of a tree or a roof and fell and died. But it is one who announced, "Look I am going to the top of the tree or the roof" and fell and died—such a person is presumed to be a suicide.[46]

In other words, the laws of evidence for a suicide are interpreted as strictly as those for a homicide. Exceptions were even found for those who announced their suicidal intentions.[47] R. Tarfon and R. Akiba, in the second century of this era, stated, on the basis of the strictness of the Jewish laws of evidence, that were they in the Sanhedrin no one would ever have been executed.[48] In our own day, in similar fashion, one prominent authority in the area of Jewish mourning law noted about the presumption of suicide:

> Our sages sought out countless times answers and exonerations for suicides to such an extent that in actual fact there were no "willful" suicides at all.[49]

In retrospect we have come full circle. Suicide is prohibited, but two categories of exceptions are noted. In analyzing those cases included in the categories of exception we have now discovered that for practical purposes every case falls under the exception and none under the rule! Although another contemporary authority recognizes this difficulty and warns about making everything the exception, thus, in effect, eliminating the rule, he is hard-put to reverse the trend noted above.[50]

Moreover, even if a suicide were validated as being "willful," most of the normal mourning rites would still apply, inasmuch as Jewish mourning law is primarily designed for the dignity and comfort of the survivors.

> R. Ishmael suggested that it be said about a suicide, "What a fool! What a fool!" R. Akiba said to him that he should simply be laid to rest, neither blessed nor cursed . . . and his survivors should be comforted as this is due dignity for the living.[51]

The law follows R. Akiba. Furthermore, most subsequent authorities follow Nahmanides over Maimonides in advocating a more lenient interpretation of the mourning honors due a suicide and his or her family. [52]

6. Suicide Before and After the Fact

Considering the development of Jewish law up to the present time, are we left with no practical insights at all as to the act of willful suicide?

At this point I believe it is necessary to further develop the Jewish law of suicide.

There must be a careful consideration of the rabbinic distinction between acts permitted before the fact (*mutar l'khat'hilah*) and acts exonerated only after the fact (*patur di'abad*). An act permitted before the fact will obviously be exonerated after the fact. However, an act exonerated after the fact will *not* necessarily be permitted before the fact. Thus, for example, after the fact, the meat slaughtered by a child is considered kosher, provided he did the act (*shehitah*) under supervision. [53] In other words, we only accept what has already been done *ex post-facto*. Nevertheless, before the fact (*ab initio*) we do not permit children to slaughter animals for food consumption. [54]

In our case of suicide, it seems to me that the same type of reasoning must also apply. Just because we exonerate most suicides after the fact does not mean we should permit them before the fact. Furthermore, before the fact we are dealing with a live actor. After the fact we are dealing with a dead victim. Suicide, then, is the most radical example of the difference between *before* and *after* in Jewish law.

Nahmanides, on the other hand, states that since Saul was "doomed" (*abud*), suicide was therefore "permitted to him" (*mutar lo*). [55] Nevertheless, on the basis of this reasoning we could not only exonerate almost every suicide but *permit* almost every suicide as well. Therefore it is important to note that the subsequent codes, *Tur* and *Shulhan Arukh*, omit the word *permitted* (*mutar*), although subsequent commentators do not emphasize the omission. [56]

Since the punishment of the act, as interpreted from Scripture, is considered to be in God's hands, the most human authorities can do is to declare that the suicide had lost his or her share in the world-to-come. And although this judgment is not found in any of the rabbinic sources, but only in comparatively recent Jewish writers, it is easy to see how it fits into the rabbinic tradition. [57]

In the case of the martyrdom of Hannah and her seven sons, as reported in the apocryphal 2 Maccabees, one of the sons declares to

Antiochus that he is not afraid of death because God gives life after death. [58] In other words, the often indistinguishable Pharisaic doctrines of the resurrection of the dead and the world-to-come constitute the ultimate rationale for martyrdom. Even the criminal sentenced to death is assured of the life of the world-to-come if he repents before his execution. [59] Suicide, on the other hand, is a rejection of the possibility of repentance; therefore it cannot bring one to the life of the world-to-come. Nevertheless, if God sees fit to make exceptions to this rule, humans cannot in humility ignore His mercy. However, one need not draw inferences from these extraordinary exceptions. The practical inference—namely, not to commit suicide—is inferred from the rule, not the exceptions.

The whole point in mentioning heavenly echoes and visions in these special cases indicates that in other cases suicide is not acceptable to God. When one eighteenth-century Jewish scholar suggested that suicide motivated by personal suffering be condoned, he was vigorously opposed. [60] Thus suicide is not permitted before the fact, but certain isolated cases were exonerated by God. The cases of self-execution discussed in rabbinic literature would fall into this category. Once one sees that these cases are not paradigmatic, the obvious contradictions within Jewish legal tradition are removed.

Here we have a clear case of the imitation of God. Before the act we imitate God's justice by prohibiting the sinner from sinning against himself or herself. After the fact we imitate God's mercy by exonerating, as best we can, the *victim* and saving his or her loved ones from the disgrace of less than complete burial and mourning honors. [61]

In terms of mental illness, for which we took the case of King Saul as paradigmatic, a broader definition of psychosis is called for. We saw that the equation of psychosis with imbecility can no longer be maintained after Freud. Furthermore, piety is no assurance against psychosis.

Happily, Jewish tradition is cognizant of advances in medical science and how these advances affect Jewish law. And we can look to Maimonides, who was both a physician and a pre-eminent Jewish legal authority, for precedents in this area. To the chagrin of many later commentators, he broadened the talmudic definition of insanity (*shoteh*), basing himself, undoubtedly, on his knowledge and experience as a physician. [62] We can certainly continue along the lines of his example.

It is a well-known fact to students of psychiatry that religious delusions often play an important role in psychoses. Indeed, coming back to King Saul, some of his most psychotic episodes are described in Scripture with the same verb used to describe "prophecy" (*niba*), except that it is used in the reflexive form. [63] If one accepts the notion that psychoses are "narcissistic neuroses" [64]—that is, that they entail the elimination of interpersonal object relations—then it can be seen how both prophecy and psychosis draw on the same psychic energies. The crucial difference between them lies not in their source but, rather, in their manifestation. Prophecy intends real objects; psychosis intends nothing outside the subject himself. Therefore, psychosis can take on religious defenses. The important thing for theologians to learn from psychiatry, however, is to be aware how religion may lend itself to psychotic thinking and not rationalize it in the same way the psychotic himself does. In other words, self-execution should be ascribed to mental illness not piety.

Both Judaism and psychiatry are concerned with the re-establishment of interpersonal object relations. Interpersonal objects transcend the subject. Repentance (teshubah) is the turning of the human person back to the person of God. As such it is the most radical transformation of personality. It must include a returning to self and to others. Here Judaism and psychiatry have something very profound to discuss in common without either losing its unique identity and function. The problem of suicide is a good place to start such discussion inasmuch as self-destruction lies at the very heart of the misery of the human condition. Judaism teaches psychiatry that self-transformation must include the perspective of the relationship with God. If Judaism said this were the only problem, then it would be attempting to eclipse psychiatry. Psychiatry teaches Judaism that certain acts, which appear religious, do not really intend God as their object at all. If psychiatry says that *every* religious act intends something other than God, then psychiatry is attempting to eclipse Judaism. [65]

Therefore, King Saul is the paradigm of the psychotic suicide. He is not subject to God's justice before the fact inasmuch as we cannot assume his motivation to be free. But he is the subject of God's mercy after the tragedy as a *fait accompli*. Since God's mercy is an attribute revealed so that it might be imitated, [66] virtually every private suicide, like King Saul, calls for our mercy to him and those close to him. For despite his psychosis he was still "the chosen of the Lord"—tragic but never forsaken.

Only the suicide knows in his heart whether his act is a rejection of God's Kingship or not. Mercy demands of the rest of us that without an almost impossible criterion of evidence, we must assume that all private suicides are like King Saul, whom we are to eulogize and not condemn. In the last analysis our practice of both justice and mercy is rooted in humility, the same humility that teaches us our lives belong to God, not to society, not even to ourselves. In the end we sympathize with the suicide's ultimate plight. In the beginning we hope that all the Torah has taught us will teach, in the moment of existential decision, that even our agony does not place us at the center of the universe, and that our death as well as our birth is the gift of the Creator of all being. [67] In the end as in the beginning the Creator and not the creature is the real I. [68]

CHAPTER 10

FUNERALS IN THE SYNAGOGUE

QUESTION: A number of rabbis and laymen have asked me the law concerning funerals in the synagogue. The question has been raised many times in the past, which only indicates that it is a perennial problem and that fundamental halakhic concepts are involved.

A synagogue funeral is considered to be a great honor. The issue of honors in the synagogue must be handled more delicately than elsewhere because of the synagogue's formality as *the* institution of Judaism. Concerning this general problem the following text is highly indicative:

> At a dinner honors may be exchanged but not in the synagogue
> for there people would tend to fight. [1]

Distribution of synagogue honors is the general problem underlying the question about synagogue funerals. Some of the more specific questions involved are: (1) Are all synagogues legally similar? (2) What is the role of the sage in the synagogue? (3) What is the definition of a eulogy? (4) When may the law be changed in cases of conflict?
Answer: The question of conducting public mourning in the synagogue is first raised in the Tosefta. There we read:

> Undignified behavior   [*kalut rosh*] is not to be carried on in
> synagogues . . . but the Scriptures are to be read, the Mishnah
> recited, and exegetical lectures given, and *public mourning* exer-
> cises   [*hesped shel rabim*] are to be held in them. [2]

In the Babylonian Talmud the baraita is presented with the added words:
" . . . *private mourning exercises*   [*hesped shel yahid*] are *not* to be held in
them." [3] This additional point is a later inference from the earlier text

as it is not found anywhere else. However, it brings out the obvious fact that indeed it was the rabbinic practice to make a clear distinction between public and private mourning exercises. [4]

What distinguishes between "public" and "private" mourning exercises and why may only the former be held in the synagogue? When the baraita is presented in the Talmud, Rashi notes about public mourning exercises that they are "for a sage" (talmid hakham) who has died; people *must* gather and mourn him, and the synagogue, being a large building, is suited for this purpose.

The Talmud then proceeds to describe public mourning exercises. [5] In an apparent example of mutual admiration, R. Hisda states that if anyone of the school of R. Sheshet died, that would surely be a public mourning exercise. R. Sheshet returns the compliment. [6] Rafram publicly mourned his daughter-in-law in the synagogue, justifying his action by noting that either because of his merit or because of the merit of the deceased a large crowd came. R. Zera and Resh Lakish publicly mourned their students for the same reason. Nevertheless, R. Nahman refused to publicly mourn a Tanna, that is, a person who had memorized large amounts of oral tradition but was lacking in any analytic ability or depth. Clearly such persons were not considered on the same level as sages. [7]

Therefore, on the basis of the development of the Tosefta in the Babli, we see that public mourning exercises are only held for sages and their close relatives. Others, even quasi scholars, are denied this privilege. Furthermore, it would seem, according to Rashi, that these exercises are held in the synagogue because this is the only place large enough to accommodate the large number of people who would attend the funeral of either a sage, his close relative, or a promising student whom a sage thought worthy enough to personally mourn. Thus, in summary, the *Tur* and the *Shulhan Arukh* state that "the funerals of sages and their wives alone may be held either in the synagogue or the House of Study, but not those of the rest of the people." [8]

In the earliest responsum I know of on the subject, Maimonides was asked about the propriety of the custom of the Jews of Alexandria, who brought the deceased into the courtyard of the synagogue until the congregational services were completed, whereupon the rabbis and officials, followed by the entire congregation, came out with the congregation reciting prayers of justification and dirges, whereafter the body was taken to the cemetery. The questioners wanted to know whether this constituted a *public funeral* and, also, whether the custom was prevalent in other communities as well. [9] Maimonides responded that this was

definitely not a public funeral and that such honors should be reserved
for one of the great people of the city where there is an *obligation on
everyone's part* to mourn him. He further extended this privilege to an
upright person, although noting that this is a permitted *option*, obviously
distinguishing this from the obligation for a sage. This slight extension
is important to note because the questioner refers to Maimonides' earlier
statement in the *Mishneh Torah*, where he limits this privilege to "the
great sages of that city." [10] However, Maimonides' slightly more liberal
interpretation of the law in his responsum is not picked up by subsequent
authorities. They all follow the lead of the *Mishneh Torah* in restricting
the privilege of a synagogue funeral to a sage or his wife. Moreover,
it seems that Maimonides, in this case, may very well be referring to
a memorial service after the burial. [11]

Finally, Maimonides referred with approval to the Egyptian custom
of constructing special places where the mourners spent the entire week
of mourning. These places, *kotel abelim*, were probably the equivalent
of the modern funeral parlor. Since these chapels were initially designated for funerals, they are not like regular synagogues, having been
initially (*metehilah*) "profaned" for such purposes. In such places, unlike
a regular synagogue, or even the courtyard of a regular synagogue,
as in Alexandria, the ban on private funerals did not apply.

The tendency among a number of later authorities was to limit the
privilege even further. For example, the sons-in-law of no less a sage
than R. Elijah, the Gaon of Vilna, were criticized by the rabbis of Vilna
for bringing the Gaon's body into the synagogue. The criticism was
certainly not due to any question about his learning or piety, but, rather,
was derived from the Gaon's own teaching that the synagogue, like
the Temple, to which it is often compared, ought not be defiled by
a corpse. [12] On the basis of this notion there would be no distinction
between a sage or anyone else since all corpses are ritually impure. [13]

Of course the comparison of the synagogue with the Temple cannot
be extended as Halakhah to exclude ritual impurity from the synagogue.
For the synagogue, as we shall see, is essentially characterized as a place
of Torah. R. Judah ben Betera authoritatively ruled that the words
of Torah do not acquire impurity, being compared to fire, which does
not acquire impurity. [14] Furthermore, R. Moses Isserles (Rema) rules
that the essential Halakhah is that a menstruant may enter the synagogue
at any time, although noting that the custom in Poland was for her
not to do so. [15] Therefore, the objection of the Gaon is at best a private
opinion, which others may adopt but which is certainly not binding
on them. [16]

Finally, a prominent authority on mourning laws in our time, the late R. Leopold Greenwald of Columbus, Ohio (d. 1955), suggests that ideally no corpse should be brought into the synagogue. As a further precedent he approvingly refers to an earlier authority, who suggests that no funerals be held in the synagogue because the privileges accorded to sages no longer apply in our time. [17]

This view has a good deal of precedent. As early as tanaitic times, the rabbis opposed the view of R. Jose ben R. Judah, holding that scholars, like ordinary people, required forewarning (hatraah) before being held culpable for a crime. [18]

Later, the talmudic suggestion that sages are excused from saying the Shema at bedtime was not followed by the subsequent Codes. [19] Again, the talmudic exemption of bridegrooms from the evening Shema until they consummated their marriages was rescinded by R. Meir of Rothenburg (d. 1293) because the original reason for the exemption was that bridegrooms were so intent on performing a mitzvah that the proper intention (kavvanah) required for the Shema could not be expected of them. However, R. Meir notes that no one has proper intention nowadays (referring of course to his own era, though his remark has even more merit for our period), so all are to be regarded equally in this respect. [20] Proper intention was considered a special virtue of sages. [21]

Therefore, on the basis of these two new concepts, R. Greenwald tightened as much as possible the old restriction of funerals in the synagogues, stopping just short of ruling them out completely. In a subsequent responsum, answering a rabbi in Peekskill, New York, he prohibits a funeral in the anteroom of the synagogue on the grounds that the sanctity of the synagogue extends to the anteroom, and that if funerals are permitted in the anteroom, they will inevitably wind up in the synagogue itself. [22] And in his earlier work, he strongly disapproved of the current practice of allowing funerals for any prominent person in the synagogue, no matter what his or her piety and learning, questioning the very sanctity of such a synagogue. [23] However, in his responsum he justifies the leniency of some authorities as to the anteroom of the synagogue on the grounds that these same rabbis did not normally pray there and this means that such places do not have the status of synagogues. [24] Nevertheless, he himself prefers the stricter view. [25]

It would seem that the question has been answered. *Ideally*, no funeral should be held in the synagogue; *practically*, only the funeral of a pious scholar or his wife.

1. A Historical Approach

As heirs of the "Historical School," we must ask ourselves a further question: Are our synagogues today the same institutions the traditional sources designated as *Bet Hakeneset?*
The rabbinic sources distinguish between two types of synagogues.

> The citizens of a city who sold the broad place of the city may purchase a synagogue with the money—they may sell a synagogue and purchase an ark.[26]

> R. Samuel bar Nahmani said that this refers to synagogues in the villages, but those in the towns, because they attract worshippers from all over, cannot be sold because they are *public property.* [27]

Furthermore, the Gemara there notes the statement of Rab Ashi that a certain synagogue had the same status as a country synagogue, even though it attracted worshippers from all over, because they came to *his synagogue,* namely, the snyagogue was under his ownership and he had the right to sell it if he so chose. In other words, the question of actual locale is simply a case of a contemporary example; [28] the essenceof the matter is either (1) the ownership of the synagogue or (2) for whose use it was established. [29] Maimonides and Asheri (Rosh) opt for the criterion of use as the sole determinant of whether a synagogue has the status of a "town synagogue" or not. [30] Rashi refers to these synagogues as "public synagogues." [31] On the other hand, the Palestinian Talmud refers to country-type synagogues as "private synagogues." [32]

By eliminating the question of ownership Maimonides and Asheri avoid the problem raised by a Mishnah that refers to the synagogue as the property of the city, namely, held in partnership by the members of the community. [33] And there a matter clearly involving ownership seems to apply to a public synagogue.

With this distinction clearly understood, we can now begin to see why the sage has a unique relationship with the public synagogue. First, since public synagogues are for the most part in the towns, they would be the natural place for sages, who for the most part were urbanites, to study and teach Torah. [34] The ignoramus (*am ha'aretz*), as his very name indicates, was primarily a rural dweller. Since the presence of the Torah was what distinguished the synagogue, the sage, as expounder of the Torah, was the natural leader of the synagogue.

For this reason, it seems to me, the sage had certain privileges in the synagogue; namely, by virtue of his leadership and his constant presence there.

> It was taught that no undignified behavior [kalut rosh] was to be conducted in synagogues or houses of study ... R. Joshua ben Levi said that synagogues and houses of study are for the sages and their students. [35]

R. David Fraenkel (d. 1762) notes that synagogues were organized ab initio for the sages and their students; therefore they are permitted to use them for their ordinary needs. [36] In other words, the presence of a sage created a community. [37] The Babylonian Talmud refers to synagogues and especially Houses of Study as "the house of rabbis." [38] R. Greenwald believed that one could gather from the Mishnah that ordinary funerals were held in the homes of the deceased. [39] If this were the case, then it would stand to reason that only a funeral for a sage could be held in the synagogue since this was indeed his "home."

With the death of a sage (or his absence due to mourning) the cohesive force of the community was severely ruptured. Since the community's raison d'être was the presence of the sage and his teaching, Nahmanides reports the specific procedure for his funeral:

> R. Hai was consulted ... a sage, outstanding and illustrious is brought into the house of study and the bier is placed in the place where he used to expound and the students and the congregation mourn him. [40]

This is based on the old rule that the study of the Torah is to be interrupted for a funeral provided that not enough people are otherwise available to provide proper escort. Proper escort for a sage was considered to be up to 600,000 people; since the Torah was given to that many people, its "removal" required as many to be present. [41] As Rashi points out, the nullification of the teaching of a sage (talmudo batel) is as if the Torah were taken back. The House of Study is out of operation for the time being. [42] This is undoubtedly why when a sage dies all are like his next of kin. [43] The reasoning is a fortiori: If our parents who gave us physical life are to be mourned, how much more so our teachers who give us the life of the world-to come? [44] If we mourn our parents in the place of our association with them, namely, the family home, then ought we not mourn the sages in the place of our association with them, namely the synagogue?

In fact, the primacy of the sage was taken so seriously that at the funeral of King Hezekiah, it is reported, a Torah scroll was placed on the bier and it was said, "This one upheld what is written here." [45] Rashi justifies this practice on the basis of the fact that the Book of Proverbs (6:23, 20:27) refers to both the Torah and the soul of man as *light*. Nevertheless, this practice was discontinued as R. Hisda reported that R. Huna did not approve of it. King Hezekiah was taken as a unique case and, besides, the practice involved other halakhic problems as well. [46]

All of this is a recognition of the fact that the living force of the sage, even more than the presence of a Torah scroll, was the condition that made the synagogue, as the center of the Jewish community, unique and holy. According to a very old baraita, Alexander Jannaeus followed the advice of the Sadducees and killed the Pharisee teachers, reasoning that anyone wanting Torah could consult the scroll placed in a corner. R. Nahman bar Isaac saw this notion as the beginning of heresy since the Written Torah is meaningless without the Oral Torah and this would be lost without the sages of Israel. [47] Rava ridiculed people who would rise before a Torah scroll but not before a sage, noting the power of the rabbis to actually change the literal meaning of the Written Torah. [48] Indeed the obligation to rise before a Torah scroll is derived *a fortiori* from the obligation to rise before a sage. [49] In short, the presence of the sage made the difference between a dead scroll and the living word of God. It almost reminds one of Plato's insistence that wise men are even more important than good laws. [50]

2. Synagogues Public and Private

The general question upon which the specific question before us rests is: Are the synagogues in America today private or public institutions? Concerning this general question in another specific context the late Professor Louis Ginzberg wrote:

> I would say that the Jewish Law is explicit on this point, discriminating between a community synagogue and a congregational synagogue. . . . congregational synagogue is one which is erected by the contributions of members of a society, primarily for their own use. . . . There are hardly any community synagogues in this sense of the law in this country. [51]

Since, unfortunately, Professor Ginzberg's responsum does not contain references, I can only surmise what sources he drew upon.

In determining what constitutes a "congregational synagogue" we must understand what constitutes a "community synagogue," since a congregational synagogue is less than a community synagogue. From the sources we have seen heretofore one can infer that there are four criteria for a community synagogue:

1. It is constructed and maintained for use by all Jews.
2. It is supported by general contributions.
3. It is organized primarily as a place for sages to study and teach.
4. There are no stipulations for its use for purposes other than study of the Torah and prayer.

The congregational synagogue in America falls short of three, perhaps all four, of these criteria for a *community synagogue*.

1. Our synagogues have distinct memberships; they charge dues from the members. Membership entitles a member to privileges not open to the general Jewish public (reserved seating, etc.).
2. Although I have never heard of a synagogue turning down a contribution from a nonmember, synagogues look to their own membership for the bulk of their support. This is why the Welfare Federations, which are truly communal, are usually loath to provide any support for congregations. Apparently Professor Ginzberg, by making this a criterion, follows Tosafot and R. Nissim over Maimonides and Asheri. However, if one followed these latter two this criterion would be irrelevant.
3. This criterion more than any other certainly does not apply to our synagogues. I am not saying our synagogues are devoid of Torah. Happily, many have excellent adult-education programs and regular classes; many rabbis are certainly scholars. But the American synagogue is not centered around the person and activity of the sage. The professionalization of the rabbinate rules this out, because the rabbi is subsequently *hired after* the establishment and incorporation of the synagogue. He is a paid employee.
4. Our synagogues are nonprofit corporations with constitutions and by-laws. I know of no American synagogue which does not stipulate use of its premises for many activities other than study and prayer.

For this last reason, especially, our synagogues are "private institutions." In fact, one early authority held that country synagogues did not have the full status of community synagogues because they stipulated that travelers could lodge in them for the night, a clearly profane activity. [52] Others held that synagogues having assigned seats are country synagogues. [53]

The question, therefore, can be asked anew, namely: May the funeral of a non-sage be held in a congregational synagogue? On this point the Talmud says something that I believe to be most germane:

> Rab Assi said that the synagogues in Babylonia were established on condition [Rashi: for general use] but even so *undignified behavior* is not to be held in them. What would there be? *Business calculations*. Rab Assi said that a synagogue where business is transacted dead bodies will be lodged there [Rashi: members of the community will die and there will be no one—i.e., next of kin—to bury them]. [54]

The question before us is: Is a private funeral an example of "undignified behavior" prohibited even in a "private" synagogue?

The Gemara seems to imply that business calculations are what is meant. However, it is difficult to determine whether the bringing of dead bodies into the synagogue is an example of even worse disrespect, [55] or perhaps a subtle indication that a synagogue whose membership is so materialistic as to engage in business dealings in the synagogue will have ultimately many *met mitzvah* cases, namely, persons whose families and neighbors have abandoned them. [56] In other words, it is hard to determine whether bringing bodies into the synagogue is an example of the *act* of disrespect or a *predicted result* of the type of disrespect specified by the Gemara. If part of the *act*, then a private funeral is prohibited even in our synagogues; if a *predicted result*, then it can be permitted although not necessarily encouraged. Finally, in the original passage in *B. Megillah* 28b, it is also doubtful whether the addition of the ban on private funerals in the synagogue to the original Tosefta passage is meant as a further example of disrespect or not.

Therefore, there seem to be sufficient halakhic grounds for a congregation stipulating that the funerals of prominent members or officers be permitted in the synagogue if this is considered an honor for service to the congregation. Furthermore, the second important point made by Maimonides in his aforementioned responsum was that the "funeral parlors" of Egypt were not the same as regular (community) synagogues because they stipulated their use for funerals *in advance*. Therefore, it would seem that our *congregational* synagogues can do the same thing in either their constitutions or by-laws.

3. The Development of the Eulogy

We have seen above that one of the reasons for restricting a synagogue funeral was to signify that in the case of the deceased sage "his Torah was nullified." In other words, a eulogy (*hesped*) was considered to be neglect of Torah (*bitul Torah*), which could only be tolerated in the synagogue, a place of Torah, when the sage, the voice of Torah,[57] had been silenced by death. For anyone not a sage, such an interruption would be intolerable.

Nevertheless, if one examines the historical development of the eulogy, the definition changes.

Originally, a hesped was an exercise in public grief chiefly characterized by histrionics. It was designed to cause weeping and wailing.[58] From the examples given in the Talmud it would seem that the hesped was a genuine emotional expression of grief with an absence of rabbinic intellectualizing, that is, exegesis.[59] Breast-beating was part of the act.[60]

In fact the Talmud specifically forbade uttering words of Torah in the presence of the deceased.[61] As Rashi explains:

> To speak of matters of Halakhah is forbidden in his presence since all are *obligated* to speak of them and the deceased is silent and this is like "Whoever ridicules the poor one reviles his Maker" [Prov. 17:5].

Tosafot limits this prohibition to the space within four cubits of the deceased, but others extend the prohibition to the same room.[62] R. Joseph Karo explains that to speak of Torah in the presence of the dead would give the appearance of ignoring the deceased.[63] The early work, *Abel Rabati*, indicates that during the period of mourning (after the funeral) neither Halakhah nor Aggadah was recited but only the laws of mourning. Although it is also noted that R. Hananyah ben Gamliel used Aggadah in his eulogies,[64] according to one commentator these eulogies took place on the Sabbath.[65] If this were so when the body was not there, how much more so when it was? However, a crucial change in the definition of hesped came with the interpretation of the talmudic passage which stated that in honor of King Hezekiah a yeshivah was erected on his grave.[66] Now Tosafot, on the basis of Rashi's earlier quoted comment, adds that it was not literally on his grave but four cubits away from it.[67] Nevertheless both R. Meir Abulafia (Ramah) and the author of *Nimukay Joseph* in the name of Asheri say that because it was done in honor of the deceased it was permitted. On the basis of their opinion R. Isaac Aboab (probably Isaac Aboab of Castile, d. 1493) takes this as ample precedent for reciting scriptural verses and sermons—that is, *exegetical eulogies*—in the presence of the dead. [68] Therefore, R. Joseph Karo, who brings this opinion in both the *Kessef Mishneh* and the *Bet Joseph,* writes in the *Shulhan Arukh*:

> It is permissible to say scriptural verses and a sermon in honor of the dead even within four cubits or in the cemetery. [69]

The only hint of the earlier ban of words of Torah in the presence of the deceased is offered there by R. David Halevi (Taz), who reminded eulogists to refrain from using the eulogy as an excuse for demonstrating their exegetical skill at the expense of honoring the deceased. This admonition was followed by many authorities. [70] However, it should be noted that ostentatious displays of learning were also discouraged in other contexts as well. [71]

Therefore, a eulogy can no longer be seen as "neglect of Torah" and thus might not be inappropriate for the synagogue. Indeed a eulogy can afford an astute rabbi the opportunity for instructing a large group of people who rarely come to the synagogue in the ways of the synagogue.

4. *Desecration of the Dead*

Finally, there is a very contemporary consideration, which did not face earlier rabbis even in the fairly recent past. Indeed it seems to be a uniquely American phenomenon. I am referring to the fact that the modern Jewish funeral-director offers, and often encourages, funerals totally against the letter and spirit of Halakhah—funerals which are literally "desecration of the dead" (*bizayon hamet*). Therefore, in many communities the result of being highly selective in allowing synagogue funerals is to give the Jewish funeral-director *carte blanche* in determining Jewish funeral procedures for the vast majority of our congregants. By insisting on the earlier ban we may very well be encouraging the much more serious transgression. Thus we are "helping transgressors," a situation the Talmud takes a dim view of. [72] Indeed the practices that take place in many modern-day Jewish funeral parlors are, in my view, nothing less than "quasi-pagan" (*darkhay Emori*) and in such cases our sages did not hesitate to take bold legal initiatives. [73]

It is also well known that the motivation for such practices is economic; a "wake" is much more expensive than an old-fashioned Jewish funeral. [74] Such a situation is not new in Jewish history.

> *In earlier times* the funeral and burial procedures were *more of a burden* for the relatives of the deceased than the death itself. It got to the point where people were *abandoning* the deceased and fleeing. Along came Rabban Gamliel and *compromised his dignity* and was buried in a linen shroud and so the people followed his lead. R. Papa said that today it is the *widespread custom* to be buried in a hemp shroud worth only a zuz. [75]

Earlier, you will recall, we saw that there is some support for the view that a "private funeral" is a case of "undignified bahavior." We now see that one no less than Rabban Gamliel himself ordered what was theretofore "undignified" when the threat of widespread desecration faced him. Our situation is very closely analogous. In conclusion, I believe this is really the most important halakhic issue in the question before us.

5. *Summary*

I present the following conclusions in summary:

1. Ideally, the only funeral that ought to be held in the synagogue is for a distinguished pious scholar or his wife.
2. There is precedent for extending this privilege to any pious person, although, perhaps, this should be restricted to a postburial memorial service.
3. There is a feeling among many later authorities that all funerals should *not* be held in the synagogue. If their reasoning concerning impurity is obscure, then the same conclusion can be reached by reasoning from democratic grounds; namely, "if we do it for one then everyone will demand the same privilege." Also there was the feeling that special privileges for sages no longer apply.
4. The contemporary American synagogue is a "congregational" as opposed to a "community" institution. As such there is serious doubt whether the ban on "private" funerals extends to our synagogues. Thus a congregation can stipulate in its constitution or by-laws privileges of membership, including the privilege of a synagogue funeral for whomever it so designates—every member, board members, officers, etc. Furthermore, the special

status of the sages in the synagogue is no longer the case *a priori*.

5. Whereas in former times the eulogy was a form of "neglect of Torah," only justified in the synagogue in the case of a sage whose death itself "nullified" the Torah, eulogies today contain exegetical content. As such they can be a useful educational device in the synagogue.

6. The scandal of the American Jewish funeral has created a situation where in many communities synagogue funerals for everyone will alone save the "dignity of the dead" and the "dignity of the living." [76] For much the same reason many communities insist that weddings be held in the synagogue, a rather new practice, to insure that the celebration not be an occasion for eating nonkosher food along with many other halakhic infractions. [77] Today in America Jewish life is virtually enclosed in the synagogue. In many communities we dare not permit any major religious function to take place outside its confines lest it be totally distorted.

7. Situations vary from community to community. I have simply tried to show that the halakhic boundaries of decision in this case are very wide indeed. [78]

CHAPTER 11

DELAYED BURIAL

In the classical rabbinic sources the great principles of the law are usually called into play when an actual case is brought for judgment (*ma'aseh she'hayah*). Although purely theoretical legal discussion is found in the Talmud, this type of discussion is mostly for the sake of ultimately arriving at some practical decision. Indeed, when a theoretical dispute is recorded, the usual question asked is: What practical difference is there between the two positions (*my ikka benayyhu*)? [1] As such the Talmud and its related literature are not only legally indispensable but also historically edifying. For in the presentation of the law we learn a great deal about its historical context and how that context influenced the development and application of the law. The law, with the exception of the Scriptures, was meant to be oral, that is, handed down by teacher to student from *memory*. [2] Only because of the dispersion of the Jewish people by the Romans during the time of R. Judah the Prince (ca. 150 C.E.), and the concomitant danger that the Law might be forgotten, was the Mishnah put into written form. However, the historical background, which always accompanied the law, could not be fully contained in any finite written work, because the history of the Jewish people is an ongoing process. While the historical factor was never ignored, it has been the privilege of the modern age to be granted the intellectual tools to more deeply appreciate the historical aspect of the Halakhah. We are the immediate heirs of the "Historial School," which flowered through the works of Frankel, Weiss, Lewy, Schechter, and Ginzberg —and more recently through the works of my own teachers, Boaz Cohen, Louis Finkelstein, and Saul Lieberman.

I emphasize the historical aspect because the following question is not only an interesting halakhic problem, but it also reflects the current state of Jewish history in the diaspora.

107

Question: In the fall of 1971 a situation arose in San Francisco which directly affected the lives of two families of the congregation I then served in Oklahoma City, Oklahoma.

At that time the gravediggers union went out on strike against all the local cemeteries. Because of a closed-shop provision no one but a union member could dig a grave. Therefore, the strike made it impossible to bury the dead in any cemetery—Jewish or non-Jewish. Literally thousands of families were directly affected. The situation became so bad that after a two-month impasse a large number of bereaved families actually picketed the authorities in Sacramento, the state capital of California. The strike was finally settled after many months and the bodies were at long last laid to rest. Among those who were finally buried were the relatives of two different families in my congregation. The sister of one of the deceased in San Francisco asked me when the period of mourning begins in such cases of delayed burial: at the time of the funeral or at the time of the final interment?

Answer: The Talmud discusses the question of when the period of actual mourning begins.

Our rabbis taught: When are the beds overturned [that is, the process of changing the normal seating arrangement for the mourners during the week of mourning (*shivah*)]? When the body is removed from the house to the cemetery.—This is the view of R. Eliezer. R. Joshua said that it is when the grave is closed. When Rabban Gamliel died they presented their conflicting views.[3]

Maimonides accepts the view of R. Joshua, writing,

Until the actual burial one is not considered a mourner [*abel*]. Therefore, King David washed and used cosmetics when his child died but had not yet been buried.[4]

The other Codes follow Maimonides: before burial the relatives of the deceased are in the category of *onen*; that is, they are preparing for the burial. Their sole responsibility is to arrange for the proper burial and they are not to be burdened or distracted with any other responsibilities, even the responsibility of such positive mitzvot as saying the Shema or studying the Torah.[5]

Nevertheless, Rashi interprets the "closing" (*she'yistom ha'gollel*) as the closing of the coffin, which would be earlier than the closing of the grave.[6] The Tosafists reject this interpretation, attempting to refute it with other passages both from Scripture and the Talmud.[7] However, in defense of Rashi, Nahmanides points out that these objections only apply where the dead body was placed on an open bier (mitah); but if it were placed in a closed casket (aron) and kept in a special place, then the period of mourning (abelut) would begin from that time. This is Rashi's view, however, and Nahmanides points out that the earlier authorities, the Geonim, held that mourning only began after the actual interment.[8] This is our normal practice as well.

However, the Shulhan Arukh recognized the following exception:

> If the body has already been placed in a coffin and had to be stored because the city was under siege, then the seven-day mourning period [shivah] and the thirty-day mourning period [shloshim] begin at once, even though they intend to bury the body in a cemetery after the siege. In this case the closing of the coffin is considered to be the beginning of the period of mourning.[9]

R. Shabtai HaKohen (Shakh) interpreted this as follows:

> Even though we normally [b'alma] hold that mourning does not begin until the grave is closed; nevertheless in case of a siege, placing the body in a special place and closing the casket is like burial because they have despaired [c'nityaashu] from burying him, even though they wanted to.[10]

Despair (yeush) is a ground for immediate mourning when the bereaved do not know when they will be able to recover the body and when they are powerless to change the situation themselves. The basis for this decision is the view of Rashi, which, although not applied in normal circumstances, is applied in abnormal circumstances (b'shaat ha'd'hak).[11]

Now it seems that the situation in San Francisco was indeed similar to a "siege" (matzor) because no one could predict if and when the gravediggers would end their strike against the local cemeteries. The bereaved were under "siege" by the union gravediggers and they were helpless to remedy the situation.

The situation called for a clear understanding of the contemporary problem of dealing with a union in a closed-shop position, where options open in the past were not available.

Three alternatives, if they had been available, would have changed the entire situation and would have made the "siege" analogy inadmissi-

ble: (1) if the gravediggers could have been bribed; (2) if there had
been a guarantee that the gravediggers would be forced back to work;
(3) if the bereaved could have buried their own dead themselves. If
any of these means were practically available, then the period of mourning would probably have to wait for actual burial. Thus R. Joseph Karo
(d. 1575), in his commentary to Maimonides' Code, emphasized that
if either bribery or an appeal to royal authority were still open options,
mourning would have to be delayed. [12]

Nevertheless, the compassion of our sages for the hardship of the
mourners undoubtedly motivated them to enunciate the principle, "In
questions of mourning the law follows the more lenient opinion." [13]
Certainly it would be a great hardship for the mourners to have to
begin their mourning period months after the actual death of their
relatives. Therefore, on the basis of this principle I tried to prove that
the San Francisco situation was indeed a siege.

None of the three options mentioned above was available to the people
in San Francisco at that time.

The strike of the gravediggers was directed against the owners of
the cemetery, not the bereaved themselves. Thus a bribe from the families
would undoubtedly have been rejected with vehemence because, from
the point of view of the union, it would not solve their labor problem
with management. Furthermore, the tradition of unionism prides itself
on obtaining an explicit contract through collective bargaining rather
than through the type of paternalism bribery involves. Finally, bribery
would create a situation where blackmail could be practiced in the future
and the Talmud ruled against bribery or ransom in situations where
this might happen. [14] The strike was indeed just like a siege, for in
a siege the attackers are not waging a war against any *particular* person
or persons who *happen* to live there, but against a city, just as the strike
was not directed against any particular mourner or mourners, but against
the cemetery management. Moreover, Nahmanides, in the strongest possible language, rules out any plan to steal the body away, fearing that
such schemes would lead to offenses far worse than lack of proper
burial. [15] He emphasizes that mourning begins when the relatives despair
of appeals to those in power who are preventing burial.

Moreover, in regard to the second option, no one could actually force
the gravediggers back to work against their will. Even a court injunction
declaring a strike illegal is no guarantee of a return to work since no
one in our democratic society can be *forced* to work by the authorities.
This is unlike the situation in the monarchies of the past, where disobedi-
ence to royal orders entailed capital punishment. This royal prerogative

was emphasized by the fifteenth-century Spanish statesman and Jewish theologian, Don Isaac Abrabanel. His remarks are in the form of a comment on a scriptural passage concerning King David's crime against Uriah, the husband of Bathsheba, but he also has in mind the political scene in his own day, as any insightful student can see.

> Even though our sages held that throughout the Torah "there is no agency for sin," in other words, the sinner and not the one who told him to sin is guilty, here is an exception ... and the reason for this is because David was a king and no one would go against his command. Hence it is as if he himself murdered Uriah. And so also is the case with Saul, who ordered the priests of Nob to be killed—it is as if he himself killed them. [16]

In our society the most the authorities can do is secure an injunction declaring the strike to be illegal (*de jure*), but this does not mean that work will actually resume (*de facto*). Thus appeals to authority, even if successful, are less effective today.

Finally, the bereaved could not bury their own dead. The closed-shop provision excluded all but union members from burying the dead, even next-of-kin. To challenge such a policy might even entail physical danger. R. Joel Serkes (d. 1640) emphasized that one need not risk his safety (*sakanah*) to bury the dead. The needs of the living always take precedence over the needs of the dead. [17]

Therefore, it seemed to me that the San Francisco situation was indeed a siege where the bereaved themselves were helpless to remedy the situation. Being helpless they *despaired*, not knowing what would ultimately happen. [18] I permitted mourning to begin as soon as the mourners left the bodies of the deceased in the morgue, where they were left to be buried when and if the strike was settled.

CHAPTER 12

A NOTE ON THE MOURNER'S KADDISH

QUESTION: A member of my congregation asked me about the length of time he was required to say Kaddish after the death of his mother. Some rabbis had told him that he should recite Kaddish for eleven months; others told him to recite it for a full twelve months, less a day or two. What is the preferred practice?

Answer: The institution of one year's mourning for a deceased parent is based on the following passage in the Talmud:

> The commandment to honor one's parents applies even after death . . . one should refer to his father (or mother) as "my father (or mother) my teacher. I am the atonement for his (or her) repose." This is the law for the first twelve months after death, but afterwards he should say, "May their memory be blessed for the world-to-come." [1]

It was believed that the child's behavior during this year affects the otherworldly status of the parent. [2] In other words, the test of a parent's influence is the life-style of his or her children. [3] Therefore, the surviving children are to engage in special mitzvot during the year of bereavement.

Originally, Kaddish was recited after a public Torah lecture as a doxology in praise of the Master of the universe, the Giver of the Torah. [4] The greatest mitzvah for the mourner would be to engage in publicly teaching the Torah, which would be followed by the usual recitation of Kaddish. However, since everyone is not a scholar, the custom gradually arose that the mourners themselves said Kaddish. Nevertheless, R. Abraham Hurwitz, in the introduction to his book, *Yesh Nohalin*,

112

emphasizes that saying Kaddish is just one mitzvah among many that ought to be specially performed during the year of mourning as proof of good parental influence. Apparently he was concerned that some people regarded Kaddish as a magical incantation having its own unique power in the world-to-come.

On the basis of all of this, it would seem to follow that Kaddish ought to be recited for the full twelve months of mourning. Indeed, all other mourning practices are required for the full twelve months.[5] Nevertheless, R. Moses Isserles, the leading authority for Ashkenazic Jewry, mentions that the custom arose to say Kaddish only for eleven months. The reason for this is that if one said Kaddish for the full twelve months, people might think that the deceased parent did not have enough personal merit to escape the judgment of hell (*Gehinnom*), which supposedly lasts for twelve months.[6]

This notion had a considerable development in the Jewish mystical tradition, the Kabbalah. However, the Zohar, the classic kabbalistic text, records an opinion that twelve months are required for a righteous person to ascend to the highest levels of heaven.[7] In other words, the twelve months of Kaddish signify the virtue, not the vice, of the departed. It seems to me, therefore, that the later kabbalist, R. Isaac Luria (Ari, d. 1572), based himself on this zoharic tradition when he urged the recitation of Kaddish for twelve months, less one week only in deference to popular custom. Other authorities follow his opinion.[8]

Therefore, the only basis for restricting the recitation of Kaddish is a popular custom loosely based on one interpretation of an aggadic statement in the Talmud. Although popular custom is important[9] and one ought not offend popular beliefs, it is clear that the mitzvah of saying Kaddish for twelve months, especially where it will aid a minyan, takes precedence.

CHAPTER 13

A JEWISH VIEW OF ABORTION

1. Abortion and Bloodshed

To arrive at a Jewish view of abortion for our democratic society, we must consider two questions: (1) Is abortion permitted to Jews? (2) Is abortion permitted to non-Jews?

Jews are bound by the commandments of the Written Torah as interpreted by the Oral Tradition, subsequently embodied in the Talmud, defined in the great medieval Codes, and continually applied to new problems by pious and learned authorities (*poskim*). Non-Jews are bound by the seven laws of the Noahide Code.

We are concerned with the morality of abortion in our democratic society. Since the non-Jewish citizens are in the overwhelming majority, we must begin with the Noahide laws, which are a Jewish expression of *jus gentium*[1]—that is, a body of norms accepted by civilized persons and binding on humanity.

Before dealing with the specific Noahide law of abortion we must answer four questions about Noahide law in general, all of which involve abortion in one way or another: (1) What is its status? (2) What is its scope? (3) How is it applied? (4) How is it related to Jewish law for Jews—that is, to the Halakhah?

Since the seven Noahide commandments are presented in the Talmud as an anonymous, publicly accepted, prescription (*tanu rabbanan*), one would assume that their source is Oral Tradition.[2]

However, in the lengthy discussion in the Gemara, six of these seven commandments are seen as based on a single scriptural verse,

> And the Lord God commanded man saying, "From every tree
> of the garden you may surely eat, but from the tree of the
> knowledge of good and evil you may not eat from it . . . " (Gen.
> 2:16-17)[3]

Therefore, in the opinion of R. Meir Abulafia these laws are actual scriptural prescriptions.[4]

Nevertheless, it is difficult to determine whether this inference means to actually *ground* Noahide law in Scripture (*gezerot haKatub*), or only uses Scripture as a description (*asmakhta*) of a body of laws grounded elsewhere. Thus, for example, R. Saadiah Gaon refers to most of these laws as rationally prescribed, without mentioning the verse from Genesis at all.[5] Considering Saadiah's eagerness to use scriptural sources whenever possible (perhaps because of his polemics with the Karaites), one can certainly assume that he held the source of these laws to be reason.

While later medieval theologians debated the scope of reason in relation to revelation, virtually all of them agreed with Saadiah that violence (*hamas*) and bloodshed (*shefikhat damim*) are rationally discernible as prohibitions for all human beings. Even such "nonrationalists" as R. Judah Halevi and Nahmanides are included.[6] Therefore, the question before us is whether or not abortion is bloodshed. Since there is virtual unanimity that reason is the source of the prohibition of bloodshed, we can conclude that the prohibition of bloodshed for Noahides is not only *jus gentium*—that is, valid by universal consensus—but also *jus naturalis*—that is, a norm valid because it is evidently rational (*ratio per se*). Since, as we will see below, normative Judaism considers abortion for Noahides within the context of bloodshed, abortion is a question which, Jewishly speaking, is within the proper range of human reason.

The scope of Noahide law is not limited to the seven prescriptions; rather, the seven laws were understood to be seven general categories, each one including a number of specific laws. Detailed presentations of this theory were made by R. Aaron Halevi (ca. 1290), R. Joseph Albo (d. 1444), and R. Azariah di Fano (d. 1620), on the basis of discrepancies in rabbinic sources as to the actual number of Noahide laws.[7]

Recognizing the essentially rational nature of the prohibition of bloodshed is the moral meaning of the general truth that human life is structured towards its own self-preservation and enhancement.[8]

As such, the category of "bloodshed" covers more cases than a specific prescription against "murder."[9]

R. Jacob bar Aha found it written in a book of the sayings [*Agadata*] of the school of Rab...that a Noahide is capitally guilty even in the case of feticide in the view of R. Ishmael. What are his grounds for this? It is written [Gen. 9:6], "Whosoever sheds the blood of a human *within* a human [*adam baadam*]." Who is "a human within a human"? This is the unborn child *within* its mother's womb.[10]

Maimonides codifies the law according to R. Ishmael's ruling and since he does not quote the verse from Genesis we can assume that he regarded the actual exegesis in the Talmud as merely descriptive of a truth grounded in reason.[11] The moral conclusion is primary; the actual exegesis is secondary.

2. Noahide Law

How is Noahide law known? How is it enforced?

The first question intrigued Moses Mendelssohn, who asked R. Jacob Emden just how the Noahides were expected to know a body of laws for which God held them responsible, if they did not have Jewish traditional teaching. But Mendelssohn already had his answer: the seven Noahide laws were rational prescriptions.[12]

If the prohibition of bloodshed is rationally evident to all (*ratio quod nos*), a fact emphasized as early as Saadiah and as late as Hermann Cohen, including virtually all the rationalists and nonrationalists in between, then is it possible to permit wanton bloodshed of any kind and still affirm the irreducible dignity of human life?

Man is not only a rational being but a historical being as well. Therefore, his cultural heritage informs him about his moral obligations, for law, which has been historically preserved, carries the assumption of its rationality unless proven otherwise. Our sages had great respect for those cultures which they believed were morally constituted, and, conversely, great contempt for those that were not. A striking example of this is the rabbis' admiration for the morality of Persian culture, which caused them to explain away the idolatrous Persian religion as a mere historical anachronism (*minhag abotehem*), no longer involving the true conviction of its adherents.[13]

Furthermore, the Hebrew Bible is morally authoritative for Christians, for they regard it as divinely revealed.[14] Indeed, although the Talmud prohibits non-Jews from studying Torah, it is permitted for the purpose of learning the Noahide laws.[15] Maimonides permits general scriptural study and instruction for Christians because they accept the Hebrew Bible as the word of God.[16] For him, Christians, and perhaps Muslims, could qualify for the bliss of the world-to-come by accepting the Noahide laws both as valid and as revealed.[17] In the Ashkenazic tradition, from as early as Rabbenu Tam up until R. Moses Isserles and R. Israel

Lipschuetz (d. 1860), the same respect for Christianity and its moral values is found. [18]

Since orthodox Christianity (whether Eastern, Western, Anglican, or Evangelical) accepts the validity of law, whether natural and revealed, or only revealed, its prescriptions should be respected as moral enlightenment for Noahides, that is, non-Jews. The stand against abortion, based as it is on Scripture, reason, and history, is a consistent application of the halakhically authoritative ruling of R. Ishmael.

The enforcement of Noahide law is left to non-Jews themselves. [19] However, Jews are to encourage non-Jews to obey and enforce their own moral code. Thus, for example, Maimonides, in presenting this category of laws, justifies the action of Simeon and Levi (Gen. 34) against the Shechemites, not as revenge for Shechem's rape of their sister Dinah, but, rather, as punishment of the people of Shechem, who stood by passively while their leader committed an outrage. On the basis of the first of the Noahide laws, the administration of justice (*dinim*), the Shechemites were guilty because of their apathy.

A rabbinic legend tells of Joshua's writing the Torah upon the stones (Deut. 27, Josh. 4) in the seventy languages to remind non-Jews of their moral obligations. [20] This is my own justification for a Jewish involvement in the prolife movement.

3. *Unanimity About Abortion*

The relationship of Noahide law to the Halakhah is of especial import for abortion legislation. As Jews, do we believe in a stricter morality for non-Jews than for ourselves, or, do we strive for a unified position synthesizing the principles of Jewish tradition and human reason?

The Talmud wrestled with this problem and later the Tosafists chose the very question of abortion as an example of a unified legal position.

> R. Jose ben Hanina said that any commandments given to Noahides and repeated at Mount Sinai apply to both Noahides and Jews. If only given to Noahides but not repeated at Mount Sinai, this is for Jews but not for Noahides . . . It would seem that the contrary should be the case [viz., if not repeated at Mount Sinai it is a commandment only for Noahides]. However, *there is nothing permitted to Jews which is forbidden to non-Jews.* [21]

In other words, Jewish revealed law presupposes Noahide law and then goes on to demand an even stricter morality for Jews. [22]

However, as the Noahide prohibition of abortion is unconditional, in that it does not admit the exception of the unborn child threatening its mother's life,[23] Noahide morality would seem to be stricter than Jewish morality. Therefore, the Tosafists proceed to use the talmudic principle quoted above in a highly ingenious way.

> In this context one could say that abortion permitted to Jews is prohibited to non-Jews. But, some say that inasmuch as a Jewish mother can be saved from a threatening fetus, *it is possible that this is also the case with a non-Jewish mother as well.*[24]

In other words, the dispensation in the case of an unborn child threatening its mother's life (*c'rodef ahareyha*) applies to both Jewish and non-Jewish mothers, just as any other abortion is prohibited to both.[25]

Actually, two options are possible: namely, either to make Jewish abortion law as unconditional as Noahide abortion law seems to be, or to make Noahide law admit the Jewish dispensation. Tosafot clearly opts for the second alternative.

The reason for this, it seems to me, stems from the principle first enunciated in the Mishnah, "One life is not destroyed for the sake of another," a principle Maimonides explicitly declared to be rational.[26] If Jewish law refuses to declare the priority of one independent life over another, then how can it possibly rule that a dependent life (the fetus) has priority over the independent life upon which it depends (the mother)? Where a fetus threatens the mother's life it is considered as part of her body and may be amputated as one would amputate a gangrenous limb.[27]

This does not mean, however, that the unborn child can be regarded as a "limb" of its mother in other situations as well. (Even if it were a "limb" in nonmortal situations, Judaism prohibits mutilation, self-inflicted or otherwise.)[28]

To illustrate, there is the well-known talmudic case of two travelers in the desert with one flask containing enough water for only one to survive. R. Akiba rules that the one with the water flask may save himself even if it results in the death of the other traveler. " 'And your brother shall live with you' [*imakh*] [Lev. 25:36]; your life takes priority [*kodmim*] over your fellow's life."[29] Why is this the Halakhah? Because the means for saving one life are *more proximate to one person than the other*. The saving of the mother's life is more proximate than saving the life of the fetus. Once the child is born, however, both mother and child are equally proximate.

The new interpretation of the Tosafists deepens the Noahide definition of feticide put forth by the Tanna, R. Ishmael, on the basis of the Halakhah's subsequent development by the Amoraim. Thus, in its relation to the developments of Jewish law, Noahide law develops a more adequate view of abortion by including the dispensation in the case of the "pursuing fetus."

Concerning the general relation of Noahide law to Jewish law, Maimonides writes:

> *Concerning six things the first man was commanded . . . until Moses our teacher came and the Torah was completed through him.*[30]

The same point has been made and developed by other traditional authorities.[31]

Thus Jewish law has illuminated Noahide law on the question of abortion. Has Noahide law returned the compliment?

I believe it has. An adulterous woman carrying another man's child petitioned R. Yair Hayyim Bacharach (b. 1639) for an abortion. Although tempted to grant her request on the grounds of certain legal technicalities, he refused such permission because "of the clear and evident consensus between us [Jews] and them [Christians] against abortion in the interest of curbing promiscuity and immorality."[32] In other words, general moral standards, universally accepted, take precedence over specific technicalities.

Indeed, R. Ezekiel Landau (b. 1713) warns against inferring any permission of abortion (where the life of the mother is not somehow at stake) from the fact that abortion is not murder in the technical sense. This is why Maimonides emphasized that the fetus is "like" a pursuer. Only in the case of mortal danger is abortion permitted; in other cases the integrity of the unborn child must be respected.[33] In the subsequent discussion R. Landau emphasized that the Noahide designation of abortion as destruction of "a human within a human" applies to Jews as well.

Finally, abortion cannot be permitted on the grounds that it is not "murder" in the technical sense, for even infanticide is not murder in the sense of a humanly prosecutable crime if the infant is under thirty days old. However, no one could possibly argue that infanticide is ever permitted. Both acts are forbidden (*assur*) even if not humanly punishable (*patur*), ex post facto.[34]

4. *A Modern Approach*

This analysis is within the scope of modern halakhic thinking, which I would characterize as not only examining the various precedents within the halakhic literature, but also taking into consideration two additional factors: (1) philosophical and theological perspectives; (2) historical background.

Many modern thinkers feel that even though authoritative conclusions cannot be inferred from Aggadah, aggadic considerations can *inform* the process of halakhic decision-making. (This is one of the most important methodological points I learned from my teachers at the Jewish Theological Seminary, especially from the late Professor Abraham J. Heschel and from Professor Seymour Siegel.) Aggadic perspective is indispensable when several divergent halakhic options are possible. [35] How does one decide a Jewish position on abortion when there are both strict and lenient trends before him? This is where a philosophy and a theology of law are required by Halakhah itself.

The philosophical question surrounding the halakhic precedents on abortion is: What is the status of human life? The theological question is: How do the covenants of God with mankind (the sons of Noah) and with the people of Israel ground the sanctity of the human person?

The irreducible status of life, namely, that life needs no justification, is a philosophical axiom which, it seems to me, underlies the opposition to the war in Vietnam, the opposition to capital punishment, and the ecology movement, which is dedicated to the integrity of all life, even nonhuman life.

An irreducible truth cannot be proven, for its truth value is not derived from a prior principle. To demonstrate an irreducible truth one must show the absurdity of anything that attempts to contradict it. [36] That life is to be preserved and not destroyed is an irreducible principle. It is the foundation of all rational human action, such as the promotion of health, the establishment of society, the worship of God, and so on. The only exceptions that are rationally justifiable arise in situations where one life is in conflict with another life. To assert, however, that life's value must be justified on the basis of something else, is, philosophically speaking, to place the cart before the horse. For if life must be justified, what principle can be objectively put forward as having greater priority? This is the basis of the philosophical insight common to the Bible, Plato, the Stoics, and the Declaration of Independence—that the natural or created order takes precedence over the conventional or humanly instituted order. [37]

The fundamental question is whether the life of a fetus may be destroyed at will. If this is permitted for utilitarian reasons (over-population, convenience, etc.), then the right to life of the severely retarded, the hopelessly psychotic, the senile, could be questioned next. Are not the senile, the retarded, and the psychotic more "trouble" than an unwanted fetus? Reverence for life is at a low ebb, and the clamor for open abortion is just one sympton of the moral climate of our times. Jews especially, who have been the most tragic victims of the contempt for life, should be the last people in the world to support legislation that would give *carte blanche* and moral sanction to abortion. There are moral considerations that transcend even the fine points of the law and that must inform the law lest legal decisions be a respectable cover for immorality.[38]

Furthermore, the covenantal theologies of both Judaism and Christianity provide a more profound basis for the "right to life" by emphasizing not only the immanent dignity of man, but even more, the transcendent sanctity of the human person, to whom, of all His creatures, God has chosen to reveal His presence. Even the unborn can be the subjects of revelation (Jer. 1:5; Ps. 139:13-16).

A modern approach to Halakhah is characterized by a concern with the historical background of the law. Jewish history is not the ground of Jewish law. That right must be reserved for revelation if Halakhah is to be morally obligatory. However, Jewish history is the indispensable context of Jewish law and conditions its application. Therefore, what is the historical background of the Jewish law about abortion?

Rabbinic sources raise only the problem of therapeutic abortion. The assumption is that bearing and raising children was a great blessing in the normative Jewish communities in Israel and Babylonia, called into question only in cases of great danger to already existing life. In the one direct scriptural treatment of abortion (Exod. 21:22) the law is presented in the context of an unfortunate accident. As such, the sources seem to assume the extraordinary, unplanned nature of the circumstances involved and take a compassionate, lenient stand.

However, in the Hellenistic sources, especially the Septuagint and Philo, a harder line is taken,[39] because in the Graeco-Roman world, where respect for life's sanctity could not be assumed, wholesale abortion and infanticide were being practiced. This is the historical background of R. Ishmael's ruling against abortion for Noahides. Dr. Immanuel Jacobovits, now Chief Rabbi of Great Britain, along with R. Isser Unterman, the former Ashkenazi Chief Rabbi of Israel, takes a "hard line" on the abortion question and explains R. Ishmael's ruling as follows:

Another view is that this extension of the Noachidic laws was intended, on the contrary, as a protest against the widespread Roman practice of abortion and infanticide. [40]

Is our society's reverence for life on any higher level?

The tendency in Jewish law has usually been to take a strict stand when general public morality has declined. [41] The proabortion movement insists that abortion be permitted on demand. It is not concerned with the *occasional* dispensations allowed in Jewish law. The issue, therefore, is whether the unborn child has any rights at all.

Historical change also has an effect on two other considerations involved in abortion: namely, (1) Is the fetus a living entity *per se*? (2) Is abortion a solution for prepartum depression accompanied by suicide threats? The assumption that the fetus is not a living entity *per se* could easily be inferred from the Mishnah in *Ohalot*, which discusses the woman in hard labor. There only the child who is born is called a person (*nefesh*) whose life cannot be violated. Furthermore, the Mishnah elsewhere notes a difference in the status of the fetus before the fortieth day of pregnancy and after. The Gemara presents various theories on the status of prenatal life based on the empirical observations of the ancient rabbis. [42] However, these theories are not directly derived from scriptural decrees, which would make them irrevocable, nor are they presented as formal rabbinic decrees (*takkanot*) requiring the complicated procedure of repeal. As such, these observations are not in themselves authoritative, but, rather, can be modified in the light of newer scientific evidence. Thus, for example, it was an empirical assumption of the rabbis of the Talmud that a child born in the eighth month of pregnancy could not possibly live. This affected the application of certain laws to newborn children where possible viability is a question. Nevertheless, subsequent evidence convinced R. Moses Isserles (Rema, b. 1520) that some eight-month children do live and, therefore, that there ought to be no distinction between them and any other newborn children. [43]

Again, it was an empirical assumption of the rabbis of the Talmud that a deaf-mute (*heresh*) was essentially the same as a mentally retarded person (*shoteh*). Nevertheless, the son of R. Moses Sofer, after a visit to an institution for the deaf in Vienna in the mid-nineteenth century, was so impressed by the responsiveness of the students that he seriously questioned whether the old empirical equation of the deaf-mute with mental retardation still applied. [44]

In other words, law based on empirical evidence admits of modification when newer empirical evidence becomes available. Even though the Jewish prohibition of nonthreatening abortion is not at question in the issue of fetal life, any inferences from rabbinic sources that belittle the status of fetal life are highly suspect on the basis of the latest scientific evidence. This evidence assigns a much higher biological status to the life of the unborn child than had heretofore been known.[45] Furthermore, as we have seen, R. Ezekiel Landau believed the very designation of the threatening fetus as a "pursuer" (rodef) ruled out any such inferences.

The second question raised, which requires the latest scientific testimony, is whether abortion is warranted in the case of the suicide threats made by a pregnant woman suffering from what is known as prepartum depression, which many psychiatrists would consider a psychotic state. Dr. David Feldman and Dr. Isaac Klein have both argued on the basis of halakhic precedents that mental health is a valid reason for abortion.

Frankly, on this issue I am in doubt. In the first place, there are situations where the mentally ill person's demands are not to be fulfilled, especially if these demands are immoral.[46] Secondly, it is often assumed in psychiatry that what the patient *wants* is not necessarily what the patient *needs*. Dr. Carl Marlow, professor of psychiatry at the University of Miami Medical School, researched the threat of suicide as a reason for psychiatric abortion. His conclusion was that there was only a minimal risk of suicide actually taking place if the demanded abortion were not performed. Further, he states, "Most abortions performed for psychiatric reasons are at best recommended on the basis of peripheral psychoses, but are generally performed for socio-economic reasons."[47]

In summary, I believe that the matter needs much more study. *Psychosis* is a term that covers as many diverse phenomena as the term *cancer*. Hence a general ruling on the whole mental health aspect of abortion would be imprudent. However, although not a psychiatrist myself, my three years as a chaplain at St. Elizabeth's Hospital, National Institute of Mental Health, in Washington, D.C., especially in working closely with several suicidal female patients, indicated to me that the guilt that might result from an abortion would hardly be therapeutic in the long run.[48]

5. Conclusion

Although my concern in this paper is with the objective moral question of abortion, it is written with deep feeling because of my own very private reasons. With one-third of our people murdered and the Jewish birthrate in both Israel and the diaspora alarmingly low, permission of abortion, for less than the most serious life-threatening reasons, is

at best insensitive. And if we permit abortion for the general pop-
ulation—*Wie es sich christelt, so juedelt es sich!*

At a time when the hold of the Torah is so weak for so many of
our people, we should by all means strengthen the only moral code
many Jews still recognize, namely, the law of the secular state.

> R. Joshua ben Levi saw a contradiction between two verses
> in Ezekiel: "And you did *not* act according to the laws of the
> nations which surround you" [5:7], "You *did* act according
> to the laws of the nations which surround you" [11:12]. He
> resolved it by saying: You did *not* act according to their good
> laws [*metukanin*]: their bad laws [*mekulkalin*] you *did* act accord-
> ing to.[49]

The question of how to do God's will in a secular world is not
easily answered. This is my response, in one specific issue, to the
ancient cry, "How shall we sing the Lord's song in a strange land?"
(Ps. 137:4).

CHAPTER 14

A JEWISH VIEW OF WAR

1. *The Nature of War*

JUDAISM, although possessing an intricate theoretical structure, has seen practice as the ultimate end of all theorizing. The ever-present require-ments of action have demanded the enunciation of intelligible principles to determine the appropriate context and final thrust of the action at hand.[1] Since the religiously involved Jew is constantly engaged in acts, he is conditioned to ask himself two questions when he approaches any new situation: (1) What is required of me at this time and place? (2) How is this specific requirement structured? In fact, the very constancy of this engagement in activity even made it necessary for the Talmud to establish several precise criteria for priority in the case of conflict of acts.[2]

It is to the credit of a number of contemporary American-Jewish leaders and thinkers that they view the Jew's involvement in war as a question demanding a religious stance. Such is the case, it seems to me, because the involvement of the United States in any war is not regarded as the policy of some remote entity, but, rather, is seen as a situation immediately present to Jewish persons—a situation calling for a judgment of conscience—similar to that involved in more traditional situations. This view assumes two things, one obvious and the other less so. The first assumption is that Jews are intimately and freely involved with a secular, non-Jewish, regime. Not only are they the subjects of government policies, as they have been in the past, or are at present in some parts of the world, but they are now constituents in the very process of policy-decision. The second, less obvious, assumption is that Judaism provides Jews with theologically significant principles, which have application in situations that in the past never called for Jewish

125

decisions at all. The first assumption is factual, but the second suggests that some sort of imperative is being sought. Therefore, the question now becomes: Does Judaism offer any criteria to the Jew, free constituent of a secular society, who is faced with the moral dilemma of how to judge his government's involvement in an offensive war, and, ultimately, what to do about it? The thesis of this chapter is that Judaism does offer the morally sensitive Jew the criteria he seeks in this particular situation. I have chosen the war in Vietnam for discussion because it, more than any other war, caught many Jews in a serious moral dilemma. However, the Vietnam War is only an example of the more general problem of participation in any offensive military action.

At first thought one would suppose that the moral question of Vietnam should be analyzed by the concept of the "just war." Although this term was formulated by medieval Catholic theology, the concept itself is found much earlier in Jewish law. The Talmud classifies war into three categories: (1) *Milhemet Hobah*, a divinely ordered war, such as the war against the Canaanites in the time of Joshua, and the war against the Amalekites in the time of Saul; (2) *Hilhemet Mitzvah*, a war of necessary Jewish self-defense; (3) *Milhemet Reshut*, a "permittted" war, where, in certain cases, Jewish national interest may be offensively pursued.[3] The deliberations necessary for the sanctioning of a "permitted" war are described in the Talmud:

> The sages of Israel approached King David and said to him, "Our royal lord, your people Israel need sustenance [*parnasah*]." He said to them, "Let them sustain one another." They said to him, "A handful of grain would not even satisfy a lion, and the wells are inadequate." He said to them, "Go and engage in plunder [*g'dud*]." Immediately they consulted Ahithophel, sought the approval of the Sanhedrin [*nimlakhin*], and inquired of the Urim and Thummin oracle.[4]

One can readily see that none of the above categories applies to the question at hand. Even the most militant religious proponent of the Vietnam War would not state that it was the direct result of a command from God. On the other hand, uniquely Jewish interests were not directly involved in the Vietnam War, as they were in World War II, and especially in the Israeli War of Independence (*Milhemet Hashihrur*). Finally, the concept of the "permitted" war, which most closely approximates this war, also does not apply, because the necessary conditions for establishing its sanction are long absent. We have neither king nor Sanhedrin. And, even if they were present, they would not be applicable anyway, because the moral decision here is that of the individual Jew, not that of a Jewish state. Thus, we see that if our search is to be successful we must be prepared to look for principles that are fundamental enough not to be solely confined within traditionally developed contexts.

We have seen that the problem in discovering the appropriate basis for moral judgment here is initially one of connection. We have not been able as yet to locate a moral connection between the individual Jew and the non-Jewish (not anti-Jewish) secular society. This context must be established before light can be thrown on the specific moral judgment required. Otherwise, any sources cited might be equivocal, that is, relevant by appearance, but irrelevant as the basis for any inference of specific conclusions from general statements. If moral decisions are to be as coherent and binding for the contemporary Jew as they were for the traditional Jew of the past, we must make sure that moral reasoning does not become logically equivocal, and, therefore, rooted in the subjective bias of the individual. The sources must be used as something more profound than illustrations. A good deal of the moral theorizing presented by Jewish thinkers today ignores the contextual issue and is thus of questionable application.[5] On the other hand, some Jewish thinkers seem to see no contextual change in Jewish moral decisions, and thus cannot face the real problems at hand.

2. Noahide Law

It is well known that Jewish tradition regarded some of the imperatives either explicitly or implicitly stated in the Torah as having an international context. While the 613 commandments are solely Jewish in context, the seven commandments of "the sons of Noah," by definition, are directed to the entire human race—to man *qua* man. Whether these laws are to be classified as "natural law" (*jus naturale*), or as "the law of nations" (*jus gentium*), or as divine law *per se* (*jus divinium*), is a disputed point among scholars.[6] However, the lack of certitude as to the appropriate classification of the seven commandments need not prevent our looking to them for guidance. For their givenness cannot be disputed, inasmuch as they are explicitly set forth in the Talmud.[7] There are many data to which we refer in making decisions without knowing their prime causality. I think the times require of Jewish theology that it determine whether the seven commandments are essentially grounded in man's reason, or in universal consent, or in the direct revelation of God's will. Surely such determination will throw deeper light on how Judaism views moral judgment. Nevertheless, a judgment is demanded of the morally sensitive Jew, here and now, and we must therefore look to what is already available for enlightenment.

However, we cannot simply infer a specific conclusion from the Noahide commandment of *shefikhat damim*, the prohibition of murder. First we must determine one final and crucial point of context. This will insure that our subsequent use of texts will not be open to the charge of equivocity.

The last problem we face in this area is that the 613 commandments regulate the life of the Jewish people, and the seven commandments regulate the life of gentiles.[8] The rabbis made it quite clear that gentiles domiciled under Jewish jurisdiction were expected to conform to their seven commandments as *enforced by the Jewish authorities*.[9] Moreover, they made it clear that certain restrictions of the seven commandments do *not* apply to Jews.[10] In other words, we seem to have clear precedents for gentiles in gentile contexts, and for gentiles in Jewish contexts. Yet we seem to be lacking precedents for Jews in gentile contexts, especially for Jews who are not only present *de facto* in a non-Jewish society, but present *de jure* as well—that is, who are free and equal constituents of that society, having full rights and responsibilities.

However, there is a relevant passage in the Mishnah. If understood in terms of its ultimate presuppositions, it can bridge the halakhic gap of the individual Jew functioning fully in a non-Jewish society. We will then be able to apply the principle embodied in the passage, which seems to me to be a basis for inferring a judgment on our involvement in the Vietnam War. Let us examine the Mishnah text and then look at the three possible interpretations, which give successively broader groundings for the Mishnah's ruling:

> All documents deposited in the gentile courts [*arkaot shelagoyim*], even though their sealing is witnessed by gentiles, are valid—except bills of divorce and manumission of slaves. R. Simon says even these are valid, for the ruling concerning invalidation only applies when the documents are deposited with individual gentiles.[11]

The simplest and most constricted interpretation of the text is given by the thirteenth-century posek (halakhic authority) R. Mordecai ben Hillel. He simply states that this is a specific rabbinic decree concerning documents. The reason he gives is that the gentiles are very careful (*makpidin*) about the signatures on documents registered in their courts.

The Gemara proper to this Mishnah[12] bases the ruling on the principle of Mar Samuel, "The law of the kindom is the law" (*Dina d'malkhuta dina*). Rashi, elsewhere, explains this principle as follows:

> All the levies and taxes and procedures regularly enacted by kings in their kingdoms are binding as law [*dina*]. For all the subjects of the kingdom *freely accept* [*mirtzonam*] *the statutes of the king and his enactments.* [13]

One can readily see that this principle is about certain positive laws; that is, it defines the right of the state to make specific decrees on the basis of popular consent and acceptance of authority. But it in no way presents any standard of judgment to determine whether these laws are right or wrong. As such it admits of no wide inference. [14]

Finally, commenting on a passage in the Gemara where our Mishnah is cited, Rashi presents the broadest and deepest basis for the specific ruling of the Mishnah:

> Although sacramental matters [*kritut*] do not concern gentiles nor matters of Jewish marriage and divorce [*gittin v'kidushin*], they are nevertheless commanded concerning the practice of justice [*dinin*]. [15]

One must realize that Rashi was presenting a more fundamental grounding for the ruling of the Mishnah than the specifics of the situation actually required. This being the case, the principle he presents here has a much wider application, and is not solely confined to the question of verification of documents with which this Mishnah deals. *Dinin* (the practice of justice) is a standard of judgment. In rabbinic Hebrew *doon* means to *logically infer*; that is, to perform an operation of rational judgment—like *krinein* in Greek, a word which has both a logical and a legal usage. [16] Rashi is presenting an extraordinary statement in depth on the role of secular order in a universe ruled by God according to His Torah. [17] His illuminating explication indicates that a non-Jewish society—in nonritual cases, of course—can be the context for Jewish action, provided that that society's legal and political order is in basic conformity with the seven Noahide commandments This is not only a *de facto* recognition of Jews being subject to a non-Jewish regime; it is a *de jure* recognition that the state's right to rule is grounded in a law directed to the conscience of man. As such, the specific policies of that state, at all times, require a judgment of conscience by its free and responsible constituents. In the absence of the full hegemony of the Torah over the life of the Jew, the Jew is not simply abandoned to pure subjectivism, nor is he forced to search for objective standards elsewhere in the area of politics. The seven commandments indicate *that even non-Jewish law has a real religious status: complete for the non-Jew,* [18] *and partial for the Jew in exile.* [19] As such, the policies of the state can and must be judged by certain standards intrinsic to Judaism. To look upon his involvement in the secular state with religious seriousness does not entail a prior alienation of the Jew from classical Judaism. On the contrary, it presupposes a Jewish quest to do what God requires of the Jew here and now. "I am a stranger in the land, do not hide Thy commandments from me" (Ps. 119:19).

3. Who Is the Pursuer?

Now that we have established an authentically Jewish context for the type of moral decision required by the situation of the Vietnam War, we are finally in a position to locate some principle of Halakhah that will directly apply to this case, and that will be binding on the Jewish conscience. Let us first see what alternatives of choice are present in this particular situation.

In wars there is a conflict between two distinct parties. Each side usually justifies its military activities by claiming that it is either defending itself against an offensive aggressor or is in imminent danger of attack. It is presupposed that the distinction of belligerent entities is at all times clear. The issues at stake in the war are between the two opposing parties. However, the Vietnam War was much more complicated.

Ostensibly, the conflict was a civil war between the Saigon government and the Communist-controlled National Liberation Front, the Vietcong, aided by the government of North Vietnam. The first problem we face is that the clear-cut division of entities, found in more conventional wars, was not found here. The question was whether the authentic leadership of the Vietnamese people was in Saigon or with the guerilla chiefs of the Vietcong. The policy of the United States government was an answer to this question. Our involvement in the war was justified as follows: The duly constituted and authorized government of South Vietnam is the government of Saigon. The guerilla forces of the Vietcong are, in effect, a group of illegal brigands, who are attempting to overthrow this legitimate polity. Over and above our strategic interests, or whatever treaty obligations we have with the Saigon government, we are, in truth, answering the cry for help of a beleaguered nation in mortal danger. In other words, the United States policy was *ultimately* justified, not in terms of national advantage, or of treaties enacted for extrinsic ends, but rather in terms of a moral principle: one is conscience-bound to act on behalf of a fellow in mortal danger. This logic can be seen in the following statement, which was issued by the State Department at the height of American involvement in Vietnam:

> Our objective in Viet-Nam is a simple one—to stop North Viet-Nam from attacking its neighbor. We believe that we can and will achieve victory in this sense. We seek only to assure that the South Vietnamese people have an opportunity to establish political and economic institutions of their own choosing while free from outside interference. [20]

Throughout the long debate as to whether the United States should or should not have been involved in the war, even the proponents of the official policy admitted that our involvement was that of a third party subsequently entering the scene. The debate centered around the question of whether or not this third-party involvement was justified. But, it should be noted, the point of morality was introduced, not by the dissenting "doves," but by those who claimed ultimate responsibility for the military action. Therefore, no one can claim that the discussion of the moral question was irrelevant or contrived, because both sides in this debate appealed for support and sympathy in moral terms. A debate presupposes that each side recognize the rationality of the other, in general if not specifically. Thus the debate over Vietnam involved an analysis of the nature of war in general. That is why this debate is paradigmatic, even after American withdrawal from actual fighting in Vietnam.

Students of the Talmud will quickly recognize the type of reasoning outlined above as identical with the rodef (pursuer) principle. The following text demonstrates this:

> These are the victimizers who may even be killed if this is required to save their victims: A person pursuing [rodef] his fellow to kill him . . . [21]

In our situation, the government equated the Vietcong with the "pursuer" and the Saigon government with the "pursued" (nirdaf). This seems, then, to be very clear. Should the American Jew have felt that he was conscience-bound to support his government's Vietnam policy? If the line of argument we have been developing in this chapter is correct, then it will seem to be at this particular juncture that the Jewish person had to exercise his faculty of moral judgment, his conscience.

However, the rodef principle is really rooted in another more fundamental principle. And when we understand what this is, we will be able
to see, in a truly Jewish perspective, the fallacy in the moral reasoning
at the very heart of the government's justification of its war policy.

As a result, a valid inference from principle to conclusion will at last
be possible. We will see that the inference is a good deal more subtle
than a simple deduction from the prohibition against murder. Rather,
this inference is based on a ·principle almost immediately present to
rational man, a principle which gives, I think, the prohibition against
murder its intelligibility and its rapid appeal to conscience.

Let us look at two texts, which although dealing with the fascinating
moral question of abortion, reveal a basis having much more general
application.

> The woman who is in extremely difficult labor: the fetus may
> be destroyed within her, and removed from her limb by limb,
> because her life has priority over its life. However, if most
> of the baby's body is already out of the womb, we may not
> harm him, because *one human life may not be sacrificed for another*
> [*ayn dohin nefesh mipnay nafesh*]. [22]

And Maimonides, in the *Mishneh Torah*, writes as follows:

> . . . because the fetus is *like a pursuer* after his mother   [*c'rodef
> ahareyha*] to kill her. [23]

Now Maimonides' comparison of the endangering fetus and the pursuer
is not easy to understand. One can only become a pursuer if he is fully
human and morally culpable. Why should Maimonides introduce this
consideration when the particular case of abortion does not even require
it? It is quite clear from several other sources that the fetus is part
of its mother's body (*yerekh immo*), and can be *amputated* when necessary. [24]
However, Maimonides, who chooses each word with care, states *c'rodef*,
"like a rodef," and thus does not use *rodef* in the complete sense of
the term. The endangering fetus is a rodef by analogy. Perhaps in the
context of abortion Maimonides is comparing the fetus to the fully human
rodef because the fetus, in essence, is more than a limb, but *persona
in potentia*. [25]

What Maimonides may also be emphasizing, if I read him correctly,
is that the principle that one life cannot be sacrificed for another is
the intelligible ground for the rodef principle *per se*. This is most important for our problem here. There are no priorities in the value of human

lives[26] unless a person (or, as in our case, a number of persons) forfeits his right to protection by denying this equality of value in his own favor. The function of society is to make this *de jure* equality *de facto* in the affairs of men. What society and any of its citizens do in the case of the pursuer is to re-establish the equality of persons which the pursuer is upsetting. To protect or ignore the true rodef would be to deny along with him this very basis of law and right. In theological terms, the pursuer is denying his creaturely status and is usurping the authority of God. Society, in acknowledging the supreme being of God, must stop this denial. Recognition of God's existence is presupposed by more than the Noahide bans on blasphemy (*birkat Hashem*) and idolatry (*abodah zarah*), but by the general category of bloodshed (*shefikat damim*) as well.[27] Actually, in the last analysis, the fundamental principle of not sacrificing one life for another is the legal ground of the famous dictum of Hillel:

> What is hateful to you do not do to your fellow. This is the whole Torah, the rest is commentary. Go and learn.[28]

This principle, then, is basic to Judaism, and common to all reasonable people.[29] Hillel had located the ultimate ground for Judaism's encounter with the world. Maimonides, too, in another text, emphasizes the fact that our principle of the equality of human life is one of natural reasoning, something universally common.

> It is a matter of rational inclination [*dabar shehadaat noteh lo*] not to destroy one life for another.[30]

Now, *rational inclination* is the very same term Maimonides uses elsewhere in referring to the seven Noahide commandments, which for him are the Torah *in potentia*.[31] In other words, this principle is the intelligible ground for the prohibition against murder, and the rodef principle is a legitimate exception by inference.

> Concerning six areas was the first man commanded: idolatry, blasphemy, murder, robbery, and administration of justice. Even though we have them by revelation [*kabbalah*] from Moses our master, they are *a matter of rational inclination* [*v'hadaat noteh lahen*].[32]

At this point we must realize that if the principle not to sacrifice one life for another is the basis, and the rodef principle is an exception by inference, the first principle is more fundamental. The benefit of a doubt (*safek*) must always be in favor of that which is more fundamental.

This is the case inasmuch as the inference is an exception; that is, a specific affirmation (rodef) inside a general negation (nonsacrifice of life). Therefore, logically, without the general negation the specific affirmation loses its validity, because a part is only meaningful where there is a whole. Thus, in case of doubt, negation (whole) takes precedence over affirmation (part) since a whole can exist without a part, but a part cannot exist without the whole. The principle of nonsacrifice of life stands alone, the rodef principle cannot. We stated above the moral claim that was made by the official spokesmen in terms of the rodef principle. However, we now know that this principle is logically derivative. We are in a position at last to discover whether a logical sleight of hand had not indeed been committed; whether, in fact, an inference was emphasized *at the expense* of its logical basis. In the context of the issue of abortion, where we first discovered the fundamental principle, the rabbis were quite aware of the tragic results that can come from faulty moral reasoning. The following question arises: If a baby, most of whom is already out of the womb, is considered to now be human, and if he is threatening his mother's life (*rodef*), why should he not be killed, if need be, on the grounds of the rodef principle? It is to this question that the Palestinian Talmud addresses itself:

> R. Jose ben R. Bun in the name of R. Hisda emphasized that this case is different from the case of the rodef, because *here we do not know who is killing whom.*[33]

In other words, where there is a doubt, the rodef principle is not involved. And the reason for this is most pertinent for our own situation. If, in a case of doubt, the rodef principle were to be applied, the intruding third party would be doing what he is accusing the "pursuer" of doing. The intruder is denying the equality of persons in his own favor. We might say, to parody a famous saying: "The arrogant rush in where the humble fear to tread."

The moral fallacy of official Vietnam policy seems to be that there was an assumption of a rodef situation, where in fact we did not know who was pursuing whom, as the Palestinian Talmud puts it so well. The distinction of entities, which is so important in any judgment of conflict, seems to absent here. Both the Saigon government and the Vietcong claimed to be the authentic leaders of the people of Vietnam. We had no way of verifying who was wrong and who was right. Finally, we ourselves were in a poor position to be an objective third party, inasmuch as Saigon was and still is as much an extension of Washington as the Vietcong seems to be an extension of Hanoi or Moscow.

And this is the point which lies behind the fallacy in moral reasoning.

Our involvement in Vietnam was, in fact, motivated by our own self-interest. As such the government erected a moral facade to justify an outright extension of American power. The much-used analogy to the Korean conflict was illegitimate. In Korea, it seems to me, we were acting in a genuine rodef situation. We were, in fact, rescuing the distinct and independent entity, South Korea (*nirdaf*), from another distinct and independent entity, North Korea (*rodef*). And if one looks for the factor of universal consent in moral reasoning, the United Nations sponsored the involvement in Korea. In Vietnam, on the contrary, we chose sides for motives extrinsic to the actual issue in the internal conflict there. We projected our own identity onto the Saigon regime, and then assumed that we ourselves were mortally threatened. This was not only the result of the logical fallacy of emphasizing a derivative at the expense of its basis, it was the direct moral vice of hypocrisy. In the light of the facts as we know them, and the Jewish principles we have seen in operation, the morally sensitive Jew had again the ancient option: "Avoid evil and do good" (Ps. 37:27). In this situation I could see no other alternative for the religiously committed Jew but to oppose the government's Vietnam policy, and to do everything in his power to stop that immoral war. Future wars will have to be judged on the basis of criteria similar to those outlined in this chapter.

4. *Conclusion*

It may seem to the reader that I have employed a very complicated and involved method for arriving at a rather simple conclusion. Perhaps this is so. But the underlying issues have demanded such elaboration. The question of how to do God's will in a secular world is not easily answered. The simple solution would be to opt either for God's will or for the secular world. However, Judaism itself would not let us do this. The Torah is not in heaven but with us on earth; we are men and not angels.[34] And to opt for the secular world would but alienate us further from our own identity as the covenanted folk. We cannot solve our problems here and now from behind elaborate disguises. Before we attempt any solution we must realize who we ourselves are. This chapter is an attempt to deal with this general problem in a particular case. In the analysis given above we are at the juncture of theology and Halakhah. We have followed the traditional method of close analysis of texts and tight logical constructions. Each discipline intimately suggests the other; the issues of one suggest questions for the other.[35] And Jewish questions have a tendency to repeat themselves. This chapter, then, like the one on abortion, is an attempt to deal with the ancient cry: "How shall we sing the Lord's song in a strange land?" (Ps. 137:4).

CHAPTER 15

BELIEF IN GOD

1. *Prescription and Description*

THE language of Scripture can be divided into two main categories: descriptive and prescriptive. There are statements describing past, present, and future states of affairs, and statements prescribing what is to be done. Beginning with the classical rabbinic sources it has been the task of normative exegetes to carefully distinguish between scriptural description and scriptural prescription. Generally, the goal of this type of exegesis was to widen the prescriptive reach of the Torah; that is, to discover as many mitzvot as possible. This resulted, at times, in sacrificing description for the sake of prescription. [1]

Nevertheless, prescription, albeit the primary interest of the Torah, could not be extended indiscriminately without sacrificing at the same time the very intelligibility of the text. If the whole text of the Torah were nothing but commandments, then these commandments themselves would be unintelligible, for they would lack a context. Without a unifying descriptive background the commandments would be a random series of isolated, atomistic, prescriptions, unrelated to one another and unrelated to the experience of the people to whom they are addressed. Thus an unintelligible *content*, a prescriptive content without a descriptive *context*, would be *inoperable*. To regard the Torah as a bare code involves an inner contradiction; namely, without descriptions prescriptions cannot prescribe.

Two brief examples from rabbinic sources will illustrate how scriptural texts are judged to be either prescriptive or descriptive.

In Exodus we learn that a Hebrew bondmaid must be relased from servitude if the master or his son does not intend to marry her, with full conjugal rights, upon her reaching puberty. Then the text states:

"She shall go free, without any payment" (Exod. 21:11). Now "going free" (*hinam*) implies "without any payment." Therefore, at first glance it would seem that "without payment" (*ayn kassef*) is a description of "going free." However, this would be redundant; therefore the Talmud infers from these extra words another prescription:

> How do we know that the betrothal money of a minor daughter belongs to her father? R. Judah said that Scripture states, "She goes out free, without payment." *"Without payment"* to this master, but *with payment* to another master—namely, her father.[2]

Thus what seems to be a description is, according to the Talmud, a prescription.

We also learn in Exodus that a burglar may be killed upon entry. Then it states: "If the sun has risen on him, there is bloodguilt in that case" (Exod. 22:2). At first glance the text seems to be specifying the right to kill a burglar at nighttime only. However, the *Mekhilta* takes the words, "if the sun has risen on him," to be a general description.

> R. Ishmael said that the sun does not only shine on him but on everyone. But the phrase means, just as the sun signifies peace in the world, so if it is known to you that the burglar has peaceful intentions, the owner is guilty if he kills him.[3]

In other words, the rabbinic interpretation takes the scriptural phrase to be a general and figurative description of intent rather than a further specification of the prescription.

To distinguish between scriptural prescription and scriptural description is a major task of normative exegesis. In this chapter I propose to demonstrate that this task necessarily involves theological insight. In other words, the determination of what is a mitzvah and what is not, is not only a question involving an exegetical framework and not only a method of halakhic reasoning, but also a systematic or philosophical theology.

Since the end of World War II there has been a steady increase of theological interest in Jewish intellectual circles in America. The subjective need of thinking Jews today for Jewish theology is clear and evident. However, unless this subjective need is correlated with an objective requirement of Judaism itself—and all such requirements must have a halakhic point of reference—then Jewish theology can still be regarded as what its detractors have always held it to be: an interesting pastime, a homiletical exercise, or apologetics. It is the thesis of this chapter that theology as a systematic discipline is, in a number of key issues, a halakhic requirement.

The objective requirement for Jewish theology was best expressed by the late Isaak Heinemann in his too little read and even less discussed *magnum opus* on the "reasons for the commandments":

> If all the commandments of the Torah were only scriptural precepts, then one commandment could not elucidate another and the rabbis would have been unable to infer one thing from another nor extend or restrict the force of the commandments as was indeed done throughout halakhic literature. [4]

Reflection along similar lines is found in the two-volume work on rabbinic theology by my late revered teacher, Professor Abraham J. Heschel, and also in his earlier study, *God in Search of Man*. [5] I present this chapter as my own modest continuation of this tradition.

The problem to be analyzed here is the root-problem of any systematic theology; namely, belief in God. I will attempt to show that this is a halakhic question and that the two leading theologians of the Middle Ages, Maimonides and Nahmanides, regarded it as such in their theological analysis of the problem. Finally, I will discuss why this problem is a perennial one for Jews, one which still confronts us and probably always will because of the nature of Judaism itself.

2. *The First Commandment.*

The question of belief in God has been the subject of the same type of dispute. In Exod. 20:2 we read:

> I am the Lord your God who brought you out of the land of Egypt, the house of bondage.

The question is: Is this a statement *about* God or a commandment *to believe in* God's existence? Both interpretations are presented in the rabbinic sources.

The *Mekhilta* interprets the scriptural proposition as a descriptive statement about God:

> Why were the ten commandments not said at the beginning of the Torah? They give a parable. To what may this be compared? To the following: A king entered a province and said to the people: May I be your king? But the people said to

him: Have you done anything good for us that you should rule over us? What did he do then? He built the city wall for them, etc. . . . Then he said to them: May I be your king? They said to him: Yes, yes. Likewise God. [6]

In other words, "I am the Lord your God" is a statement about God as Israel's Redeemer from Egypt.

However, in the Babylonian Talmud we find the contrary:

R. Simlai interpreted that 613 commandments were given to Moses . . . R. Hamnuna said, What is the meaning of the verse: "A Torah Moses commanded us . . . ?" [Deut. 33:4]. The numerical value [*gematria*] of Torah is only 611. However, "I am the Lord your God" and "You shall have no other gods" they heard directly from the mouth of God. [7]

Here "I am the Lord your God" is explicitly designated as the first positive commandment; that is, it prescribes belief in the existence of God.

To opt for either view requires analysis of a fundamental theological problem: Can belief in God be prescribed or only described? Can one be commanded to believe in God's existence or must all the commandments presuppose this very belief? In the rabbinic sources dealing with this verse we find no such analysis, although the implications are clear. Such analysis had to wait for another exegetical epoch.

3. *Maimonides.*

Maimonides codified the talmudic text as follows:

The first commandment prescribes belief in the Divine, namely, that we are to believe that there exists a first, prime Cause who creates all existents, as it says, "I am the Lord your God" . . . Thus let it be evident to you that this is included as one of the 613 commandments. [8]

As we have seen, Maimonides was certainly not the first to designate belief in God's existence as a positive commandment. Nevertheless, he had to bear the brunt of the criticism against this designation, although his predecessor, R. Abraham ibn Ezra, had already criticized the talmudic sources Maimonides drew upon. [9] The reason the criticism is directed against Maimonides directly, it seems to me, is that he was a *systematic*, a philosophical, theologian. A system by definition is consistent. Therefore, if an inconsistency is presented, the first reaction is to direct criticism against the most systematic person who proposes the inconsistency—in our case, Maimonides. The designation of belief in God as a commandment is contradictory. The problem with Maimonides' statement lies in its logic.

A mitzvah as a commandment presupposes the prior existence of one who commands (metzaveh). Thus the talmudic view holding that the sufficient fulfillment of the commandments requires intention (kavvanah) is interpreted as requiring that this intention intend the act to be done as a mitzvah.[10] The other talmudic view, which holds that the commandments do not require intention, is interpreted as only requiring self-consciousness of the act itself (peulah). Obviously, then, intention of the source of the commandment, God, is required by the stricter view but not by the more lenient view.

Now as regards most commandments there are three components: (1) God who gives, (2) man who upholds, and (3) an object to be achieved. For example, one is required by God to eat matzah on the first night of Passover. In this case an act can be accomplished with the second and third components: the man consciously eats the matzah. The act itself can be accomplished without intending God as its source. Whether this is sufficient to fulfill the Torah's prescription or not is indeed subject to debate.[11] However, there is no inconsistency in positing that an instance of self-conscious behavior fulfills the legal obligation, in this case, without intending its source.

In the case of the commandment to believe in the existence of God, on the other hand, we have only two components: man and God, because God is both source and object of the commandment. Therefore, it is impossible not to intend the source of the commandment since the source is identical with the object, and no self-conscious act can ignore its object. Furthermore, in this case, to recognize the source of the commandment is to *already* recognize the object. In an act the object is that which *is to be done*. In an experience the object is that which is *already* present. To see belief in God as a commandment presupposes the very relationship to be accomplished. Thus it would appear that Maimonides is in fact *describing* belief about God rather than prescribing it. He has confused an act to be done with an experience that has happened. It seems as though we are involved in a vicious circle and that Maimonides' statement of the first commandment is literally absurd.

This logical objection was most cogently raised by R. Joseph Albo. In this criticism he follows the precedent of his teacher, Don Hasdai Crescas.[12] However, for Crescas the criticism plays an introductory role in his larger criticism of Maimonides' Aristotelian proof of the existence of God, and the presuppositions of Aristotelian philosophy in general. But now our concern is with the logic of Maimonides' statement in *Sefer HaMitzvot* and Albo seems to be primarily concerned with the logical problem. He writes:

> According to Maimonides, who includes specific command-ments among his principles, counting in his list the first of the Ten Commandments ... it is strange that the other princi-ples are not mentioned in the ten commandments. But accord-ing to our view there is no difficulty here. For our idea is that no specific command is a principle. [13]

This criticism is within the task Albo set up for himself in his *Sefer HaIkkarim:* to determine the basic principles of "natural religion" and then of "revealed religion"—concentrating, of course, on Judaism. What Albo did in the course of his theological project was to examine the Torah as a whole, deciding what is primary and what is derivative. On the basis of this delineation he could systematically criticize the logic of anyone who seemed to ignore this fundamental order. Maimonides received much logical criticism from Albo on various points. [14] Therefore, if we accept the logical criticism of Albo (and Crescas) we might as well accept their judgment that belief in God can only be described; that is, it is an experience, not an act to be done.

However, if we do not accept this logical criticism it must then be shown how Maimonides' statement is not guilty of such an obvious logical fallacy. It is only when we surmount this seemingly reasonable criticism that we can see the fundamental assumptions behind Maimonides' con-clusion that to believe in God's existence is a positive commandment. [15]

The fact that Albo sees principles as prior to commandments means that he sees *belief*, whereby we relate to principles, as prior to *action*, whereby we relate to commandments. Our task must be to show that for Maimonides there is a state of religious consciousness prior to *both* belief and action. Because of this priority, both belief and action can be seen as operating *together* for the sake of this highest state of religious consciousness. This, then, will show why Maimonides can speak of action in terms of belief and of belief in terms of action; for they are not related to each other as principle and derivative where careful distinctions must at all times be maintained. Actually, they are both derived from something more prior and, hence, careful distinctions must be main-tained between this superior state on the one hand and *action and belief* together on the other hand.

In dealing with the philosophical assumptions of Maimonides, especially concerning the relationship with God, which for him is most important, we must ask: (1) How does man seek a relationship with God? (2) What does he do to realize it? Only this twofold question will get us to the heart of Maimonides' theology.

4. *Metaphysics and Theology*

A Jew may well feel strange if his God is referred to as *First Cause*, but this feeling of strangeness is more for the concept than for the reality it conceptualizes. To affirm God as First Cause is to simply acknowledge that nothing or no one is prior to God. Of course Judaism affirms God as First Cause, it is just that historical revelation has enabled Jews to use more personal, less abstract, names for God. The question is whether man can intelligently relate to God as First Cause. To this question a good deal of Maimonides' theology is addressed.

It would seem, at first glance, that man cannot intelligently relate to the First Cause of the universe, because our ability to observe the process of cause and effect is quite limited. If one thinks of causality in terms of efficient causes, for example, "A makes B," then the relation of the cause (A) and the effect (B) is only intelligible if directly experienced. For there is nothing in either the cause or the effect alone that could indicate with certainty what relation there is between them. Experience is not equal to the structure of the universe, as Koheleth observed:

> All things are tiresome, one cannot put them into words, and
> so the eye is never satisfied with seeing nor the ear filled with
> hearing. (Eccls. 1:18) [16]

It is only when causality is understood in terms of final causes that a cause and effect relation can be intelligently predicted. The entity itself carries within itself the seeds or potential for its own fulfillment. It intends its end. The relation is one of attraction. This definition of primary causality and its development was the main contribution of Aristotle to the history of thought. Thus the *function* of an entity is correlated with its end. Concentration on the function of any entity necessarily involves a search for that end towards which it is attracted. When this is ascertained, the intellect can discover those *laws* which determine the activity of the entity in relation to its final cause. All being is teleological in nature.

For Aristotle, who was primarily a natural scientist, the chief concern was with the teleology of the universe. This is the subject matter of both the *Physics* and the *Metaphysics*. For Maimonides, who was primarily a Jewish theologian, the chief concern was with human activity, with human teleology or purposiveness. This Jewish interest in anthropology is very important to bear in mind, because it enables us to accept the truth in Maimonides' theology without being forced to accept an archaic Aristotelian cosmology. [17] Thus, early in his theological career, Maimonides wrote about the end of man:

> It is necessary for man to exercise all his spiritual powers for the sake of knowledge . . . and he should always place before his eyes one end, namely, to reach God to the extent it is possible to know Him. He should direct all his activities, both at rest and at work, everything, to this end so that none of his activities be without purpose, that is, inconsistent, with this end. [18]

Here he says that all human activity has for its proper end the knowledge of God. The function of man, therefore, is seen in the activity which God affects by His attractiveness. Since man is essentially an intellectual being, [19] this causes him to direct all of his respective energies towards the knowledge of the Supreme Object, God. Human nature is perfected by this activity. This perfection is for the sake of prophecy, the summit of human life. [20]

It is highly significant that Maimonides sees the means for prophecy in the statements of *Abot*, to which his work, *Shemonah Perakim*, from which the above quotation is taken, is an introduction. For the maxims of *Abot*, for the most part, are applicable to man in general, irrespective of his religious tradition. [21] In other words, the contemplation of the nature of man involves more than the acceptance of traditional authority. All human activity finds its rightful definition as the *means* for man to come close to knowing God. This is the state of prophecy. Just as the intellect can discover the laws of the physical universe by determining its final cause, so it can also discover the laws of human nature by determining the ultimate object towards whom man is attracted.

The designation of knowledge of God as the final cause of all human activity enables Maimonides to assign reasons to the various commandments of the Torah. Since the mitzvot are seen as essentially rational, and since rationality intends a teleological order, the value of the mitzvot is seen in their function in a hierarchy of ends. In addition to having specific purposes their most generic function is seen in how they enable man to reach this ultimate end of knowledge of God. Maimonides emphasizes this most lucidly in the *Moreh Nebukhim*, but there are many antecedents in his earlier writings. [22]

> The Law as a whole aims at two things: the welfare of the
> soul and the welfare of the body. As for the welfare of the
> soul, it consists in the multitude's acquiring correct opinions
> corresponding to their respective capacity. Therefore some of
> them (namely, the opinions) are set forth explicitly and some
> of them are set forth in parables. For it is not within the nature
> of the common multitude that its capacity should suffice for
> apprehending the subject matter as it is.[23]

Time and time again Maimonides emphasized that even though all
men are not capable of abstract philosophical reasoning, it is nonetheless
necessary for them to receive correct opinions about God.[24] This can
be seen as the touchstone of Maimonides' political philosophy. Following
Aristotle in the view that human nature is social, and, moreover, maintain-
ing independently that the end of all ends for man is prophecy, it becomes
necessary for society itself to be ordered towards this ultimate end.[25]
Since the mundane function of society is to provide stabilizing authority
in the lives of men, such a transcendentally oriented society as the Torah
prescribes must supply epistemological authority in addition to legislating
social laws and mores.[26] It must inculcate correct opinions by the power
of conventional authority. The highest exercise of this authority is
pedagogy. Conventional ideas in a religious context are *dogmas*. Early
in his career Maimonides formulated a simple dogmatic creed. Dogma
satisfies the popular need for immediate certitude and Maimonides was
afraid that if the Torah did not fulfill this need, the impressionable
masses would turn to idolatry, which has always had great imaginative
appeal.[27] The most evident meaning of the Torah is *natural*—concerned
with society as the fulfillment of man's social needs. However, the highest
meaning of the Torah is *supernatural;* that is, the prophetic consciousness
of God.[28]

Thus we see that *both* practice and belief are prescribed for the end
of knowledge of God. Neither practice nor belief is that knowledge
which has God as its total and immediate object. Therefore, on the
basis of the foregoing philosophical assumptions, there is nothing illogical
in Maimonides' expression of the prescription to believe in the existence
of God. For all prescriptions, whether pertaining to practice or to belief,
are *mediated* by the authority of the Torah-constituted society. Although
God is the *ultimate* source of the commandments, He is not their
immediate source, because they are addressed to the people of Israel
as a constituted society before being upheld by individual Jews. The
society can direct prescriptions to the people to believe *that* God exists,

but they cannot create for the potential prophets in their midst the experience of *what* God is. As Jeremiah put it:

> ... and they shall no more teach every man his neighbor, and every man his brother, saying: "Know the Lord"; for they shall all know Me ... (Jer. 31:34)

The commandment is to believe that God exists so that one might ultimately experience God's presence directly. Thus the ultimate object of the commandment, knowledge of God as He is, is not *already* presupposed by the commandment. The experience of God's presence is greater than His prescription of the Torah's authority, which comes first. The immediate presupposition of the commandments, both practical and dogmatic, is the *social* authority of the Torah, This is the *conditio sine qua non* for the ultimate *personal* experience of God's presence.

The mitzvot, as regulations of both action and belief, are ultimately grounded in the prophetic experience of God's presence, which is their end. The immediate condition of these commandments is, however, the Torah-constituted society. The ground is transcendent; the condition immanent. Belief in God is a presupposition for knowledge of God. Like everything else in the world, the commandment to believe in the existence of God is unintelligible if isolated from its teleological frame of reference.

The commandments of the Torah are expressed in terms readily describable. "The Torah speaks in the language of man." [29] As for the ultimate experience of God's presence, however,"No eye has seen but thine, O God, what Thou will do for those who wait for Thee."[30] It is with this background in mind that the text in *Sefer HaMitzvot* can now be seen as logically cogent and theologically profound.

5. Nahmanides

Nahmanides, in his commentary on *Sefer HaMitzvot*, ostensibly accepts the view of Maimonides that to believe in the existence of God is a positive commandment. However, upon closer examination of what he says, two factors indicate that he is laying the groundwork for a profound departure from Maimonides' theology.

First, Nahmanides shows the earlier position of R. Simon Kairo (Behag) in his *Halakhot Gedolot*, a position from which Maimonides departed. In elaborating this earlier position Nahmanides expresses ideas curiously similar to his own:

> It seems to be the view of the *Halakhot Gedolot* that . . . the belief in God's existence which comes from the signs and won-

drous demonstrations and the revelation of His presence [*giluy Shekhinah*] to our eyes—this is the fundamental principle, the root from which the mitzvot are derived. Therefore it cannot be numbered among the other 613 commandments of the Torah . . . this is the view of the *Halakhot Gedolot* and it has exegetical merit [*panim*].[31]

Nahmanides also bases this objection on the well-known statement of R. Joshua ben Levi in the Mishnah, which declares that the acceptance of the "yoke" of God's kingship must precede the acceptance of the "yoke" of the specific commandments.[32] At this point we seem to have the argument of Crescas and Albo by anticipation; namely, belief in God is the principle presupposed by all the subsequent commandments.

Second, in his presentation of his own opinion of the meaning of "I am the Lord your God," Nahmanides reasons as follows:

It seems correct to me in this entire matter to include "I am the Lord your God" among the commandments according to Maimonides' opinion. . . . For they already believed in God in Egypt as it says, "They believed in the Lord" [Exod. 14:31]. This act of faith [*emunah*] is now a recollection [*zekhirah*] . . . that is, a reaffirmation to strengthen their faith that there is a God and that He is the liberator from Egypt.[33]

Here Nahmanides grounds faith in history. Thus, although his understanding of the status of "I am the Lord your God" is technically similar to that of Maimonides, we shall see that his theological assumptions are radically different. Nahmanides differed with Maimonides on many points, but this, it seems to me, is the fundamental point of difference.

For Nahmanides, as for Maimonides before him, the mitzvot intend a relationship beyond mediated prescription. If the knowledge of God is the End of all intelligent human striving, then this relationship, although first in importance, is last in time. For Maimonides, the *telos* (intelligible end) and the *eschaton* (temporal end) are identical. However, if one understands God's causal action as dynamic rather than teleological, then man's relationship with God is grounded in experience that *precedes* his action. Hence man's first experience of the presence of God must be *before* his observance of any specific mitzvot. This difference in understanding the relationship of God and man is what prompts Nahmanides to take strong issue with Maimonides on the question of the first commandment. The belief in the existence of God is a presupposition *in time* for the observance of any specific mitzvah.

In examining the roots of Nahmanides' theology we must ask: (1)

What enables man to become aware of the power of God? (2) How does this state of awareness involve man's activity?

Being within the theological tradition of Judaism, both Maimonides and Nahmanides acknowledge the doctrine of *yesh me'ayin* (*creatio ex nihilo*); that is, entities in the universe exist because God alone wills their existence in every aspect. However, as we saw earlier, the ordinary experience of the world only deals with causal relations within its own narrow purview. This means that one cannot relate to the First Cause of the universe, who is held to be a dynamic power (*poel*), because causality of this type transcends the range of normal experience. Medieval Jewish theologians were aware of this fact long before Kant's critique of causality and causal inferences of the existence of God.

Therefore, how does man relate to God? Maimonides' answer is that we begin with the function of entities within the universe, primarily man, and discover the teleological intent of their function. By changing our causal orientation we can remain within the range of ordinary experience. Although Maimonides does not allow his Aristotelian frame of reference to imply rejection of the traditional Jewish doctrine of creation, he does notground the relationship of man with God in this doctrine. [34] For if creation is the point of contact between man and God, then ordinary experience of the natural world can no longer be the starting point for that relationship.

For Nahmanides, who insists that we relate to God as a creative Power, ordinary experience no longer suffices as a beginning. The alternative, which he developed with the greatest consistency and insight, is that this relationship calls for *extraordinary* experience at its very inception, experience that transcends the ordinary sequence of events and through which God manifests Himself to man. Traditionally, these extraordinary experiences have been called "miracles," but, especially after Hume's critique of the concept of miracle, I think the modern theological concept of *Heilsgeschichte* better explains the meaning *nes* has, for the most part, in the classical Jewish sources. These experiences are special occasions when God does the unexpected in order to enable His people to become immediately aware of His lordship. They are what Nahmanides called "public manifestations" (*nissim mefursamim*) of God's creative power. [35]

Since these manifest experiences are the sole occasions for man to become aware of God's lordship, it follows that they are the grounds for any subsequent relationship. This is the point Nahmanides emphasizes in his note to Maimonides' text. The emphasis is seen again very clearly in his Torah commentary to the verse, "I will be [*ehyeh*] what I will be [*asher ehyeh*]" (Exod. 3:13):

God answered Moses *I will be with you* in this sorrow. . . .
And this will be *the* great proof that God is with Israel whenever
we call unto Him. However, Maimonides interprets this verse
in the *Moreh Nebukhim* [1. 63] as "I am absolutely self-sufficient
Being"; . . . but this is not the meaning of this statement.

Both the views about God reflected in this exegetical dispute have many
precedents in earlier theological works.[36] Nevertheless, the best restate-
ment of Nahmanides' theological approach, it seems to me, occurs in
the Buber-Rosenzweig Torah translation of Exod. 3:13:

God spoke to Moses: "I will be there as THE ONE WHO WILL
BE THERE . . . I am there sent me to you."[37]

In other words, we do not relate to God in His *Sein* (being *per se*) but
in His *Dasein* (being-there), in His own manifestation of a direct relationship with us. God's historical presence is, for Nahmanides as for Judah
Halevi before him, the proof of His existence.[38] Man's primary relationship with God is grounded in the historical manifestation of Presence;
namely, in the *Heilsgeschichte* of Israel.

These events force the Jew to recognize the creative power of God
as if he were present at creation itself; for they bridge the otherwise
infinite gap between ordinary experience and God. The *Heilsgeschichte*
is itself an act of creation by God for the benefit and comprehension
of man.[39] This primary experience, the exodus and deliverance from
Egypt, results, then, in an *imperative* for man to believe in God. This
imperative is a mitzvah, but Nahmanides differs from Maimonides in
refusing to designate it as a prescription, that is, as similar in kind to
the 613 commandments. Prescriptions, as we have seen, presuppose
one immediate source of authority and another ultimate object of the
act to be done. But, for Nahmanides, to believe *that* God exists is a
response to some direct experience of the presence of God. Being the
direct result of a personal experience, such a response cannot very well
be authoritatively prescribed as something *to be done*.[40] Rather, it must
spontaneously arise in direct response to something that has already
happened. This is why the manifestation of God in the exodus from
Egypt is the foundation of all the other commandments. The imperative,
which this direct experience engenders, is the irreducible point of reference for all subsequent prescriptions, for the prescriptions prescribe
acts that are symbolic participations in the primary experience. The
meaning of the mitzvot, especially the positive ritual ones, is cultic.[41]
In other words, the acts the Torah prescribes are subsequent experiences

of the events the Torah describes. These events entail immediate imperatives. Thus, later in his note on Maimonides, Nahmanides, interpreting the earlier source, writes:

> Nevertheless, if there is such a commandment which says, "Know and believe that I am the Lord who has brought you out of the land of Egypt, and do My commandments," it would not be included in the 613 commandments, because it is the foundation [ikkar] and they are derivative [toldot].

For Nahmanides, to believe in God's existence is a mitzvah, but it is a mitzvah in the sense of a direct response to a personal experience (imperative), not the fulfillment of an act authoritatively presented (prescription). In other words, mitzvah has for him a twofold meaning. Thus, in his Torah commentary to Exod. 20:2 he writes:

> This is a positive commandment. He said, "I am the Lord" who instructs [yoreh] and commands them to know and believe that the Lord is God, namely, Prime Being, from whose will and power everything is derived. He is God whom they are obliged [hayyabim] to serve.

The exodus from Egypt engenders faith. Faith is not the voluntary affirmation of a Reality *not yet* experienced; rather, it is an inescapable imperative to respond to an event *before* one's eyes. Faith is an imperative but not a prescription. [42]

Whereas for Maimonides belief precedes knowledge, [43] for Nahmanides the experience of God precedes the faith that commemorates it.

6. The Obligation of Theology

In the difference between Maimonides and Nahmanides concerning a seemingly technical problem of Halakhah, we see the presentation of two different theories of the nature of faith for Jews. Both deal with the question: What is a Jew's relationship with God? This question includes two subquestions: What role does the historical community of Israel play in that relationship? What role does the Torah play in it? This fundamental question and its corollaries have not been obscured by the passing of Jewish history. Quite the contrary, they have been deepened by it. The systematic theologies of Maimonides and Nahmanides are indispensable models for any believing Jew who desires to understand the structure and content of his faith.

Both theologians were passionately concerned with what is good for man, what God requires of us. Since man is an intelligent creature, his faith must inevitably require the search for its own intelligibility. They have shown that the fullest exercise of our powers of philosophical analysis is one of the offerings with which we must approach God. Philosophical theology is not just an optional gift dependent on our own particular, subjective mood, it is a halakhic requirement. [44]

NOTES

NOTES

All sources quoted and referred to in the text are fully documented in the notes. All translations, unless otherwise indicated, are by the author.

CHAPTER 1

1. For the precise meaning of Halakhah as law, see S. Lieberman, *Hellenism in Jewish Palestine*, 2d imp. ed. (New York: Jewish Theological Seminary of America, 1962), p. 83, n, 3. For the meaning of Aggadah as theology in the widest sense of that word, note: "If you desire to know God, study Haggadah." *Sifre*, Ekeb. ed. Friedmann, no. 49.

2. See L. Wittgenstein, *Tractatus Logico-Philosophicus*, 4.2-4.23, trans. D. F. Pears and B. F. McGuiness (London: Routledge & Kegan Paul, 1961), pp. 58-61.

3. *God in Search of Man* (New York: Farrar, Straus & Cudahy, 1955), p. 337.

4. "If all the commandments of the Torah were only scriptual precepts, then one commandment could not elucidate another and the rabbis would not have been able to infer one thing from another nor extend or restrict the force of the commandments as was indeed done throughout halakhic literature." Isaak Heinemann, *Taamay HaMitzvot b'Sifrut Yisrael*, 4th ed. (Jerusalem, 1959), 1:29.

5. "Ish HaHalakhah, " *Talpiot* 1, no. 3-4 (1944): 665.

6. *The Rabbinic Mind* (New York: Jewish Theological Seminary of America, 1952), p. 89.

7. "Moralization and Demoralization in Jewish Ethics," *Judaism* 11, no. 4 (Fall 1962):297.

8. See *Mishneh Torah*, intro., beg. following B. Berakhot 5a. Also, see M. Lazarus, *The Ethics of Judaism*, trans. H. Szold (Philadelphia: Jewish Publication Society of America, 1900), 1:272-73.

9. *Crescas' Critique of Aristotle* (Cambridge: Harvard University Press, 1929), p. 26. Along the lines of our analogy, note: " . . . total science is like a field of force whose boundary conditions are experience. A conflict with experience at the periphery occasions readjustments in the interior of the field. . . . But the total field is so undetermined by its boundary conditions, experience, that there is much latitude of choice as to what statements to reevaluate in the light of any contrary experience." W. V. Quine, "Two Dogmas of Empiricism," *From a Logical Point of View*, 2d rev. ed. (New York: Harper Torchbooks, 1961), pp. 42-43.

10. Wolfson, *op. cit.*, p. 25

11. See Bertrand Russell, *Mysticism and Logic* (Garden City, N.Y.: Doubleday Anchor Books, 1957), pp. 200-201.

12. B. Kiddushin 13a.

13. Rashi thereto; also, see Rashi on B. Kiddushin 6a, s.v. "b'teeb."

14. R. Samuel Edels (Maharsha) thereto.

15. For a liberal rabbi's critique of the lack of halakhic considerations among liberal rabbis, see J. J. Petuchowski, "Plural Models Within the Halakhah," *Judaism* 19, no. 1 (Winter 1970): 85-86. For a more traditional rabbi's critique of the conceptual insensitivity among

153

traditional rabbis, see S. Greenberg, "And He Writes Her a Bill of Divorcement," *Conservative Judaism* 24, no. 3 (Spring 1970): 91-92.

16. *Hakdamah L'Mishnah,* ed. Rabinowitz (Jerusalem: Mosad HaRav Kook, 1961),pp. 50-51.

17. See B. Kiddushin 5a and parallels. Cf. B. Baba Kama 2a, Rashi and Tosafot, s.v., "hashor."

18. See B. Nedarim 11b.

19. M. Gittin 9.10. See Albeck's note in his commentary, *Seder Nashim* (Jerusalem: Mosad Bialik, 1955), p. 407, and S. Rosenblatt, *The Interpretation of the Bible in the Mishnah* (Baltimore: Johns Hopkins University Press, 1935), p. 46. Also, see B. Cohen, *Law and Tradition in Judaism* (New York: Ktav Publishing House, 1959), p. 105.

20. B. Gittin 90a. See Lev. 18:6 ff. Both Ben Sirach (25:24-26) and Josephus, *Antiquities* 4.253, seem to present the law according to the Hillelite position. The view of Philo sounds like the Hillelite position, for in alluding to the grounds for divorce he speaks of "any reason [*prophasis*] which might occur [*kath ayn tyche*]." *De Specialus Legibus* 3.5, Loeb Classical Library (Cambridge: Harvard University Press, 1937), p. 492. The New Testament, on the other hand, definitely presents the Shammaite position; see Matt. 19:3-6 and Mark 9:12, 10:2. Cf. Tob. 6:18.

21. See, e.g., B. Sanhedrin 4a.

22. *Gerushin* 10.21. See *Tur,* Eben HaEzer 119. R. Joseph Karo in the *Bet Joseph* to this section of the *Tur* explains that even according to Maimonides actual law still follows the Hillelites. See Rashi to B. Gittin 90b, s.v. "im."

23. In his commentary to the Mishnah, Maimonides writes: "What R. Akiba said is by no means the law ... because she has committed no sin and she complies with his objective standards." Cf. B. Shabbat 64b.

24. B. Erubin 13b. For various interpretations of the essential differences between the two schools, see L. Ginzberg, *On Jewish Law and Lore* (Philadelphia: Jewish Publication Society of America, 1955), pp. 88-123; N. N. Glatzer, *Hillel the Elder* (New York: Schocken Books, 1966), pp. 56-63.

25. *Tur,* Eben HaEzer 119. See Serkes (Bach) thereto.

26. B. Gittin 90b. Cf. B. Kiddushin 50a and B. Sanhedrin 22a.

27. *Bamidbar Rabah* 3.4. See *Vayikra Rabah* 8.1. Cf. B. Sotah 3a. For a discussion of the many texts where this story is found, see *Vayikra Rabah,* ed. M. Margoliot (Jerusalem, 1953), 1:166, no. 4. On non-Jewish agreement with the scriptural account of creation in six days, see *Midrash Tehillim* 19.1, ed. Buber, p. 162. For other related texts, see I. Abrahams, "Marriages Are Made in Heaven," *The Book of Delight and Other Papers* (Philadelphia: Jewish Publication Society of America, 1912), pp. 178-183, 307.

28. Concerning rabbinic disapproval of the unmarried, see, e.g., B. Kiddushin 29b.

29. For an example of halakhic encouragement without specific prescription, see B. Baba Metzia 92a and Asheri (Rosh), chap. 7, no. 11.

30. B. Moed Katan 18b. See B. Hagigah 8b.

31. Cf. M. Berakhot 9.3.

32. See B. Moed Katan 18b, Tos., s.v. "umi"; B. Sotah 2a, Tos., s.v. "ha"; and Maharsha to B. Moed Katan 18b.

33. See Deut. 25:5-10; B. Yebamot 29b, 52a; B. Kiddushin 14a; Maim., *Yibum ve' Halitzah* 1.1., 2.1.

34. The parallel text in *Vayikra Rabah* 8.1 adds the words, "without their good will [*shelo b'tobatan*]." The text in *Midrash Tanhuma,* Ki Tissa, 5 adds "attaches a yoke [*kolar*] on each one's neck." Cf. *Seder Eliahu Zuta,* chap. 3.

35. See P. Kiddushin 1.1 where a tradition is reported that only Jews are dispensed from the full ramifications of predestined marriage by the institution of divorce. See R. David Fraenkel, *Korban HaEdah,* s.v. "shelo." However, this text reflects the difference between Jewish marriage as a sacrament and Roman marriage as a civil contract. Note B. Cohen, *Law and Tradition in Judaism,* pp. 279 ff.

36. This translation follows LXX: *Kat' auton*. See B. Yebamot 63a.

37. See Maim., *Ishut* 1.1-4; *Tur*, Eben HaEzer, beg.

38. See Maim., *Shemonah Perakim*, chap. 8, ed. Rabinowitz (Jerusalem: Mosad HaRav Kook, 1961), pp. 204-6 and *Teshubah* 5.1-4. Cf. Kant, *Critique of Practical Reason*, Preface, for the distinction between grounds and conditions in practical reason. My identification of moral grounds is different from Kant's, but the conceptual distinction is extremely useful even for non-Kantians.

39. See, e.g., B. Yoma 18b and Tos., s.v. "yihuday" and B. Nedarim 20b and R. Nissim (Ran) thereto.

40. See Maim., *Yesoday HaTorah* 8.1-3; Nahmanides, "Vikuah," sec. 39, *Kitbay Ramban*, ed. C.B. Chavel (Jerusalem: Mosad HaRav Kook, 1963), 1:308-9; *Encyclopedia Talmudit*, 1:60-62, s.v. "Aggadah."

41. "R. Judah said in the name of Rab that a man is forbidden to marry a woman before he has seen her lest she be repulsive to him [*dabar meguneh*], thus causing him to violate the command, 'You shall love your neighbor as yourself.' " B. Kiddushin 41a. Cf. B. Niddah 17a. However, the purely legal ruling of the Halakhah, emphasized on that very page, permits marriage by proxy.

42. This would also explain the following: "Whoever vows not to have intercourse with his wife, his wife has to wait two weeks before petitioning for a divorce—according to the School of Shammai." M. Ketubot 5.6. However, this is because he has denied her her Torah-guaranteed rights of cohabitation. See B. Nedarim 81b and I. H. Weiss, *Dor Dor veDorshav* (Jerusalem: Ziv, n.d.), 1:172 and 2:20.

43. Cf. *Sifra*, ed. Weiss, p. 27a, viz., R. Akiba commenting on Lev. 5:21 concerning interhuman breach of faith as a sin against the All-Present God.

44. On the need for mutuality as a property distinguishing man from God, see Rashi to Gen. 2:18, quoting *Pirkay d'Rabbi Eliezer* 17.5.

45. See R. David Kimhi (Radak) thereto. Thus Hosea's marriage and reunion with the promiscuous Gomer is sanctioned by a command of God, who chose this *particular* situation to illustrate His own faithfulness and forgiveness of His unfaithful people. See Hos. 1:2, 2:21, 3:1, B. Pesahim 87a-87b. Maimonides explains the problem away by interpreting the whole episode as a parable. See *Moreh Nebukhim* 2.46.

CHAPTER 2

1. " 'But God does not let him eat from it' [Eccles. 6:2]: this is the aggadist, for he does not forbid nor permit; he does not declare anything to be impure or pure." P. Horayot 3.5. R. Moshe Margolis, *P'nay Moshe*: "He has no authority [*shelitah*] in ritual or civil matters." See *Encyclopedia Talmudit*, 1:62, n. 66.

2. See Maimonides' introduction to *Perek Helek*, end. Even though others differed with Maimonides as to the number and selection of dogmas, the dogmas themselves were not challenged; see Albo, *Ikkarim* 1.3. Max Kadushin writes: "Rabbinic dogmas are beliefs which the Rabbis have singled out as those to which all must ascribe." *The Rabbinic Mind*, p. 365. Cf. S. Schechter, *Studies in Judaism*, 1st series (Philadelphia: Jewish Publication Society of America, 1920), pp. 156-59. Nevertheless, Franz Rosenzweig was correct, I believe, when he wrote, "Das Judenthum hat naemlich zwar Dogmen, aber keine Dogmatik." *Kleinere Schriften* (Berlin: Schocken Verlag, 1937), p.31. I think one could say that Jews sought the systematic order one would associate with "dogmatics" in the realm of Halakhah.

3. *Bereshit Rabah* 17.12.

4. P. Shabbat 2.6; also, *Tanhuma*, Noah 1.

5. *Shabbat* 5.3. Cf. B. Shabbat 32a and Rashi, s.v. "harayny."

6. See *Otzar Vikuhim*, ed. J. D. Eisenstein (Israel, 1959), p. 89.

7. *Students, Scholars and Saints* (Philadelphia: Jewish Publication Society of America, 1928), p.117; Cf. *On Jewish Law and Lore*, p.78.

8. B. Baba Kama 15a.

9. See Aristotle, *Nicomachean Ethics* 1133a30; also, Ibn Ezra to Exod. 21:24.

10. See Maim., *Ishut* 23.1-7.

11. See B. Pesahim 25b.

12. M. Kiddushin 1.7.

13. See B. Kiddushin 30b.

14. *Ibid.* 34a.

15. *Tefillah* 1.2 following B. Berakhot 20b.

16. See B. Berakhot 20b. For a discussion of the difference between male and female roles in the ritual domain, see D. M. Feldman, "Woman's Role and Jewish Law," *Conservative Judaism* 26, no. 4 (Summer 1972): 29-39.

17. See B. Baba Batra 119a and Tos., s.v. "yodea."

18. B. Erubin 96a-96b.

19. B. Hagigah 16b.

20. Cf. Rashi to Exod. 38:8.

21. *Tosafot*: B. Erubin 96a-96b, s.v. "dilma"; B. Rosh Hashanah 33a, s.v. "ha"; B. Kiddushin 31a, s.v. "dela." See Asheri, Kiddushin, chap. 1, no. 49. Nevertheless, cf. *Shulhan Arukh* O.H. 38.3 and Isserles, thereto.

22. B. Sukkah 51b-52a.

23. T. Megillah 4.11 and B. Megillah 23a. Cf. Esther 1:11-12.

24. B. Yoma 69a-69b. See Maim., Hagigah 3.4

25. T. Abodah Zarah, chap. 8 and B. Sanhedrin 56a-56b.

26. M. Berakhot 3.3 and B. Hagigah 4a and parallels.

27. *Siddur Kol Bo*, ed. Vilna, 1914, quoting M. Berakhot 9.5.

28. *Siddur Derekh HaHayyim of R. Jacob Lissa*, ed. New York, 1971, p. 40b.

29. *Kitabim Nibharim* (Jerusalem: Mosad HaRab Kook, 1969), 1:21-22. See Ben Zion Bokser, *High Holy Day Prayerbook* (New York: Hebrew Publishing Co., 1957), p. 66. Cf. *Sabbath and Festival Prayerbook* (New York: United Synagogue of America and Rabbinical Assembly, 1946), p. 45. Nevertheless, in Menahot 43b the blessing is considered mandatory (see Rashi thereto and Maim., *Tefillah* 7.6). However, considerations of *kabod haberiyot* could apply here inasmuch as the obligation is not scriptural. See *supra*, n. 31. Also, it is a question of omission (*sheb v'al taaseh*), which is a valid consideration even in cases of scriptural law, much less rabbinic law.

30. *HaSiddur HaShalem* (New York: Hebrew Publishing Co., 1949), p. xi.

31. See B. Berakhot 19a-20b and Menahot 37b-38a. Maim., *Kelayim* 10.29.

32. See B. Gittin 2b-3a and B. Kiddushin 70b-71a.

33. B. Pesahim 66a.

34. *Bereshit Rabah* 48.21. See B. Yebamot 65b.

35. For another liturgical change undoubtedly brought about through similar concerns, see M. Bikkurim 1.4, P. Bikkurim 1.4, and Maim., *Bikkurim* 4.3.

CHAPTER 3

1. See *Jewish Encyclopedia*, 10, s.v. "Sambation" and L. Ginzberg, *Legends of the Jews*, 6:407-8, n. 56. Concerning the behavior of oxen on the Sabbath, see M. Baba Kama 4.2 and Bertinoro thereto. For the notion of universal Jewish Sabbath observance, see B. Shabbat 38a and Rashi, s.v. "dela atay."

2. See Zechariah Frankel, *Darkhay HaMishnah* (Tel Aviv: Sinai, 1959), p. 20; I. H. Weiss, *Dor Dor veDorshav*, 1:69 ff.

3. M. Shabbat 7.2.

4. Exod. 35:1-3; *Mekhilta*, ed. Horovitz-Rabin, p. 345, B. Shabbat 97b.

5. Expanded ed., New York: Meridian Books, 1963.

6. This seems to me to be the meaning of the famous Aggadah at the beginning of *Bereshit Rabah*, namely, God used the Torah and His masterplan to create the universe.

The Torah, therefore, precedes history and is not its product. See, also, Ibn Habib, *Ayn Yaakob*, introduction. Concerning the Sabbath law, see B. Shabbat 31b commenting on Num. 9:23 and Rabbenu Hananael thereto.

7. See B. Kiddushin 29a.

8. B. Shabbat 2b and B. Baba Kama 2a-2b.

9. See the comment of R. Akiba on B. Kiddushin 37a.

10. See the *Proceedings of the Rabbinical Assembly of America* 14 (1950): 138-64.

11. B. Shabbat 94a, Tos., s.v. "Rabbi Simon." Also, see *ibid.* 31b, Tos., s.v. "vesoter," *ibid.* 46b.

12. *Proceedings*, 14:130-31.

13. See Maimonides' comment to M. Shabbat 10.5.

14. See R. Nissim on B. Shabbat 93b; B. Shabbat 30a. Cf. Maimonides, *Shabbat* 1.3, 7.

15. B. Shabbat 93b, Rashi, s.v. "Rabbi Simon."

16. Cf. *ibid.* 31b.

17. See Aristotle, *Physics* 263a5 ff.

18. M. Shabbat 13.3, B. Shabbat 105b; Maim., *Shabbat* 8.8 and 10.10.

19. *Proceedings*, 14:126.

20. According to M. Eduyot 1.5-6 minority views were recorded in the Mishnah so that subsequent generations would *not* follow them. (However, note Rabad thereto, who reads the text contrarily.) Nevertheless, in an emergency (*sh'at hadehak*), the Talmud in B. Berakhot 9a and parallels accepts a minority opinion, but the opinion only applies to an individual situation, not a specific law. See T. Eduyot 1.4 and Maim., *Mamrim* 1.2.

The interpretation of Ri's interpretation of the view of R. Simon satisfies neither of these criteria. Ri's view is not held by either Rashi or Maimonides. Furthermore, it seems to me that the best interpretation of R. Simon's view is given by R. Yom Tob ben Abraham Ishbili (Ritba, ca. 1342), who wrote: "The principle of *an act not required for its own sake* applies to any act where one does not benefit [*neheneh*] from the act itself [*megufah*], but only removes himself from something harmful [*heyzek*]." *Hidushay Ritba* to B. Shabbat 94a, ed. New York, 1970, p. 65.

21. See Maim., *Shabbat* 7.5-7. A *toldah* accomplishes the same end as an *ab* through different means. *Shebut* closely resembles an *ab* or a *toldah* in terms of its means, but accomplishes a different, scripturally permitted end. Because of its similarity the rabbis forbade acts of *shebut* as inconsistent with the spirit of the Sabbath.

22. See B. Baba Kama 2a.

23. See L. Nemoy, *Karaite Anthology* (New Haven: Yale University Press, 1952), p. 116.

24. B. Erubin 51a.

25. See M. Erubin 3.4 ff.

26. *Mishpatay Uziel*, O.H. 1 (Jerusalem, 1935), sec. 9, pp. 27-28.

27. *Hatam Sofer* VI, sec. 93.

28. *Mishpatay Uziel*, O.H. II (Jerusalem, 1947), sec. 41, p. 109.

29. Hullin 11a interpreting Exod. 23:2.

30. B. Betzah 36b.

31. Cf. B. Hagigah 15a where R. Meir is walking beside Elisha ben Abuyah (Aher), who was riding on a horse on the Sabbath. Here the rider tells the pedestrian that they have approached the *tehum*. However, there was apparently no marker because Elisha says, "Meir, turn back, for I have already measured by the paces of my horse that the *tehum* only extends so far." Elisha ben Abuyah was an unusually perceptive person who would notice things overlooked by ordinary people.

32. See, e.g., *Proceedings*, 14:174-76.

33. B. Rosh Hashanah 29b.

34. However, certain positive commandments do take precedence over negative commandments, e.g., *milah* is performed on the Sabbath. See B. Shabbat 132a-132b.

35. Menahot 29b interpreting Prov. 3:34.

36. B. Yebamot 65b interpreting Prov. 9:8.

37. Eli Ginzberg, *Keeper of the Law: Louis Ginzberg* (Philadelphia: Jewish Publication Society of America, 1966), p. 242.

38. B. Pesahim 22b interpreting Lev. 19:14.

39. "Our rabbis did not make decrees [*lo gazru*] for uncommon cases [*dela shekhiha*]." B. Erubin 63b and parallels.

40. In modern times, when many Jews live nonobservant, but not non-Jewish, lives, one must make a clear distinction between apostates and the religiously lax (see Hullin 4a and B. Abodah Zorah 26b). For the views of several later authorities (*aharonim*) on this problem, see Louis Jacobs, *Principles of the Jewish Faith* (New York: Basic Books, 1964), p. 311.

CHAPTER 4

1. B. Gittin 2b-a. Rabbenu Tam (d. 1171) in *Tosafot,* s.v. "ed" justifies this by stating that this type of testimony is a point of information (*giluy milta*), not formal testimony where two *bona fide* witnesses are required. See, also, Maim., *Gerushin,* end. The whole question of testimony in agunah cases is dealt with in the thorough study of I. Z. Kahana, *Sefer HaAgunot* (Jerusalem: Mosad HaRav Kook, 1954). Cf. B. Shabbat 145a-b.

2. See B. Shabbat 56a and Rashi and Tos., s.v., "get"; B. Gittin 73a.

3. See Chapter 1.

4. See B. Yebamot 89b-90b. No rabbinic changes of scriptural laws were ever made on the grounds that the scriptural laws were outdated or imperfect. The criteria for change were themselves scriptural. Only man-made rabbinic law is subject to repeal; see M. Eduyot 1.5.

5. Even so astute and sensitive a scholar as Dr. Louis M. Epstein overstated the rationale for his own moral zeal about the agunah problem when he wrote: "I hope I will not be accused of irreverence when I admit the truth that Jewish law as relates to the family is inferior to our own moral level and less just than the laws of domestic relations of the gentiles." "A Solution to the Agunah Problem," *Proceedings of the Rabbinical Assembly* 4 (1930-32): 83.

6. See P. Kiddushin 1.1. Cf. Josephus, *Antiquities* 15.7, 10 and 17.5,4. Also, note B. Gittin 88b: "Rab Masharshya said that according to scriptural law [*d'bar Torah*] a get forced [*meuseh*] by non-Jews is valid. Why, then, did the rabbis invalidate it [*pasul*]? So that any woman could not go to the gentiles and free herself from her husband." Rashi: "She hires a gentile hoodlum [*onas*] to force her husband to divorce her by dubious [*b'akifin*] means." Nevertheless, despite the acquisitory language used in the Mishnah (Kiddushin 1.1) to describe marriage, the woman was not regarded as her husband's property; see B. Gittin 85b.

7. See Chapter 1.

8. M. Ketubot 5.6, B. Ketubot 77a. Also, see Isserles' note to *Shulhan Arukh,* E.H. 154.1, where he eliminates the "double standard," viz., whereas a husband is obliged to divorce his promiscuous wife (M. Sotah 6.1; B. Gittin 46a), so now the wife can petition the court to force her promiscuous husband to divorce her.

9. See, e.g., *Shulhan Arukh,* E.H. 115.4 and Isserles' note thereto; also, *Encyclopedia Talmudit,* s.v. "zakhin," 12:165-66.

10. The notion of the woman paying her husband to divorce her was well known in talmudic times. See M. Gittin 7.5 and B. Gittin 74b.

11. Quoted in W. Gunther Plaut, *The Rise of Reform Judaism* (New York: World Union for Progressive Judaism, 1963), 1:223.

12. Deut. 23:3 and B. Kiddushin 73a.

13. "Plural Models Within the Halakhah," *Judaism* 19, no. 1 (Winter 1970): 85-86.

14. "... most of us are trying to persuade prospective applicants that we cannot officiate without a Get having been obtained. ... I foresee the development of a Reform Bet Din, knowledgable in gittin, which will produce a religious divorce either in cooperation with the Conservative movement or in some other way. Certainly we are headed in that direction." From a letter to the author by Dr. W. Gunther Plaut, Rabbi of the Holy Blossom Temple in Toronto, Canada, dated March 28, 1973.

15. See B. Gittin 79b and Rashi, s.v. "gita," who says that a child born out of wedlock has a "stigma" (*pegam*); however, this stigma is not the same as *mamzerut*, which has definite legal consequences. See Asheri, *Gittin,* chap. 8, no.8 and, also, Taz to Y.D. 195, n. 7.

16. See, esp., B. Kiddushin 6b ff.

17. "Marriage Annulment," *Proceedings of the Rabbinical Assembly* 2 (1928): 71.

18. B. Gittin 81b.

19. *Iggrot Mosheh,* E.H. (New York, 1961), sec. 74, p. 173 and sec. 75, p. 177, following Radbaz quoted in Rozanis, *Mishneh L'Melekh* to Maim., *Gerushin* 10.18. Concerning the same problem note the responsum of R. David Hoffmann (d. 1921) in *Melamed L'Ho'il* 3 (New York, 1954), sec.20, pp. 32-33, which, although accepting the same conclusion as R. Feinstein, raises a number of serious reservations. Concerning marriages of nonobservant Jews, see Jehiel J. Weinberg, *Seriday Esh* 3 (Jerusalem: Mosad HaRav Kook, 1966), E.H., sec.28, pp. 82-83.

20. Feinstein, *Iggrot Mosheh,* E.H., sec. 75, p. 177. Cf. Karo, *Kessef Mishneh* to Maim., *Ishut* 1.4, end.

21. *Ibid.,* sec. 76, p. 178. See M. Kiddushin 4.10 and Rashi and B. Kiddushin 79b-8a for the discussion of when presumption (*hazakah*) or when proof (*rayah*) is required for determining familial status.

22. Following this to a logical conclusion, Dr. Solomon Freehof, the leading Reform halakhist, writes: "... it would seem that consideration for the religious scruples of Orthodox and Conservative congregations should impel the Reform rabbi to refuse to marry members of other congregations whose rabbi refuses to marry them." *Reform Jewish Practice and its Rabbinic Background,* rev. ed. (Cincinnati: Hebrew Union College Press, 1948), 1:109-110. In a later work Dr. Freehof answers the objections of those who claim Reform marriages are invalid. See *Recent Reform Responsa* (Cincinnati: Hebrew Union College Press, 1963), pp. 194-203.

23. *Proceedings of the Rabbinical Assembly* 5 (1933-38): 485. Also, see Boaz Cohen, *Law and Tradition in Judaism,* pp. 239-43. Cf., however, B. Gittin 89a-89b.

24. See Maim., *Ishut* 1.1, 4.

25. *Melakhim* 9.8.

26. *Seriday Esh* 3, E.H., sec. 22, pp. 46-47. The only problem with this argument is that it seems to recognize the reality, but not of course the value, of concubinage in a way contrary to Maimonides, who refused to recognize it. See *Ishut* 1.4 and Rabad's note thereto. Maimonides seems to recognize no middle ground between marriage (*kiddushin*) and fornication (*zenut*). See *Melakhim* 4.4.

27. Weinberg, *op. cit.,* E.H., sec. 18, pp. 41-42.

28. "Kedat Moshe veYisrael," *Proceedings of the Rabbinical Assembly* 15 (1951): 132.

29. *Ibid.,* p. 138.

30. "And He Writes Her a Bill of Divorcement," *Conservative Judaism* 24, no. 3 (Spring 1970): 83 ff.

31. B. Yebamot 110a.

32. B. Baba Batra 48b.

33. *Responsa RIBASH,* ed. Jerusalem, 1967, no. 399, pp. 252-54.

34. M. Gittin 3.1.

35. B. Gittin 33a and Rashi and Tos. thereto for various queries and reservations.

36. See Aronson, *op. cit.,* p. 133.`

37. B. Ketubot 2b-3a; cf. P. Gittin 4.2.

38. *Bet Joseph* to *Tur,* E.H., 28, end, and Isserles to *Shulhan Arukh,* E.H., 28, end.

Moreover, note the various responsa cited in *Otzar HaPoskim* E.H. 11 (Jerusalem, 1968), pp. 93-112. Also, see B. Cohen, *Law and Tradition in Judaism*, pp. 110-14, and J. J. Weinberg, *Seriday Esh* 3, sec. 114, pp. 328-30. Note B. Nedarim 29a, which is the basis for the reluctance to apply *afka'at kiddushin*.

39. Greenberg, *op. cit.*, pp. 136-37.
40. M. Kiddushin 2.3.
41. *Tenay beNissuin ubaGet* (Jerusalem: Mosad HaRav Kook, 1966), p. 2.
42. Quoted in Alfred Freimann, *Seder Kiddushin veNissuin* (Jerusalem: Mosad HaRav Kook, 1945), p. 390.
43. Published in Vilna in 1930.
44. See Berkovitz, *op. cit.*, pp. 57 ff.
45. See *Jewish Encyclopedia*, 9:46 f., s.v. "Sanhedrin, French."
46. Berkovits, *op. cit.*, pp. 165-66.
47. *Ibid.*, p. 58.
48. *Ibid.*, p. 70.
49. See Freimann, *op. cit.*, pp. 391-94.
50. Berkovitz, *op. cit.*, p. 67 referring to B. Yebamot 107a and Tos., s.v. "Bet Shammai."
51. *Proceedings of the Rabbinical Assembly* 32 (1968): 241.
52. *Ibid.*, p. 240. Cf. Berkovits, *op. cit.*, p. 69.
53. M. Gittin 9.8.
54. See, e.g., B. Nazir 43b and Tos., s.v. "v'hay"; B. Kiddushin 12b.
55. Greenberg, *op. cit.*, p. 91.
56. Quoted in Eli Ginzberg, *Keeper of the Law: Louis Ginzberg*, p. 293.
57. *Proceedings of the Rabbinical Assembly* 4 (1930-32): 86-87.
58. New York: Jewish Theological Seminary of America, 1927; esp., chap. 1.
59. B. Gittin 71b.
60. Epstein, *Proceedings*, 4:233. His proposal is presented more fully in a Hebrew pamphlet, *Hatza'ah L'Ma'an Takanat Agunot* (New York, 1930), which he sent to various rabbis throughout the world for their opinion. See, esp., pp. 19-22.
61. See, e.g., B. Berakhot 45a and B. Baba Batra 60b.
62. Epstein, *Proceedings* 4:235.
63. The whole issue and its precedents are dealt with in Dr. Epstein's book, *L'She'elat HaAgunah* (New York, 1940). For the reservation of his teacher, Prof. Louis Ginzberg, see *Keeper of the Law*, pp. 225-6.
64. *L'She'elat HaAgunah* pp. 15-21.
65. *Ibid.*, p. 19.
66. B. Baba Kama 89b; cf. B. Ketubot 57a.
67. *Proceedings of the Rabbinical Assembly* 17 (1954): 67-68.
68. Maim., *Ishut* 3.1; B. Ketubot 8b.
69. Printed in *A Rabbi's Manual*, ed. Jules Harlow (New York: Rabbinical Assembly, 1965), pp. 37-8.
70. M. Gittin 9.8.
71. B. Gittin 88b and Rashi, s.v. "kedin." See Cohen, *Law and Tradition in Judaism*, pp. 54-55.
72. Tos., *ibid.*, "ubaAkum."
73. *Gerushin* 2.20 following M. Arakhin 5, end. See Cohen, *op. cit.*, pp. 106-7.
74. M. Gittin 9.9.
75. This was the practice of R. David Hoffmann. See *Melamed L'Ho'il*, 3, sec. 22, p. 36.
76. "Recent Additions to the Ketubah," *Tradition* 2, no. 1 (Fall 1959): 113-14. Also, see the article of R. B. Rabinowitz-Teomim, *Noam* 1, no. 1 (1958): 287 ff., which emphasizes most of the same arguments in greater detail.
77. A. Gulak, *Yesoday HaMishpat Halbri* (Berlin: Dvir, 1922), 1:66-67; I. H. Herzog, *The Main Institutions of Jewish Law*, 2d ed. (London: Soncino Press, 1967), 2:71-92.
78. See *Targum Jonathan* to Deut. 32:8 wherefrom the phrase is taken.

79. See *Sifre*, Deuteronomy, ed. Friedmann, no. 144, p. 103a and B. Yebamot 90b; also, *Responsa RIBASH,* no. 399.

80. See B. Sanhedrin 6a-6b and Maim., *Sanhedrin,* 22.4-6.

81. Lamm., *op. cit.,* p. 117, n. 35 (sec. 6), referring to Isserles to *Shulhan Arukh,* H.M., 207.15.

82. *Ibid.,* p. 109.

83. A. Leo Levin and Meyer Kramer, *New Provisions in the Ketubah* (New York: Yeshiva University, 1955). Also, see *Proceedings of the Rabbinical Assembly* 17 (1953): 76 ff. and 18 (1954): 69 ff. However, Dr. W. Gunther Plaut called to my attention a recent ruling of a Canadian court ordering a Jewish husband to comply with the ruling of a Bet Din that he give his wife a get, on the grounds that when he accepted the provisions of the ketubah he obligated himself to the Jewish law of matrimony. I subsequently received a copy of this ruling from Mr. M. F. Garfinkel, attorney for the applicant, Roberta Morris. The judgment was rendered by Mr. Justice Wilson of the Manitoba Court of Queen's Bench on March 16, 1973. Mr. Garfinkel informed me in a letter dated April 9, 1973, "We expect that the appeal will be heard in the fall of 1973 or in January, 1974."

84. Although such problems are considerably less common in Israel than in the diaspora, even there they are not completely absent. See R. Elyakim Elinson, "Sirub La'tet Get," *Sinai* 69, no. 3-4 (1971): 135 ff. His most valuable study suggests further ways to strengthen the power of the Bet Din.

85. See *Shir HaShirim Rabah* 1.43 and *Seder Eliahu Raba,* chap. 30.

86. Of course, the biggest such problem is that of *mamzerut.* For a novel solution to the problem, see the open letter of retired Israeli Supreme Court Justice Moshe Silberg to the new Ashkenazi Chief Rabbi Shlomoh Goren, "Bitul HaHok L'Ma'an Kiyumo," *Panim el Panim* no. 705 (Jan. 12, 1973): 14 ff.; also, Jacob Chinitz, "Yesh Koah biYday Hakhamim," *HaDoar* 52, no. 15 (Feb. 16, 1973): 232-34.

CHAPTER 5

1. The term *hadesh* means, for the most part, *renew* rather than *anew.* Thus, e.g., "...let us renew [*un'hadesh*] there the kingship" (1 Sam. 11:14) refers to reconfirming Saul, who already was king. Even the celebrated, "There is nothing new [*hadash*] under the sun" (Eccles. 1:9) refers to the unrewardability and boredom of life as opposed to a lack of innovation. This verse and its immediate context reflect Koheleth's own subjective ennui; they are not objective statements about the universe *per se.*

2. Cf. the case of R. Elisha ben Abuyah, whose alienation was moral not intellectual. See B. Hagigah 15b and Hullin 142a.

3. B. Shabbat 68b.

4. Actually they are compared to converts hastily converted. Thus their initiation into Jewish practices, like that of converts, is also gradual. See Maim., *Issuray Biah* 14.2.

5. B. Sanhedrin 56a-56b. For certain very technical differences between this law for Jews as opposed to non-Jews, see Hullin 121a-121b.

6. See Maim., *Melakhim* 9.1.

7. B. Baba Kama 80b.

8. B. Sanhedrin 15b.

9. See Rashi, *ibid.,* s.v. "yesh"; Maim., *Sanhedrin* 5.2 and Rabad thereto.

10. B. Shabbat 121b and Tos., s.v. "col."

11. B. Erubin 63b and parallels.

12. *Sefer HaMitzvot,* Neg. no. 57. Also, see *Melakhim* 6.8.

13. See B. Baba Metzia 32b-33a.

14. B. Baba Metzia 32b, Tos., s.v. "medibray," and B. Abodah Zarah 11a, Tos., s.v. "okrin."

15. *Noda BiYehudah* 2, Y.D., sec. 10.

16. See Louis Ginzberg, *Legends of the Jews,* 7 (Index), s.v. "Esau." Also, note B. Baba Metzia 85a and B. Baba Batra 73b.

17. See S. B. Hoenig, "The Sport of Hunting: A Humane Game?", *Tradition* 11, no. 3 (Fall 1970): 13-21. Jews are characterized as merciful; see B. Yebamot 79a.

18. B. Shabbat 105b and Maim., *Shabbat 8.8; 10.10.*

19. B. Shabbat 156a.

20. See, e.g., *Abodah Zarah* 11.8-9.

21. *Hidushay Aggadot* to B. Shabbat 156a.

22. See B. Kiddushin 30b and, also, B. Berakhot 5a.

CHAPTER 6

1. *Jewish Antiquities* 18.3, 1, trans. L. H. Feldman, Loeb Classical Library (Cambridge, Mass.: Harvard University Press, 1965), 9:42-43. Cf. *ibid.* 17.6, 2.

2. See *ibid.,* pp. 43-45, note h.

3. B. Abodah Zarah 43a-43b. For the similar view of Philo, see H. A. Wolfson, *Philo* (Cambridge, Mass.: Harvard University Press, 1947), 1:29-30, n. 22.

4. *Abodah Zarah* 3.10. Nevertheless, note B. Yoma 54a-54b, Tos., s.v. "cherubim," which permits paintings and possibly relief work on walls. The only objection to this permitted art is that it should be absent from the synagogue lest it distract the attention of the worshippers from God. See Karo, *Bet Joseph* to *Tur,* Y.D. 141, end. Indeed, distraction from God as the Object of worship caused some authorities to criticize overveneration of the Holy Ark. See J. D. Eisenstein, *Otzar Dinim uMinhagim* (New York, 1922), p. 29.

5. *Ibid.,* 3.11.

6. Quoted in Eli Ginzberg, *Keeper of the Law: Louis Ginzberg,* pp. 233-34. Also, for the possible rabbinic disapproval of the obscene nature of some non-Jewish pictorial art, see B. Sanhendrin 39b, commenting on 1 Kings 22:38.

7. However, R. Moses Schreiber banned the use of sun-rays in the stained-glass windows of a synagogue because he noticed the same motif in Christian contexts. See *Responsa HATAM SOFER,* Y.D., no. 129.

8. Yoreh Deah 141, end.

9. "The Concept of Man in Jewish Thought," *The Concept of Man: A Study in Comparative Philosophy,* ed. S. Radhakrishnan and P. T. Raju (London: George Allen & Unwin, 1960), p. 138. See Louis Ginzberg, *Legends of the Jews,* 1:122-23, 5:150-51, n. 54.

10. Note: "Just as God sees but is not seen, so the soul sees but is not seen." B. Berakhot 10a. Cf. *Vayikra Rabah* 4.8. However, even the body has an invisible sanctity. See *Vayikra Rabah* 34. 3; also, Maim., *Shemonah Perakim,* chap. 1, ed. Rabinowitz, p. 157.

11. B. Rosh Hashanah 24b. See B. Abodah Zarah 43b for the parallel. This interpretation of this passage is taken from Professor Heschel, *op. cit.,* p. 140. Although his citation (n. 51) is of the text in Rosh Hashanah, it seems that his interpretation of the passage is based on the comment of Rabbenu Hananael to the text in Rosh Hashanah, viz., "You shall not make My symbol [*otti*], namely, the image of man that I show to the prophets in their visions."

12. As Plato well noted: "The art of representation, then, is a long way from reality; and apparently the reason why there is nothing it cannot reproduce is that it grasps only a small part of any object, and that only an image." *Republic* 598 B, trans. F. M. Cornford (New York: Oxford University Press, 1945), p. 328.

13. See Maim., *Abodah Zarah,* beg., who characterizes idolatry as human self-deception. In *Moreh Nebukhim* 3.39 ff. he analyzes the recurrent manifestations of idolatry.

14. Maim., *Melakhim* 11.1. However, the restoration of the Jewish nation to political

sovereignty in the Land of Israel is a legitimate human ideal. See M. M. Kasher, *Passover Haggadah* (New York: Shengold Publishers, 1964), p. 274.

15. B. Abodah Zarah 43a. Note Josh. 22 and 2 Kings 4:10. Cf. M. Yoma 3.10, T. Megillah 3.3, and *Hidushay Ritba* to B. Abodah Zarah 43a.

16. B. Megillah 29a.

17. Thus, e.g., the custom of separate seating of the sexes in the synagogue is not based on the fact that there was a separate women's section (*ezrat nashim*) in the Temple, but, rather, on the fact that dignity (*kobed rosh*) required this in *any* place of Jewish worship. See B. Sukkah 51b-52a and B. Litvin, *The Sanctity of the Synagogue* (New York, 1959).

18. See Maim., *Moreh Nebukhim* 3.32. Cf. Nahmanides to Lev. 1:9, who criticizes Maimonides' historical treatment of the sacrificial system in that it seems to make a sacred institution historically relative. However, if one remembers that for Maimonides idolatry is a *perennial* issue, then its antidotes are by no means limited to any finite period in history.

19. When the Temple was used for purposes contrary to God's will, it was destroyed. See Jer. 7:3-16. The Jewish people, on the other hand, transcends the Temple. See B. Gittin 56b and B. Makkot, end.

20. B. Berakhot 34b commenting on Isa. 64:3.

CHAPTER 7

1. See Halevy, *Sefer HaHinukh*, no. 2. Cf. Maim., *Sefer HaMitzvot*, Pos. no. 215. For the question of a danger to health postponing circumcision, see M. Shabbat 19.5.

2. Yoreh Deah 260.1.

3. See M. Nedarim 3.11.

4. B. Kiddushin 29a.

5. Keritot 9a and B. Yebamot 46a; Maim., *Issuray Biah* 13.6.

6. P. Berakhot, end; cf. T. Berakhot, end, and Menahot 43b.

7. *Perush meSefer HaHaredim.*

8. B. Kiddushin 29a.

9. Isserles, note to Yoreh Deah 264.1.

10. B. Abodah Zarah 26b.

11. *Ibid.*, 27a and Rashi and Tos., s.v. "rofe."

12. Rashi, *ibid.*, s.v. "l'HaShem himol."

13. Note B. Erubin 63b and parallels.

14. Taz to Yoreh Deah 264.1, n. 3.

15. B. Abodah Zarah 26b.

16. Isserles and Shakh to Yoreh Deah 264.1 contra Taz in the name of Rashba. For the indispensability of *hatafat dam* for a convert already circumcised, see B. Shabbat 135a and *Tur*, Y.D. 268, beg.

17. Karo, *Kessef Mishneh* to Maim., *Milah* 2.1.

18. B. Nedarim 32a and Rashi to Exod. 4:24.

19. B. Abodah Zarah 27a.

20. Cf. B. Baba Kama 10a.

21. *Arukh HaShulhan*, Y.D. 264.8.

22. P. Shabbat 19.2. See M. Shabbat 19, end.

23. B. M. Levin, *Otzar HaGeonim* 2 (Jerusalem, 1930), Shabbat, p. 134.

24. *Edut L'Yisrael* (New York, 1955), p. 144.

25. Note Hullin 10a: "A danger to life [*sakanta*] is graver than ritual infraction [*issura*]."

26. B. Abodah Zarah 26b.

27. B. Sanhedrin 17b.

28. *Melamed L'Ho'il* 2, sec. 80, p. 86.

29. See Meiri to B. Abodah Zarah 26b, ed. Schreiber, p. 62.
30. B. Gittin 70a, Tos., s.v. "Rab Shimi."
31. M. Nedarim 3.11.
32. B. Nedarim 31b-32a. For the Christian rejection of circumcision as a necessity for conversion, see Rom. 2:25-29. Cf. Acts 15:6 ff.

CHAPTER 8

1. According to the Talmud (B. Kiddushin 18a) a Jew who abandoned Judaism for another faith (*mumar*) still is his Jewish father's son and inherits his estate. Note: " . . . the ties of blood binding the Jew to the Jewish people can never be loosened . . . on the other hand, by becoming a Jew, a pagan severs his national connections with those to whom he previously belonged." Louis Ginzberg, *Students, Scholars and Saints*, p. 123.
2. For a thorough presentation of the various classical sources, see B. Bamberger, *Proselytism in the Talmudic Period* (New York: Ktav Publishing House, 1968); also, *Encyclopedia Talmudit*, 6, s.v. "ger."
3. B. Yebamot 22a and parallels.
4. M. Bikkurim 1.4.
5. P. Bikkurim 1.4.
6. *Bereshit Rabah* 39.14; also quoted in Rashi to Gen. 12:5.
7. *Bikkurim* 4.3. See *Teshubot HaRambam* 2, ed. J. Blau (Jerusalem, 1960), no. 448, pp. 725-28. The surprising thing is that Maimonides contradicts the earlier decision of Rab Ashi recorded in B. Makkot 19a. See Rozanis, *Mishneh L'Melekh*, thereto. However, the problem only concerns the first fruits, not the wording of the Amidah, which was the practical issue in Maimonides' time and our own. See B. Baba Batra 81a.
8. See M. Negaim 7.1 and M. Zabim 2.3. Cf. *M. Pesahim,* 8.8.
9. Sometimes the term *cemo* can mean "indeed" in the sense of *member of a class,* and sometimes it can mean "like" in the sense of *similar but not identical* (see, e.g., B. Berakhot 28a and P. Berakhot 1.6). However, since the Talmud uses the comparative term *dami* in addition to the prefix *caf,* it obviously is meant in the latter sense. The principle is more of a general description than an absolute rule; hence the many exceptions. For a similar situation with a general description and its many exceptions, see M. Kiddushin 1.7 and B. Kiddushin 33b-34a. For important exceptions to halakhic analogies see, e.g., Landau, *Noda BiYehudah* 2, ed. Paris, 1947, H.M., no. 59.
10. B. Yebamot 62a; Karo, *Bet Joseph* to *Tur,* E.H. 1 and Ashkenazi, *Be'er Heyteb* to *Shulhan Arukh,* E.H. 1.7.
11. B. Yebamot 22a.
12. See, esp., B. Sanhedrin 59a.
13. *Ibid.*
14. Indeed R. Saadiah Gaon gives the following rationale for the prohibition of sexual immorality: " . . . in order that men might not become like the beasts with the result that no one would know his father so as to show him reverence in return for having raised him. . . . A further reason was that a human being might know the rest of his relations . . . and show them whatever tenderness he was capable of." *Emunot ve Deot* 3.2, trans. S. Rosenblatt, *The Book of Beliefs and Opinions* (New Haven: Yale University Press, 1948), p. 141.
15. B. Kiddushin 17b and B. Abodah Zarah 64a. See Maim., *Nahalut* 6.10.
16. Rashi, B. Kiddushin 17b, s.v. "mishum."
17. See B. Baba Metzia 72a; also, Maim., *Issuray Biah* 13.14.
18. See Maharsha to B. Kiddushin 17b, who emphasizes the strong probability of error in such cases. Conversely note Matt. 8:21-22: "Another of his disciples said to him, 'Lord,

let me first go and bury my father.' But Jesus said to him, 'Follow me and let the dead bury their own dead.' " See *ibid.*, 10:37-39. Disciples of Jesus were considered "born again" [*anagennasas*] — 1 Pet. 1:3. Also, see W. D. Davies, *Paul and Rabbinic Judaism* (London: S.P.C.K., 1958), pp. 119 ff.

19. B. Gittin 45b.

20. For the nonsacred status of a Torah scroll written by a heretic or apostate, see Maim., *Tefillin* 1.13.

21. Rashi, B. Gittin 45b, s.v. "mishum."

22. *Mishnah Berurah* to O.H. 39.6.

23. Act I, scene iv.

24. See Maim., *Deot* 6.4.

25. B. Sanhedrin 94a. See M. Baba Metzia 4.10. Cf. B. Kiddushin 70b, Tos., s.v. "kashim."

26. M. Gittin 5.8 and *Shulhan Arukh*, Y.D. 151.12.

27. *Abel* 2.3. Also, see Halevi, *Sefer HaHinukh* no. 264.

28. See *Kessef Mishneh* and *Shulhan Arukh*, Y.D. 374.5; also, Radbaz to Maim. thereto.

29. Note no. 4 to Y.D. 374.5.

30. *Mordecai*, Moed Katan, no. 906; in the digest of R. Joseph Ottiling, no. 142.

31. *Mamrim* 5.11.

32. I have been unable to see the original text of this responsum. It is summarized by S. Freehof, *Recent Reform Responsa*, pp. 136-37.

33. See B. Kiddushin 31b.

34. Ibn Ezra to Deut. 21:13; see B. Yebamot 47b and B. Kiddushin 22a, Tos. s.v. "shelo."

35. B. Kiddushin 31a.

36. Bereshit Rabah 39.7, quoted in Rashi to Gen. 11:32.

37. B. Kiddushin 31b.

38. See B. Sanhedrin 104a.

39. Note Ganzfried, *Kitzur Shulhan Arukh* 144.21: "Whoever really wants to honor his father and mother should engage in the study of the Torah and good deeds, because this is the greatest honor to parents that people should say, 'happy are the father and mother who raised a son like this!' "

40. See B. Berakhot 3a, Tos., s.v. "ve'onin."

41. Quoted in D. de Sola Pool, *The Kaddish* (New York: Bloch Publishing Co., 1964), pp. 104-5.

42. See, e.g., B. Erubin 96a, Tos., s.v. "dilma," where Rabbenu Tam permitted women to say the blessing before commandments they do not have to keep. Also, see B. Kiddushin 31a, Tos., s.v. "dela."

43. See Yoreh Deah 341 ff.

44. *MiMa'makim* 3 (New York, 1969), pp. 69-72. R. Oshry refers to R. Aaron Walkin of Pinsk, *Responsa Z'kan Aaron* Y.D., no.877.

45. *Seder Eliahu Zuta*, chap. 25.

46. *Zohar*, Bereshit, p. 78b.

CHAPTER 9

1. *Kuzari* 1.1, 98, 103. See Leo Strauss, *Persecution and the Art of Writing* (Glencoe, Ill.; Free Press, 1952), pp. 95 ff.

2. B. Baba Kamma 17a and parallels. See Tosafot thereto, s.v. "v'ha'amar." Cf. M. Abot 1.17.

3. See B. Berakhot 3b.

4. M. Sotah 9.12. See B. Yoma 73a-73b and P. Yoma 7.3 for the rabbinic description of how the oracle worked.

5. *Bereshit Rabah* 22.4.

6. See C. W. Reines, "The Jewish Attitude toward Suicide," *Judaism* 10, no. 2 (1961): 165, n. 20. Cf. Augustine, *De Civitate Dei* 1.20, who includes the ban on suicide in the sixth commandment of the Decalogue.

7. B. Baba Kamma 91b. See Maim., *Hobel u'Mazeek* 5.1; also, *Shabuot* 5.17 and Radbaz thereto.

8. *Bereshit Rabah* 34.19.

9. See Chapter 1.

10. See A Perls, "Der Selbstmord nach der Halacha," *Monatschrift fuer Geschichte und Wissenschaft des Judenthums* 55 (1911): 288, n. 6.

11. A. Schechter, *Dobeb Siftay Yeshanim* (Jerusalem, 1957), p. 244. Cf. *Midrash Bereshit Raba* 2d printing, ed. J. Theodor and Ch. Albeck (Jerusalem: Wahrmann Books, 1965), 1:324, note.

12. B. Sanhedrin 74a-74b. See Maim., *Yesoday HaTorah* 5.1 ff. Cf. B. Ketubot 33b.

13. *Ekhah Rabati* 1.53.

14. *Encyclopedia Judaica*, 15:490.

15. B. Sanhedrin 74a.

16. *Ibid.*, 74b.

17. B. Abodah Zarah 18a. See Schechter, *op. cit.*, p. 245. For the historical background of this incident, see S. Lieberman, "The Martyrs of Caesarea," *Annuaire de Philologie et d'Histoire Orientales et Slaves* 7 (1939-44): 419 ff. Cf. B. Berakhot 61b.

18. Cf. Plato, *Phaedo* 62C; Thomas Aquinas, *Summa Theologica* 1-2. 64,5. These sources and others are dealt with in my forthcoming book, *Suicide and Morality.*

19. B. Gittin 57b. Cf. B. Ketubot 3b and Tosafot, s.v. "u'lidrosh."

20. See Abraham ibn Daud, *Sefer HaKabbalah*, ed. G. D. Cohen (Philadelphia: Jewish Publication Society of America, 1967), pp. 46-47 (Heb.), 63-64 (Eng.). The poet H. N. Bialik wrote an epic poem about the incident, "Megilat HaEsh," trans. B. Aronin in *Complete Poetic Works of Hayyim Nahman Bialik*, ed. I. Efros (New York: Histadruth Ivrith of America, 1948), pp. 156-201. Also note the suicide of ninety-three Jewish girls in Warsaw in 1944, by the same motivation, recorded in Ben Zion Bokser, *High Holy Day Prayerbook* (New York: Hebrew Publishing Company, 1959), pp. 434-36. See G. D. Cohen, "The Story of Hannah and Her Seven Sons in Hebrew Literature," *Mordecai M. Kaplan Jubilee Volume* (Heb. sec.) (New York: Jewish Theological Seminary of America, 1953), pp. 109 ff. for other related sources.

21. B. Gittin 57b, Tosafot, s.v. "kaftzu"; B. Abodah Zarah 18a, Tosafot, s.v. "v'al." See Shalom Spiegel, *The Last Trial*, trans. J. Goldin (New York: Schocken Books, 1969), pp. 130 ff.

22. B. Sanhedrin 74b and Tosafot, s.v. "v'ha." Cf. however, *Seder Eliahu Raba*, chap. 21.

23. *Bellum Judaicum* 3. 8,5, trans. H. St. John Thackery, Loeb Classical Library (Cambridge, Mass.: Harvard University Press, 1927), 2:678-79. Cf. Augustine, *De Civitate Dei* 1.27. As for the whole recent debate over the death of the Masada defenders, I accept the views of S. B. Hoenig, "Historic Masada and the Halakhah," *Tradition* 13, no. 2 (1972): 100 ff.

24. See R. Jacob ibn Habib, *Iyun Yaakob* to B. Gittin 57b for an even more lenient interpretation.

25. For examples of other suicides of this type, see B. Ketubot 103b and P. Ketubot 11.3; B. Taanit 29a; B. Abodah Zarah 18a; Rashi, B. Abodah Zarah 18b, s.v. "v'ika"; and F. Rosner, *Modern Medicine and Jewish Law* (New York: Yeshiva University, 1972), pp. 177-93.

26. Maim., *Sanhedrin* 18.6 and Radbaz thereto, who quotes Ezek. 18:4, "Behold the lives are Mine." See A. Kirschenbaum, *Self-Incrimination in Jewish Law* (New York: Burning Bush Press, 1970), pp. 72-79. Also, see Reines, *op. cit.*, pp. 167-68 and M. Zucker, *Rav Saadya Gaon's Translation of the Torah* (Heb.) (New York: Philipp Feldheim, 1959), p. 320.

27. *Midrash Tehillim* 11.7, ed. Buber, pp. 103-4; cf. B. Abodah Zarah 10b. Note the New Testament account of the suicide of Judas Iscariot in Matt. 26:24, 27:5.

28. B. Baba Metzia 59b.
29. R. Eliakim Goetz, *Responsa Eben HaShoham* (Dyhernfurth, 1733), no. 44; R. Isaac Lampronti, *Pahad Yitzhak* (Venice, 1750), s.v. "m'abed"; R. Moses Schreiber, *Responsa Hatam Sofer* (Pressburg, 1864), Yoreh Deah, no. 326.
30. B. Gittin 57b and Rashi, s.v. "bar"; cf. Marharsha thereto.
31. *Arukh HaShulhan*, Y.D. 345.5. See J. M. Tuktzinsky, *Gesher HaHayyim* (Jerusalem, 1960), 1:273, n. 2. Also, see Josephus, *op. cit.* and R. Saadia Gaon, *Emunot v'Deot* 10.11.
32. *Abel Rabati* 2.3, ed. D. Zlotnick (New Haven: Yale University Press, 1966).
33. "Torat HaAdam," *Kitbay Ramban* 2, pp. 83-84.
34. Rosh, Moed Katan, no. 33. One could categorize the suicide attempts recorded in B. Kiddushin 40a and 83b as hysterical. Also, Schechter, *op. cit.*, p. 248, considers the talmudic report of Hannah's suicide (B. Gittin 57b) as a case of mental derangement due to the shock of seeing her seven sons martyred one after the other.
35. Nahmanides, *op. cit.*
36. *Tur*, Y.D. 345, adds the word *anoos*—"under duress," viz., without any free choice. See *Encyclopedia Talmudit*, 2, s.v. "anoos."
37. B. Berakhot 12b.
38. B. Yebamot 78b; B. Moed Katan 16b. See L. Ginzberg, *Legends of the Jews*, 6:238-39, n. 80.
39. Nahmanides, *op. cit.*
40. R. Solomon Luria, *Yam shel Shlomoh* to B. Baba Kamma, chap. 8, no. 59.
41. Commentary of the Tosafists (*Da'at Zekenim*) to Gen. 9:5. Also, see commentary of R. Levi ben Gershon (Ralbag) to 2 Sam. 1:14. Cf. B. Gittin 58a.
42. 1 Sam. 16:14-15, 23; 18:10; 19:9.
43. Abrabanel to 1 Sam. 28:11 ff.
44. Abrabanel to 1 Sam. 31:4, following R. David Kimhi (Radak) thereto.
45. Schechter, *op. cit.*, p. 253.
46. *Abel Rabati* 2.2; *Shulhan Arukh*, Y.D. 345.1-3. For the presumption of sanity *before the fact* in such cases, see M. Gittin 6.6 and B. Gittin 66a; M. Gittin 7.1 and P. Gittin 7.1.
47. See R. Leopold Greenwald, *Kol Bo al Abelut* (New York, 1947), p. 319, n. 31. Only Josephus, probably basing his view on contemporary Roman practices, advocates disgracing the body of the suicide. See *Bellum Judaicum, op. cit.*, pp. 682-83 and Heb. trans. with notes by J. N. Simhoni (Warsaw, 1923), p. 453.
48. M. Makkot 1.10; B. Makkot 7a.
49. Greenwald, *op. cit.*, p. 319. For a very recent halakhic treatment of suicide, see the responsum of R. Judah Girshuni in *Or HaMizrach* 21, no. 4 (June 1972): 218-22.
50. Tuktzinsky, *op. cit.*, p. 273.
51. *Abel Rabati* 2.1.
52. See the note of R. Shabati HaKohen (Shakh) to Y.D. 345.1, referring to R. Solomon ibn Adret (Rashba), *Responsa*, no. 763. For the tendency, however, to avoid an actual funeral oration, see Eisenstadt, *Pithay Teshuba* to Y.D. 345.1.
53. M. Hullin 1.1, Hullin 2b.
54. Hullin 12b and Meiri, ed. Masorah (New York, 1945), p. 12.
55. Nahmanides, *op. cit.*
56. E.g., Karo, *Bet Joseph* to *Tur*, Y.D. 345.
57. See Perls, *op. cit.*, p. 289, Greenwald, *op. cit.*, p. 318; Tuktzinsky, *op. cit.*, p. 210, n. 1—all of whom suggest possible sources for this popular saying.
58. 2 Macc. 7:9.
59. M. Sanhedrin 6.2.
60. *Responsa Besamin Rosh* (Berlin, 1793), no. 345, attributed to Asheri (Rosh) but actually written by R. Saul Berlin (d. 1794)—see *Encyclopedia Judaica*, 4:663, s.v. "Berlin, Saul." For the unanimous rejection of this view, see Schechter, *op. cit.*, p. 246; Tuktzinsky, *op. cit.*, p. 273; Reines, *op. cit.*, p. 170.
61. Often considerations of the feelings of survivors led to exonerations *ex post facto*.

See, esp., *Mordecai,* Moed Katan, no. 686. *Hatam Sofer, op. cit.,* emphasizes that nothing should be omitted that would besmirch the honor of the family of the suicide (*pegam mishpahah*).

62. The main talmudic definition is found in B. Hagigah 3b. Maimonides' more general definition is found in *Edut* 9.9. See Karo, *Bet Joseph* to *Tur,* Eben HaEzer 121. For other examples of Maimonides' recognition of scientific progress, see *Hakdamah L'Mishnah,* ed. Rabinowitz, p. 74; *Shehitah* 10.12-13.

63. 2 Sam. 10:10-12, 19:23-24. See A. J. Heschel, *The Prophets* (Philadelphia: Jewish Publication Society of America, 1962), pp. 405 ff. Cf. B. Baba Batra 12b.

64. See Sigmund Freud, "The Unconscious" (1915), *The Complete Psychological Works of Sigmund Freud,* trans. J. Strachey (London: Hogarth Press, 1957), 14:196 ff.

65. This is precisely what Freud tried to do in *The Future of an Illusion.* Two fairly recent secularist Jewish treatments of suicide are presented in essentially psychological terms; viz., Hayyim Greenberg, *The Inner Eye* (New York: Jewish Frontier Publication Association, 1953), pp. 146-56; Nisson Touroff, *Be'ayot HaHitabdut* (Tel Aviv: Dvir, 1953), esp., p. 5.

66. See B. Shabbat 133b; Maim., *Deot* 1.6, *Moreh Nebukhim,* end.

67. M. Abot 4, end.

68. Exod. 3:14, Isa. 44:6. See A. J. Heschel, *Man Is Not Alone* (Philadelphia: Jewish Publication Society of America, 1951), pp. 125-29.

CHAPTER 10

1. B. Gittin 59b.

2. T. Megillah 2, end, ed. Lieberman, p. 353. See *Tosefta Kifshuta,* Moed 5 (New York: Jewish Theological Seminary of America, 1962), p. 1163.

3. B. Megillah 28b.

4. Lieberman, *op. cit.*

5. B. Megillah 28b.

6. See R. Nissim thereto. Also, see B. Sanhedrin 46b.

7. See B. Sotah 22a. Cf. Menahot 29b; B. Baba Kama 114b.

8. Yoreh Deah 344.19. See Orah Hayyim 151.1.

9. *Responsa PE'ER HADOR* no. 77, ed. Amsterdam, 1764.

10. *Tefillah* 11.6-7. Cf. B. Shabbat 105b.

11. L. Greenwald, *Kol Bo al Abelut,* p. 100.

12. *Ibid.,* pp. 99-100, based on *Hokhmat Adam* 155.18.

13. M. Kelim 1.4; Rashi, B. Baba Kama 2b, s.v. "vetame met."

14. B. Berakhot 22a; Maim., *Keriat Shema,* end.

15. Note to *Shulhan Arukh,* O.H. 88, end.

16. See M. Betzah 2.6.

17. *Responsa MAHARAM SCHICK* Y.D. 345 quoted in *Kol Bo al Abelut,* p. 100, n. 7. See Isserles' note to *Shulhan Arukh,* Y.D. 243.2 and Eisenstadt, *Pithay Teshubah* thereto. See *Melamed L'Ho'il* 2, sec. 106, p. 110 for a number of significant examples of synagogue funerals for prominent rabbis.

18. B. Sanhedrin 8b; Maim., *Sanhedrin* 12.2 and Karo, *Maggid Mishneh* to Maim., *Issuray Biah* 1.2; B. Makkot 9b.

19. B. Berakhot 4b-5a; see Maim., *Tefillah* 7.2, and, esp., Kagan, *Mishnah Berurah* O.H. 239, end. For another example see B. Sotah 39a and Tos. s.v. "kevan."

20. M. Berakhot 2.5; B. Berakhot 16a-16b; Rashi, *ibid.,* 11a, s.v. "hakones"; *Tur,* O.H. 70.

21. M. Berakhot 5.1 and P. Berakhot 5.1.

22. *Kol Bo al Abelut,* Responsa (New York, 1951), 2:35-36.

23. *Kol Bo al Abelut,* quoting *Responsa Bet Ab Hamishai,* end.

24. *Magen Abraham* O.H. 154.

25. *Kol Bo al Abelut,* 2:36.

26. M. Megillah 3.1.

27. B. Megillah 26a. See B. Yoma 11b-12a.

28. See, e.g., M. Shabbat 6.6.

29. B. Megillah 26a, Tos., s.v. "kevan." See Ran thereto and B. Shabbat 11a.

30. Maim., *Tefillah* 11.6 and Karo, *Kessef Mishneh* thereto.

31. B. Megillah 26a, Rashi, s.v. "derabbim."

32. P. Megillah 3.3. See *Penay Mosheh* thereto.

33. M. Nedarim 5.5 and Rashi thereto. Regarding the synagogue as a public center see B. Ketubot 5a. However, cf. B. Shabbat 32a and Rashi, s.v. "Bet Am."

34. See Louis Finkelstein, *The Pharisees* (Philadelphia: Jewish Publication Society of America, 1938), 1:82 ff.

35. P. Megillah 3.3. Some synagogues were more intellectually oriented than others; see B. Berakhot 8a.

36. See *Penay Mosheh* to the text in P. Megillah 3.3.

37. See B. Berakhot 61b: "R. Akiba gathered large crowds and engaged in teaching Torah."

38. B. Megillah 28b; see Karo, *Kessef Mishneh* to Maim., *Tefillah* 11.6; also, B. Moed Katan, end. For the role of the *Bet HaKnesset* as an elementary school, see B. Gittin 58a and M. Shabbat 1.3.

39. *Kol Bo al Abelut,* p. 96, referring to M. Ketubot 2.10. The reference in the Mishnah, however, is to an unspecified place. Nevertheless, since no place is specified it may very well have been the home.

40. Torat HaAdam, *Kitbay Ramban* 2:88; also quoted in *Tur,* Y.D. 344.

41. B. Ketubot 17a-17b. See Maim., *Abel* 14.11 and B. M. Levin, *Otzar HaGeonim* 8: Ketubot, p. 56.

42. Tos., B. Moed Katan 27b, s.v. "assurin."

43. T. Moed Katan, end. See *Tosefta Kifshuta* Moed 5, p. 1263; B. Moed Katan 25a.

44. See B. Baba Metzia 2.11.

45. B. Baba Kama 17a; Rashi, B. Moed Katan 25a, s.v. "apuray."

46. B. Moed Katan 25a and Rashi and Tos., B. Baba Kama 17a, s.v. "ella."

47. B. Kiddushin 66a; cf. Josephus, *Antiquities* 13.10, 5. See B. Shabbat 31a.

48. B. Makkot 22b.

49. B. Kiddushin 33b; cf. *ibid.,* 32a-32b.

50. See *Statesman* 294A ff.

51. Quoted in Eli Ginzberg, *Keeper of the Law: Louis Ginzberg,* p. 229.

52. *Nimukay Joseph,* Hilkhot Mezuzah, end; reference in *Encyclopedia Talmudit,* 3:198.

53. Meiri and Ritba; reference, *ibid.,* p. 202.

54. B. Megillah 28b.

55. For other examples of this concept see M. Abot 3.13 and B. Sukkah 51b-52a.

56. See Weil, *Korban Nathaniel* to Asheri, B. Megillah 28b. For the connection between materialism and weakened interpersonal ties, see M. Sotah 9.6 and Rashi to Num. 32:16; L. Ginzberg, *Legends of the Jews,* 1:179. Also B. Nazir 43b, Tos., s.v. "vehai."

57. See *Bereshit Rabah* 65.16.

58. B. Berakhot 6b and Rashi, s.v. "daluyay." See B. Shabbat 153a; *Tur* Y.D. 344, beg.

59. E.g., B. Megillah 28b.

60. B. Moed Katan 27b.

61. B. Berakhot 3b. Cf. P. Berakhot 3.1, end.

62. Tos, B. Berakhot 3b, s.v. "ayn"; *Tur* Y.D. 344 in the name of Rab Hai Gaon; also, Asheri quoted in *Bet Joseph* thereto.

63. *Bet Joseph, ibid.*; See Maim., *Abel* 13.9.

64. Semahot 10.14, ed. Zlotnick, p. 31 (Heb.). See Nahmanides, Torat HaAdam, *Kitbay Ramban,* 2:89.

65. Naumburg, *Nahalat Yaakob* to Semahot 10.11.
66. B. Baba Kama 16b-17a.
67. Tos., *ibid.*, s.v. "shehoshibu."
68. Karo, *Kessef Mishneh* to Maim., *Abel* 13.9. See *Bet Joseph* to *Tur* Y.D. 344, n.19.
69. Y.D. 344.17.
70. See Mendel, *Be'er Heyteb.*
71. See, e.g. Tos., B. Kiddushin 30a, s.v. "al."
72. See M. Gittin 5.10; B. Abodah Zarah 55b.
73. See B. Shabbat 67a and *Sifra* to Lev. 18:3, ed. Weiss, p. 86a. Cf. M. Berakhot, end.
74. See S. Dresner, "The Scandal of the Jewish Funeral," *The Jew in American Life* (New York: Crown Publishers, 1963), pp. 20 ff.
75. B. Moed Katan 27b.
76. See Semahot 2.1.
77. The late R. Ben Zion Uziel, as well as other *aharonim,* prohibited synagogue weddings in very strong terms, emphasizing the non-Jewish origins of this custom. See *Mishpatay Uziel* E.H. (Jerusalem, 1964), sec. 60-61, pp. 248-53. However, R. Uziel does noᴋ deal with our alternative, viz., a synagogue wedding or no authentic Jewish *simhah* at all!
78. For a Reform treatment of synagogue funerals, see S. Freehof, *Reform Jewish Practice* (Cincinnati: Hebrew Union College Press, 1952) 2:54-58.

CHAPTER 11

1. See, e.g., B. Gittin 2b.
2. *Ibid.*, 60b. However, private notebooks were not banned, only publication was. See B. Shabbat 6b and Rashi, s.v. "megilat starim."
3. B. Moed Katan 27a.
4. *Abel* 1.2. The reference to King David is based on 2 Sam. 12:20.
5. See M. Berakhot 3.1.
6. Rashi, B. Ketubot 4b, s.v. "gollel."
7. Tos., *ibid.*, s.v. "ad."
8. Torat HaAdam, *Kitbay Ramban,* 2:146-47.
9. Yoreh Deah 275.4.
10. Shakh thereto. See *Be'er Heyteb* and *Shiltay Giborim* to Alfasi, Moed Katan 27a.
11. Cf. M. Eduyot 1.5-6.
12. Karo, *Kessef Mishneh* to Maim., *Abel* 1.3.
13. B. Erubin 46a and parallels. See L. Greenwald, *Kol Bo al Abelut,* pp. 257-58.
14. M. Gittin 4.6 and see B. Gittin 45a.
15. Torat HaAdam, *Kitbay Ramban,* 2:157, and the notes of Dr. Chavel thereto.
16. Comment to 2 Sam. 12:9, referring to B. Kiddushin 43a. The Talmud there indicates that rebellion or even disrespect for royal authority (*mored b'malkhut*) was deserving of death.
17. Bach to *Tur* Y.D. 375.
18. See Taz to Y.D. 375.6 n. 2. The key concept is that of *yeush,* viz., despair of recovery of an object. See Epstein, *Arukh HaShulhan* Y.D. 375.8. For other uses of this concept, see B. Baba Metzia 21b; for a general discussion, see I. H. Herzog, *The Main Institutions of Jewish Law,* 2d ed., 1:281 ff.

CHAPTER 12

1. B. Kiddushin 31b.
2. B. Sanhedrin 104a.
3. See Ganzfried, *Kitzur Shulhan Arukh* 144.21.

4. See B. Berakhot 3a, Tos., s.v. "v'onin." Also, for background on this whole subject, see David de Sola Pool, *The Kaddish* (New York: Bloch Publishing Co., 1964).

5. See J. M. Tuktzinsky, *Gesher HaHayyim*, 1:250, 327.

6. Note to *Shulhan Arukh*, Y. D. 376, end. See Rashi, B. Kiddushin 31b, s.v. "mikan." Also, see M. Eduyot 2.10 and the comment of Rabad thereto and B. Shabbat 33b and Rashi, s.v. "mishpat reshayim."

7. *Zohar*, Bereshit, p. 68a.

8. Greenwald, *Kol Bo al Abelut*, pp. 369-70, n. 19. Cf. Taz, Y.D. 240.9.

9. See M. Pesahim 4.1.

CHAPTER 13

1. See Boaz Cohen, *Jewish and Roman Law* (New York: Jewish Theological Seminary of America, 1966), 1:271 ff.

2. B. Sanhedrin 56a following T. Abodah Zarah, chap. 8, ed. Zuckermandl, pp. 473-74.

3. B. Sanhedrin 56b.

4. *Yad Ramah* thereto.

5. *Emunot veDeot* 9.2. See *The Book of Beliefs and Opinions*, trans. Samuel Rosenblatt, pp. 327-28 and esp. n. 16.

6. *Kuzari* 2.48; Nahmanides' comment to Gen. 6:13.

7. Aaron Halevi, *Sefer HaHinukh*, no. 416; Albo, *Ikkarim* 3.7; Azariah di Fano, *Assarah Maamarim*, ed. Frankfurt-am-Main, 1698, 3.21. See Louis Ginzberg, *Legends of the Jews*, 5:92-93, n. 55.

8. Cf. Thomas Aquinas, *Summa Theologica* 1-2, q. 94, aa. 2-3.

9. See *Sefer HaHinukh*, no. 186:

10. B. Sanhedrin 57b; cf. *Sifra* to Lev. 12:3, ed. Weiss, p. 48a.

11. *Melakhim* 9.4. See Maim., *Sefer HaMitzvot*, shoresh 3.

12. Mendelssohn, *Schriften*, Jub. ed. 16:178-80; 3:43-44. Later, Hermann Cohen developed the Mendelssohnian notion of Noahide law along the lines of his neo-Kantian ethics. See *Juedische Schriften* (Berlin: C. A. Schwetschke und Sohn, 1924), 1:179-83; 3:345-51; *Religion der Vernunft aus den Quellen des Judenthums* 3d ed. (Darmstadt: Joseph Melzer Verlag, 1966), pp. 381-87.

13. Hullin 13b. Concerning pro-Persian views, see B. Berakhot 8b; B. Baba Kama 117a and R. N. Rabinowicz, *Dikdukay Sofrim*, for the textual variants; B. Baba Metzia 70b, 119a and Rashi and Tosafot, s.v. "Shbor Malka."

14. See Thomas Aquinas, *Summa Theologica* 1-2, 22'. 98-100.

15. Sanhedrin 58b-59a.

16. *Responsa Pe'er HaDor*, ed. Amsterdam, no. 50.

17. See *Melakhim* 8, end and Karo, *Kessef Mishneh*. For the fullest discussion of the dispute surrounding the correct reading and meaning of this passage, see Leo Strauss, *Spinoza's Critique of Religion* (New York: Schocken Books, 1965), pp. 23-24, 273, 293.

18. For the Ashkenazic sources, see Jacob Katz, *Exclusiveness and Tolerance* (Oxford: Clarendon Press, 1961). Also see *Tiferet Israel* to M. Baba Kama 4.3 and M. Abot 3.14.

19. B. Sanhedrin 56b; Maim., *Melakhim* 9, end; Nahmanides, comment to Gen. 34:13.

20. T. Sotah 8.6, ed. Zuckermandl, 310-11; P. Sotah 7.5.

21. B. Sanhedrin 59a.

22. See B. Yebamot 22a and Tosafot, s.v. "ervah"; B. Baba Metzia 72a; B. Kiddushin 13b and Tosafot, s.v. "malveh."

23. B. Sanhedrin 72b.

24. B. Sanhedrin 59a, Tosafot, s.v. "leyka." Cf. P. Shabbat 14.4. •

25. See Hullin 33a, Tosafot, s.v. "ehad"; Isaac Klein, "Abortion and Jewish Tradition," *Conservative Judaism* 24, no. 3 (Spring 1970): 26-33; G. G. Grisez, *Abortion: The Myths, the Realities and the Arguments* (New York: World Publishing Co., 1970).

26. M. Ohalot 7.6; Maim., *Yesoday HaTorah* 5.7.

27. B. Sanhedrin 80b and Tosafot, s.v. "ubar." Cf. B. Pesahim 25a-25b.

28. Baba Kama 91a; Maim., *Sefer HaMitzvot,* neg. no. 57.

29. Baba Metzia 62a and Rashi, s.v. "imakh"; B. Abodah Zarah 6a, Tosafot, s.v. "vehashata."

30. *Melakhim* 9.1; cf. *Vayikra Rabah* 9.3.

31. This is especially true in the Sephardic tradition. See Halevi, *Kuzari* 2. 48; Albo, *Ikkarim,* Book 1; Meiri to B. Baba Kama 38a (in *Sheetah Mekubetzet*) and to B. Sanhedrin 57b, ed. Schreiber, pp. 226-27; Elie Benamozegh, *Israel et L'Humanité* (Paris, 1914), pp. 457 ff.

32. *Responsa Havot Yair,* ed. Lemberg, 1896, no. 31. Cf. Kiddushin 12b; B. Sotah 47b; *Genesis Rabah* 51.1. See *Zohar,* p. 3a to Exod. 1:7. Cf., however, R. Jacob Emden, *Responsa YABETZ,* ed. Lemberg, 1884, 1: no.43.

33. *Noda BiYehudah* 2, ed. Vilna, 1904, Hoshen Mishpat, no.59. Cf. Heller, *Tosfot Yom Tob* to M. Niddah 5.3.

34. See M. Niddah 5.3; B. Niddah 44b; Maim., *Rotzeah* 2.6, *Abelut* 1.7 and Karo, *Kessef Mishneh,* thereto.

35. See Chapter 1. For the various halakhic options, both lenient and strict, see David M. Feldman, *Birth Control in Jewish Law,* 2d ed. (New York: New York University Press, 1970), pp. 284-94.

36. See Aristotle, *Metaphysics* 1005b29; Thomas Aquinas, *Summa Theologica* 1-2, q.94, a.2; Ludwig Wittgenstein, *Tractatus Logico-Philosophicus* 5.133.

37. See Shalom Spiegel, *Amos versus Amaziah* (New York: Jewish Theological Seminary of America, n.d.).

38. Nahmanides to Lev. 19:2; also, the responsum of R. Solomon ibn Adret (Rashba), quoted by Karo, *Bet Joseph* to *Tur,* Hoshen Mishpat 2.1; cf. B. Abodah Zarah 55b.

39. See Feldman, *op. cit.,* 257-62.

40. *Jewish Medical Ethics* (New York: Bloch Publishing Co., 1959), p. 181. This is based on I. M. Weiss, *Dor Dor veDorshav,* 2:22.

41. See, e.g., B. Sukkah 51b-52a; B. Kiddushin 12b and M. Berakhot, end.

42. M. Niddah 3.7; B. Niddah 30a-31b.

43. Note to *Shulhan Arukh,* E.H. 156.4. However, some authorities tried to explain this not so much as a change in our knowledge of the evidence, but as a change in the nature of the evidence itself. See Kagan (Hafetz Hayyim), *Mishnah Berurah* to O.H. 173.2, n.3.

44. *Shibtay Sefer* 2.21. I found this reference in Louis Jacobs, *Principles of the Jewish Faith,* pp. 310-11. For the earlier attitude toward the deaf-mute, see, e.g., M. Baba Kama 6.4, 8.4.

45. See the brief and motion filed *amicus curiae* before the Supreme Court of the United States, October term, 1971, no.70-18.

46. B. Sanhedrin 75a; Maim., *Yesoday HaTorah* 5.9. Cf. M. Yoma 8.6 and B. Yoma 83a-83b.

47. Quoted in "Abortion's Psychological Price," *Christianity Today* 15, no.18 (June 4, 1971): 41 ff.

48. At present I am researching this question in the psychiatric literature. The phenomenon of suicide, which has, I think, important light to throw on the question of abortion, is the subject of my forthcoming book, *Suicide and Morality.*

49. B. Sanhedrin 39b. Cf. Abot 2.1 and commentators.

CHAPTER 14

1. Note M. Abot 1.17: "Simon ben Rabban Gamliel said . . . not learning [*hamidrash*] but doing [*hamaaseh*] is the chief thing [*ikkar*]." Even the celebrated "intellectualist"

statement, "Greater is the study of the Torah [than doing] for it brings one to doing," (B. Baba Kama 17a and parallels) justifies itself on practical grounds. cf. Maim., *Hakdamah L'Mishnah*, ed. Rabinowitz, pp. 79, 88.

2. Such principles as "One engaged in one mitzvah is exempt from other mitzvot at the same time" (B. Sotah 44b and parallels), and "One must not do mitzvot in bundles" (B. Pesahim 102b and parallels), were necessitated by the continuous imperatives present to Jews.

3. See M. Sotah 8.7 and B. Sotah 44b. For a concise collection of many of the pertinent sources see *Torah Studies in the Light of the Halakhah* (Heb.), no. 8, "Wars," ed. J. Copperman (Jerusalem: Kiryat Noar, 1962).

4. B. Berakhot 3b and B. Sanhedrin 16a.

5. See J. Neusner, "What Is Normative in Jewish Ethics," *Judaism* 16, no. 1 (Winter 1967): 3-20.

6. See Boaz Cohen, *Jewish and Roman Law*, 1:107, 271, 281, 338-39, 380, 386. For a concise background of all these terms, see A. P. d'Entrèves, *Natural Law* (New York: Harper Torchbooks, 1965). For an attempt to see the importance of this material for contemporary Judaism, see R. Gordis, *The Root and the Branch* (Chicago: University of Chicago Press, 1962), pp. 204-35.

7. T. Abodah Zarah 8.4, ed. Zuckermandl, p. 473; B. Sanhedrin 56a.

8. Cf. B. Baba Kama 38a.

9. Note B. Sanhedrin 56b: "Concerning a gentile: crimes which the Jewish courts punish by death, a gentile [*ben Noah*] is considered forewarned [*muzhar*]; matters which the Jewish court does not punish by death, a gentile is not considered forewarned."

10. See B. Sanhedrin 59a and Rashi, s.v. "mishum" and Albo, *Ikkarim* 3.19.

11. M. Gittin 1.5.

12. B. Gittin 10b.

13. B. Batra 54b. See L. Landman, *Jewish Law in the Diaspora: Confrontation and Accommodation* (Philadelphia: Dropsie University, 1968).

14. See B. Bab Kama 113a.

15. Rashi, B. Gittin 9b, s.v. "hutz."

16. See Liddell and Scott, *Greek-English Lexicon*, s.v. "krino" and "krima." For the use of *doon*, see, e.g., B. Sanhedrin 54a.

17. Cf. *Bereshit Rabah*, beg.

18. Maim., *Melakhim* 8.11.

19. B. Sanhedrin 39b.

20. *U.S. Objectives in Viet Nam*, Public Information Series (Washington, D.C.: Department of State, 1967), p. 8.

21. M. Sanhedrin 8.9. See B. Sanhedrin 73a, which attempts to find either immediate or inferred scriptural basis for this law.

22. M. Ohalot 7.6 and B. Sanhedrin 72b. Also, see M. Niddah 5.3.

23. *Rotzeah* 1.9.

24. See B. Sanhedrin 80b and Maim., *Nizkay Mammon* 11.2. Note the earlier sources, e.g., *Mekhilta*, Nezikin 8, ed. Horovitz-Rabin, pp. 275-76; B. Niddah 44b; B. Baba Kama 42b.

25. See R. Ezekiel Landau, *Noda BiYehudah* 2, H.M. no. 59.

26. See B. Pesahim 25a-25b.

27. See Albo, *Ikkarim* 3.7.

28. B. Shabbat 31a.

29. Over and above the acknowledgment of this by Christianity (Matt. 7:2; *Didache* 1.2; Gratien, *Init. D.* 1), the very same idea is found in Greek texts written long before any direct encounter between the two civilizations can be verified. See Herodotus, *Persian Wars* 3.142, 3; Aristotle, *Nicomachean Ethics* 1132b25.

30. *Yesoday HaTorah* 5.7.

31. *Melakhim* 9.1.

32. *Ibid.* Cf. Thomas Aquinas, *Summa Theologica* 1-2, q.94, a.2: "Omnia illa quae habet

naturalem inclinationem, ratio naturaliter apprehendit ut bona ..." a.3: "Multa enim secundum virtutem fiunt ad quae natura non primo inclinat; sed per rationis inquistionem ea homines adinvenerunt quasi utilia ad bene vivendum."

33. P. Shabbat 14, end and P. Abodah Zarah 2.2. See B. Shabbat 129a and parallels.

34. See B. Baba Metzia 59b and B. Kiddushin 54a.

35. See A. J. Heschel, *God in Search of Man*, pp. 320-47.

CHAPTER 15

1. The most famous example of this tendency is found in Rashi's opening remarks in his Torah commentary, viz., that the Torah could have begun with the first mitzvah, i.e., Exod. 12:1 ff. Also, according to the Talmud (Menahot 45a), the Book of Ezekiel was only admitted to the canon because its descriptions of the future service of the Temple were interpreted in such a way as not to contradict the prescriptions of the Torah on the same subject.

2. M. Ketubot 4.4 and B. Ketubot 46b.

3. *Mekhilta*, Nezikin 13, ed. Horovitz-Rabin, p. 293. Cf. B. Sanhedrin 72b. Also, see *Sifre*, Deuteronomy, ed. Friedmann, no. 237, p. 117b.

4. *Taamay HaMitzvot b'Sifrut Yisrael*, 4th ed., 1:29.

5. *Torah min HaShamayim b'Ispaklariah shel HaDorot* (London: Soncino Press, 1962), 1:i ff.; *God in Search of Man*, pp. 320 ff.

6. *Mekhilta*, DibaHodesh 5, ed. Horovitz-Rabin, p. 219.

7. B. Makkot 23b-24a.

8. *Sefer HaMitzvot*, Pos. no. 1, ed. Heller (Jerusalem: Mosad HaRav Kook, 1946), p. 35 and see n. 1 thereon. See also *ibid.*, shoresh no. 9; *Yesoday HaTorah*, beg.; *Hakdamah L'Perek Helek*, ed. Rabinowitz (Jerusalem: Mosad HaRav Kook, 1960), 13 foundations, no. 1, pp. 136-37; *Moreh Nebukhim* 2.33.

9. "How can the statement, 'I am the Lord your God,' be included in the ten commandments as a commandment, for surely it is neither a positive nor a negative prescription." Ibn Ezra commenting on Exod. 20:2.

10. For the background and development of this crucial dispute, see M. Rosh HaShanah 3.7; B. Rosh HaShanah 28a-29a; Maim., *Shofar* 2.4 and esp. Karo, *Maggid Mishneh* thereto; *Shulhan Arukh* O.H. 60.4 and Kagan, *Mishnah Berurah* thereto; J. B. Soloveitchik, "Ish HaHalakhah," p. 689; A. J. Heschel, *God in Search of Man*, pp. 317-19; M. Kadushin, *Worship and Ethics* (Evanston, Ill.: Northwestern University Press, 1964), pp. 197 ff.

11. See B. Pesahim 114b.

12. *Or HaShem*, Ferrara ed., pp. 3a-3b. See H. A. Wolfson, *Crescas' Critique of Aristotle*, pp. 114 ff.

13. *Sefer HaIkkarim* 1.14, ed. and trans. Isaac Husik (Philadelphia: Jewish Publication Society of America, 1946), 1:128.

14. E.g., *ibid.*, 1:4.

15. The recent interpretation given by Dr. Louis Jacobs in his *Principles of the Jewish Faith*, p. 54, does not, I believe, recognize the theological root-problem with which Maimonides deals. Dr. Jacobs holds that Maimonides means by *mitzvah*, a "good deed," viz., belief in God is not really a prescription. However, if this is the case, why does Maimonides include this "good deed" as the first of all positive *commandments*?

16. Trans. R. Gordis, *Koheleth: The Man and His World* (New York: Bloch Publishing Co., 1955), p. 136.

17. For a discussion of the problem of the interrelationship of teleology with ethics and cosmology, see Leo Strauss, *Natural Right and History* (Chicago: University of Chicago Press, 1953), pp. 7-8; Ernst Cassirer, *The Logic of the Humanities*, trans. C.S. Howe (New Haven: Yale University Press, 1961), pp. 165-78.

18. *Shemonah Perakim*, chap. 5, beg., ed. Rabinowitz, p. 184.

19. *Moreh Nebukhim* 1.2.

20. *Shemonah Perakim,* intro., ed. Rabinowitz, p. 154.

21. This fact proved embarrassing to some theologians. See the comment of R. Obadiah di Bertinoro on M. Abot 1, beg.; also, Isaak Heinemann, "Die Lehre vom ungeschriebenem Gesetz im juedischen Schriftum," *Hebrew Union College Annual* 4 (1928):166-67.

22. See *Me'ilah,* end; *Iggeret Teman,* chap. 1, ed. Rabinowitz (Jerusalem: Mosad HaRav Kook, 1954), pp. 123-24.

23. *Moreh Nebukhim* 3.27, trans. S. Pines (Chicago: University of Chicago Press, 1963), p. 510. Earlier Maimonides played down the physical end of the Torah more than in the *Guide;* see *Hakdamah L'Mishnah,* ed. Rabinowitz, pp. 77-78.

24. See *ibid.* 3.27; *Hakdamah L'Perek Helek,* ed. Rabinowitz, pp. 117 ff. Cf. R. Hananiah Kazis, *Kinat Sofrim* to Maim., *Sefer HaMitzvot* Pos. no. 1, who holds that the first commandment is a prescription to rationally prove what has been traditionally received, viz., belief in God's existence. He sees this as Maimonides' theological legacy from R. Saadiah Gaon and R. Bahyah ibn Pakudah. Although he does not quote the Zohar, a precedent for R. Kazis's view is to be found there. "When God gave the Torah on Mount Sinai to Israel the first statement was, 'I am the Lord your God' ... This is the esoteric meaning of the 'I' [*anokhi*] of the first commandment, to know Him generally ... viz., that there is a higher power ruling the world ... To know him particularly is the meaning of 'the Lord your God.' " Zohar to Exod. 20:2, p. 25a.

25. *Moreh Nebukhim* 2.40.

26. *Ibid.,* 2.39.

27. *Ibid.,* 3.29; *Abodah Zarah,* beg.; Commentary to M. Abodah Zarah 4.7.

28. "Therefore I say that the Law, although it is not natural, enters into what is natural. It is a part of the wisdom of the deity with regard to the permanence of the species of which He has willed the existence, that He put into its nature that individuals should have the faculty of ruling." *Moreh Nebukhim* 2.40, Pines trans., p. 382.

29. For Maimonides' use of this principle, see *ibid.,* 1.26. In the Talmud the principle had a somewhat more technical use; see, esp., B. Abodah Zarah 27a and Tos., s.v. "dibra." As far as I know, the first theologian to use this principle in a specifically theological way was R. Abraham ibn Ezra; see his comment to Gen. 1:26. Also, see Isaak Heinemann, *Darkhay HaAggadah* (Jerusalem: Hebrew University, Magnes Press, 1954), pp. 12 ff. Cf. A. J. Heschel, *Torah min HaShamayim,* 1:3 ff.

30. *Teshubah* 8.7 and *Hakdamah L'Perek Helek,* ed. Rabinowitz, p. 127. This is a significant midrash on Isa. 64:3 based on B. Berakhot 34b and parallels.

31. Note to *Sefer HaMitzvot* Pos. no. 1.

32. M. Berakhot 2.2.

33. Note to *Sefer HaMitzvot* Neg. no. 1.

34. See *Moreh Nebukhim* 2.13 ff.

35. Nahmanides' commentary to Exod. 13:16; Num. 21:8; Torat HaShem Temimah, *Kitbay Ramban* 1:150-55.

36. As precedents for Maimonides' view, see R. Saadiah Gaon as quoted in Nahmanides' comment; Philo, *Quod. Det.* 44.160; LXX thereto. As precedents for Nahmanides' view, see Halevi, *Kuzari* 4.3; Shemot Rabah 3.7; B. Berakhot 9b.

37. "Gott sprach zu Mosche: Ich werde dasein, als der dasein werde. Und sprach ... ICH BIN DA schickt mich zu euch." Note Franz Rosenzweig's polemic against Moses Mendelssohn on this point in *Kleinere Schriften,* pp. 185 ff. and Martin Buber, *Zur einer neuen Verdeutschung der Schrift* (Olten: Verlag Jakob Hegner, 1954), pp. 28-29.

38. See *Kuzari* 1.35 ff. Halevi's influence on Nahmanides is evident in many places. For an explicit recognition of this influence by Nahmanides himself, see his comment to Deut. 11:22.

39. See Nahmanides' comments to Exod. 4:3, Num. 4:3, Num. 16:30, and Deut. 5:15.

40. Cf. Franz Rosenzweig, *The Star of Redemption,* trans. W. W. Hallo (New York: Holt, Rinehart & Winston, 1970), pp. 176-77.

DAVID NOVAK

41. See Nahmanides' note to *Sefer HaMitzvot* Neg., no. 2; comment to Exod. 13:8; cf. Rashi to Exod. 13:8 and Deut. 11:13, 24:18.

42. Cf. Sefer HaEmunah vehaBitahon, *Kitbay Ramban* 2:397, 429-30.

43. Cf. Plato, *Republic* 477C ff.

44. See Leo Strauss, *Philosophie und Gesetz* (Berlin: Schocken Verlag, 1935), pp. 48 ff.; J. B. Soloveitchik, "Ish HaHalakhah," pp. 659-60.